Homeland Security

▲▼ ▲▼ ▲▼

LEGAL AND POLICY ISSUES

Joe D. Whitley and Lynne K. Zusman, Editors

Section of Administrative Law and Regulatory Practice

Defending Liberty
Pursuing Justice

Cover design by ABA Publishing

13 12 11 10   5 4 3

Cataloging-in-Publication data is on file with the Library of Congress

Homeland Security: Legal and Policy Issues / Whitley, Joe and Zusman, Lynne, eds.

ISBN: 978-1-60442-462-1

Discounts are available for books ordered in bulk. Special consideration is given to state bars, CLE programs, and other bar-related organizations. Inquire at Book Publishing, ABA Publishing, American Bar Association, 321 North Clark Street, Chicago, Illinois 60654.

www.ababooks.org

Contents

Chapter 8
Succession Planning and Business Continuity **141**
James P. Gerkis and Adam Klepack

Chapter 11
Maritime Security Developments and TWIC
Jonathan K. Waldron

Chapter 14
Export Control Enforcement Developments 253
Thomas E. Crocker

Dedication

This book is dedicated to the men and women who serve in the U.S. military together with those who serve as first responders, in emergency services, and in law enforcement.

Thank you for protecting us each and every day. May God bless you.

Foreword

by the Hon. Lee H. Hamilton*

The economic challenges America presently faces are great and complex, dominating the congressional and presidential agendas. Nonetheless, the continued threats of terrorism and natural disasters demand vigilance—in both the private and public sectors—in protecting America's people and critical infrastructure.

The 9/11 Commission, at its core, sought to recommend practical, lawful, and effective approaches to securing the homeland in the twenty-first century. In the aftermath of Hurricane Katrina, it became clear that similar efforts with regard to natural-disaster response were appropriate.

As a legal discipline, Homeland Security Law has gained traction with the American Bar Association in recent years, as evidenced by its Annual Homeland Security Law Institute. Over the last four years, private practitioners and public lawyers, along with many others, have benefited from this program's legal and policy resources addressing man-made and natural disasters.

As a result of the Institute's work, the ABA developed *Homeland Security: Law & Policy* to encourage discussion beyond the Institute's walls of the legal and policy challenges related to homeland security. The topics addressed in the following chapters reflect the diversity of those challenges. The book is a useful resource for those seeking greater understanding of the dynamic threats to America—from both within and without.

I congratulate the ABA Administrative Law and Regulatory Practice Section, the editors of this book—Joe Whitley and Lynne Zusman—and the authors for developing an excellent resource for lawyers and others interested in the importance of the law, and public policy more broadly, in protecting America.

---

* Lee H. Hamilton is president and director of the Woodrow Wilson International Center for Scholars and director of the Center on Congress at Indiana University. Hamilton represented Indiana's Ninth Congressional District for 34 years beginning in 1965. He served as chairman and ranking member of the House Committee on Foreign Affairs and chaired the Subcommittee on Europe and the Middle East, the Permanent Select Committee on Intelligence, the Select Committee to Investigate Covert Arms Transactions with

Iran, the Joint Economic Committee, and the Joint Committee on the Organi-
zation of Congress. As a member of the House Standards of Official Conduct
Committee, Hamilton was a primary draftsman of several House ethics re-
forms. Since leaving the House, Hamilton has served on several commissions.
He served as vice chair of the National Commission on Terrorist Attacks upon
the United States (the 9/11 Commission) and as co-chair of the Iraq Study
Group, the National Commission on the War Powers of the President and the
Congress, and the Congressional Commission on the Strategic Posture of the
United States. He is currently a member of the FBI director's Advisory Board,
the defense secretary's National Security Study Group, and the U.S. Department of Homeland Security Task Force on Preventing the Entry of Weapons of
Mass Effect on American Soil. Hamilton is a graduate of DePauw University
and Indiana University Law School, and studied for a year at Goethe University in Germany. Before his election to Congress, he practiced law in Chicago
and Columbus, Indiana.

Acknowledgments

The authors and editors of this book are grateful for the support and encouragement of many colleagues and friends. We have a few words of thanks to numerous individuals for helping us with the book from conception to publication.

First, we would like to thank Randolph (Randy) May, the American Bar Association's (ABA) former Administrative Law and Regulatory Practice Section chair. Randy first envisioned the Section developing a monograph or book on homeland security issues when he chaired the Section's Publications Committee several years ago, and continued to support the vision of the Section in establishing accessible avenues of education in this area.

Next, we are indebted to Richard Paszkiet, deputy director of ABA's Publications Department; Anna Shavers, the Section Publications Committee chair of recent years along with recently appointed co-chair Bill Jordan; and various practitioners and committee members, who have provided useful insight and direction on the book's content and structure. Alphabetically, Section Chairs Michael Asimow and Russell Frisby and incoming chair Bill Luneburg have provided invaluable support and leadership to this effort. William Morrow, the Section's budget officer, has provided his usual visionary advice and counsel.

We are appreciative of the work of ABA staff members Kimberly Knight, Sarah Orwig, Catherine Kruse, Anne Kiefer, and Katrina Pariera, who have all played essential roles in this endeavor. Additionally, we are grateful for the work of Holly Hampton of Greenberg Traurig.

Finally, we would like to thank the Sections and committees of the ABA that make the ABA's Homeland Security Institute the success it has become over the last four years. This book, in many ways, is a reflection of the Institute and should prove to be a useful resource for the lawyers and others who work in this exciting new legal discipline.

About the Editors

Joe Whitley is a shareholder in both the Atlanta and Washington, D.C., offices of Greenberg Traurig LLP. He had a wide-ranging career in the Department of Justice. In the George H.W. Bush administration, Joe served as the Acting Associate Attorney General, the third-ranking position in the Department of Justice. He was appointed by Presidents Reagan and Bush, respectively, to serve as U.S. Attorney in the Middle and Northern Federal Districts of Georgia. Throughout his career, Joe served under five United States Attorneys General in a number of key operational and policy positions. In 2003, Joe was appointed by the President as the first General Counsel of the United States Department of Homeland Security (DHS), the highest-ranking legal official in DHS. He held that position for two years before his departure and return to private practice. Joe has represented numerous individuals and corporations in major government investigations throughout the United States and internationally. He is a frequent speaker and lecturer on white-collar, compliance, and corporate governance issues. Recently, Joe has been chosen for listing in the 2009 edition of *The Best Lawyers in America*® and has been recognized as one of *Georgia Trend's 2008 Elite*.

Lynne Zusman is an experienced litigator and negotiator in Washington, D.C. and has been a solo practitioner since 1986. She drafted housing regulations at the Department of Housing and Urban Development. She has litigated appellate cases in the U.S. Department of Justice's Criminal Division, as well as civil cases, including those involving national security issues, in the U.S. Department of Justice's Civil Division. Lynne also managed 60,000 cases for Health and Human Services as Deputy General Counsel for Litigation. She served in the U.S. Attorney's Office for the District of Columbia, was inside corporate counsel to a NASDAQ mini-conglomerate, and practiced law in Alexandria, Virginia. Lynne graduated from Bryn Mawr College in Bryn Mawr, Pennsylvania, with a B.A. *cum laude* with honors in political science and graduated from the Yale Law School. She is admitted to practice in Washington, D.C., Maryland, Virginia, and California. Her firm, Lynne K. Zusman and Associates, P.C., serves clients throughout the country and overseas.

About the Authors

Mahsa Aliaskari is of counsel at Greenberg Traurig, LLP. She leads the business immigration and compliance practice in the firm's Los Angeles office, where she counsels multinational corporations on a variety of issues relating to U.S. immigration laws, I-9 due diligence, best business practices, and employment compliance matters. She develops immigration-related compliance strategies and programs designed to minimize exposure and liabilities. Mahsa has performed internal and government initiated I-9 and H-1B compliance audits. She also focuses her practice on business immigration matters and provides strategic immigration planning to address the visa and work authorization needs of U.S. and global personnel, including professionals, managers, and executives, treaty investors/traders, essential workers, persons of extraordinary ability, corporate trainees, and students. Her practice encompasses assisting companies in a variety of industries, including health care, pharmaceutical, technology, entertainment, sports, retail, manufacturing, trade, and financial services.

Mark J. Biros is a partner in the Washington, D.C., office of Proskauer Rose LLP and co-founded the firm's Corporate Defense and Investigations Group in 1997. Mark has nearly 35 years of investigative experience as a legislative counsel, former prosecutor, and defense counsel, his current role. On the federal level, he served as an assistant U.S. attorney for the District of Columbia from 1977 through 1988. He has tried over 100 jury trials. For a time, he was deputy chief of the Felony Trial Division. Later, he became a member of the Special Prosecutions Unit, which concentrated on complex international and domestic federal criminal investigations. His investigative experience began as an assistant counsel to the U.S. Senate Committee on Presidential Campaign Activities, known informally as the "Watergate Committee." His international practice has taken him to the United Kingdom, Germany, Italy, Belgium, Ireland, Mexico, and Argentina, while focusing on activities in Europe, the Middle East, South America, the Far East, and Africa. At the state level, he investigated and prosecuted political and police corruption in Philadelphia, Pennsylvania, where he was an assistant attorney general for several years. In private practice, he has conducted internal investigations in defense of government allegations of violations of the Foreign Corrupt

Practices Act, domestic and foreign tax laws, money-laundering provisions, bribery, insider trading, anti-trust laws, and government contract fraud, as well as U.S. Customs and environmental law violations. He has helped clients identify internal control issues and establish procedures for compliance under Sarbanes-Oxley, SEC, and other regulatory provisions. He has represented organizations and individuals that have been the subject of congressional inquiries. Mark has been an adjunct professor at Georgetown University Law Center for 25 years. Presently, he teaches advanced criminal procedure. He has lectured on criminal law issues to federal judges at the Federal Judicial Center, and to bar associations and meetings of private and government attorneys. He provides the firm's clients with training on how to conduct internal corporate investigations. Mark is a contributing author to two books: *Corporate Counsel's Guide to Handling Government Investigations* and *Business & Legal Guide to Online Internet Law*. He has written numerous articles for a variety of publications, including in-depth articles on internal investigations and white-collar crime. Mark graduated *cum laude* from Princeton (1970) and received his law degree from Georgetown University Law Center (1973), where he was an editor of the *American Criminal Law Review.*

Jonathan G. Cedarbaum is a partner in the law firm of Wilmer Cutler Pickering Hale & Dorr LLP in Washington, D.C., where he is a member of the Litigation Department and the Defense and National Security Practice Group. Jonathan joined WilmerHale in 2002. Previously he spent two and a half years as an attorney-adviser in the Office of Legal Counsel, Department of Justice, specializing in international and national security matters, and a year as a Bristow Fellow in the Office of the Solicitor General. Jonathan clerked for Justice David H. Souter on the U.S. Supreme Court and Judge David Tatel on the U.S. Court of Appeals for the D.C. Circuit. Earlier in his career, he served as a legislative assistant to a member of Congress. In addition to representing clients before the interagency Committee on Foreign Investment in the United States (CFIUS), Jonathan has a diverse litigation practice and heads the firm's False Claims Act Practice Group.

James W. Conrad, Jr., is the principal of Conrad Law & Policy Counsel, Washington, D.C., founded in 2007. Jamie represents businesses, associations, and coalitions before federal agencies and Congress in the areas of homeland security; environment, health, and safety; and science policy/information quality. He spent the previous 14 years at the American Chemistry Council (ACC), where he had legal responsibility for security issues after 9/11. He organized and has counseled the Chemical

Sector Coordianting Council and has been centrally involved in chemical security legislation and regulation since 9/11. He also led the ACC's advocacy regarding information quality, science policy, regulatory enforcement, and a range of other environmental issues, and ACC's environmental legal staff. In 2001, he founded the Performance Track Participants Association. Jamie has also practiced with the Washington, D.C., offices of Davis, Graham & Stubbs and Cleary, Gottlieb, Steen & Hamilton. He has chaired the city of Alexandria, Virginia, Environmental Policy Commission and was one of the few Democrats on the Bush-Cheney Transition Advisory Committee for EPA. He was secretary of ABA's Section of Administrative Law and Regulatory Practice from 2005 to 2008, currently serves on its governing council, and has also held leadership positions in the Section of Environment, Energy and Natural Resources. Jamie developed and edits the *Environmental Science Deskbook* (http://west.thomson.com/store/product.aspx?r=5051&product_id=16624886). He has testified before Congress and the U.S. Sentencing Commission and is a frequent speaker. His work has appeared in a peer-reviewed scientific journal, numerous law reviews, and trade journals, as well as *The New Republic* and *The Washington Post*. He graduated with high honors from the George Washington University Law School, where he was a member of the *Law Review* and the Order of the Coif. He received a B.A. and the Department Prize in Philosophy from Haverford College.

Tom Crocker, a partner in Alston & Bird, LLP, is co-chair of the firm's International Trade and Regulatory Group based in Washington, D.C. His practice focuses on regulatory and legislative aspects of international business and financial services. He specializes in Foreign Assets Control sanctions and embargoes, export controls, foreign direct investment reviews by the Committee on Foreign Investment in the United States (CFIUS), encryption, anti-money laundering, Foreign Corrupt Practices Act, and technology cooperation issues. Tom has particular expertise in the Office of Foreign Assets Control (OFAC) regulations and programs, Export Administration Regulations (EARs) governing dual-use exports (including anti-boycott and Chemical Weapons Convention compliance), and the International Traffic in Arms Regulations (ITAR) governing the export of defense articles and services. For over 25 years he has assisted clients from a broad range of sectors—including some of the largest global financial institutions, as well as U.S. and foreign companies in the technology, pharmaceuticals, medical products, biotechnology, chemicals, telecommunications, defense, aircraft, and space sectors—in transactional compliance and in developing export management systems and compliance policies. He has represented numerous companies in internal investigations, voluntary disclosures, and civil penalty enforcement cases. In addition, Tom maintains an active practice counseling and representing clients before the U.S. government on the USA Patriot Act, Bank Secrecy Act, homeland security, payments systems, data management, and electronic signatures.

James Gerkis is a partner in the Corporate Department of the New York office of Proskauer Rose LLP. James has extensive experience in sophisticated domestic and international corporate, financing, securities, and real estate transactions. His practice expertise includes mergers and acquisitions and leveraged buyouts; private equity and venture capital transactions; real estate transactions, including joint ventures and hotel and resort developments; various financing transactions; and securities experience, representing both issuers and underwriters. He is co-chair of the Securities, Commodities and Exchanges Committee and vice-chair of the Homeland Security Committee of the ABA's Section on Administrative Law and Regulatory Practice. He has made presentations relating to securities law and homeland security at several ABA conferences and is the author of many articles on various aspects of securities law, homeland security, and related subjects. James received his law degree from Columbia University School of Law in 1983, where he was a Harlan Fiske Stone Scholar and a Teaching Fellow. He did his undergraduate work at Columbia University where, having been admitted without finishing high school, he received a Bachelor of Arts degree in Political Science in 1980.

Michael Greenberger is the director of the Center for Health and Homeland Security (CHHS) at the University of Maryland and a professor at the School of Law. CHHS works on a broad range of homeland security and emergency response issues for federal, state, and local governmental agencies. Michael teaches classes on emergency management and the law of homeland security, as well as on constitutional and securities law. Prior to coming to the University of Maryland, he worked as a top official at the U.S. Justice Department, where he had responsibility for several counterterrorism projects, and as director of the Division of Trading and Markets and the Commodity Futures Trading Commission. Before entering government service, he was a partner for over 20 years in the Washington, D.C., law firm of Shea & Gardner, where he served as lead litigation counsel before courts of law nationwide, including the U.S. Supreme Court. Michael is a Phi Beta Kappa graduate of Lafayette College and the University of Pennsylvania Law School, where he served as editor-in-chief of the *Law Review*. He is a life member of the American Law Institute, has served on the board of governors of the D.C. Bar and the D.C. Circuit Advisory Committee on Procedures, and has served as a mediator for the U.S. Courts for the District of Columbia.

Jessica R. Herrera-Flanigan is a partner at the Monument Policy Group in Washington, D.C., where she advises clients on national security, law enforcement, cybersecurity, media, intellectual property, trade, and technology issues. Before joining Monument Policy in 2008, she served as the staff director and general counsel for the House Committee on Homeland Security, where she directed, supervised, and managed the legislative, policy, and oversight activities of the committee's staff. Prior to her work on Capitol Hill, Jessica served as senior counsel at the Computer Crime & Intellectual Property Section, Criminal Division, of the U.S. Department of Justice, where she led a team of prosecutors who specialized in cybercrime. She was one of the government's leading experts on critical infrastructure protection, the Committee on Foreign Investment in the United States (CFIUS), and electronic evidence–gathering issues. She also served as vice-chair on the U.S. delegation to the Organization for Economic Cooperation and Development Experts Group on international information security. Jessica also has worked as an associate at Crowell & Moring LLP and as a special assistant U.S. attorney in the Fraud and Public Corruption Division of the U.S. Attorney's Office in Washington, D.C. She has taught courses on cybercrime, information security, and criminal law as an adjunct professor at the Washington College of Law at American University and at the American Military University. Jessica is a native of Port Arthur, Texas. She received her B.A. in American studies from Yale University and her J.D. from Harvard Law School.

Jeffrey Kaliel served from 2005 to 2007 as an Honors Program attorney-advisor in the Department of Homeland Security's (DHS) Office of the General Counsel. In addition to his DHS tenure, he served as a special assistant U.S. attorney in the Southern District of California. Jeffrey is a former U.S. Army Psychological Operations soldier and served in Iraq in 2003. Jeffrey received his J.D. from Yale Law School and B.A. *summa cum laude* from Amherst College. He also studied at Cambridge University, where he completed a dissertation in philosophy.

Adam Klepack is an associate in the New York office of Proskauer Rose LLP in the firm's Corporate Department. His practice focuses primarily on corporate finance and general securities and corporate law matters. He has represented both issuers and investment banks in a variety of publicly and privately placed debt and equity securities offerings, including high-yield debt financings. He has also represented clients in connection with debt tender offers, exchange offers, and consent solicitations. Adam received his J.D. *cum laude* from New York University School of Law and his B.A. from New York University.

Dawn Lurie is a shareholder based in the Tysons Corner, Virginia, office of Greenberg Traurig LLP. She advises multinational corporations on a variety of employment-related issues, particularly I-9 alien employment verification matters and minimization of exposure and liabilities. She develops immigration-related compliance strategies and programs as well. Dawn has performed internal I-9 compliance reviews and defended businesses involved in government audits. She has also published articles and frequently lectures on I-9 issues, including penalties for failure to act in accordance with government regulations, antidiscrimination laws, and employers' responsibilities upon receiving Social Security "no-match" number letters. Dawn also focuses her practice on business immigration matters and provides strategic immigration planning to address the visa and work authorization needs of U.S. and global personnel, including professionals, managers, and executives, treaty investors/traders, essential workers, persons of extraordinary ability, corporate trainees, and students. Dawn concentrates her practice on global immigration and provides outbound (non-U.S.) assistance to U.S. and foreign companies. She also has experience in legislative policy, specifically with essential guest-worker issues. Moreover, Dawn has provided pro bono legal assistance to unaccompanied minors and those seeking immigration relief on the basis of extreme hardship, and has successfully represented individuals applying for special immigrant status under the Violence Against Women Act. Her practice also includes a specialization in consular processing issues, and she has particular expertise before U.S. Consulates in the Middle East and North Africa.

Lieutenant Colonel Jeanne M. Meyer is the legal advisor for the United States Northern Command Standing Joint Force Headquarters and a member of the Staff Judge Advocate office of North American Aerospace Defense Command and United States Northern Command. Following law school and admission to the Texas State Bar, Jeanne entered active duty in January 1994 as an Air Force judge advocate. She has served as a staff judge advocate for the 8th Fighter Wing, Kunsan Air Base, Korea, in Kuwait in support of Operation SOUTHERN WATCH, and Afghanistan in support of Operation ENDURING FREEDOM. She was an instructor in international and operations law at the Army's Judge Advocate General's School. Jeanne has also served on the Joint Staff and as a

Deputy Staff Judge Advocate. She has published in the *Air Force Law Review* and *The Reporter*, an Air Force JAG publication. She was a senior editor for the Army JAG school's *Operational Law Handbook*. Jeanne holds degrees from Duke University, Duke University School of Law, American Military University, and the Army Judge Advocate General's School.

Stephen W. Preston is a partner with the law firm of Wilmer Cutler Pickering Hale and Dorr LLP in Washington, D.C. He is co-chair of the Defense and National Security Practice Group and a member of the firm's Regulatory and Litigation Departments. Stephen joined WilmerHale in 1986 and returned to the firm in 2001 after more than four years at the Pentagon and three years with the Justice Department. From 1993 to 1995, he was the principal deputy general counsel of the Department of Defense, serving an extended period as acting general counsel. He served as deputy assistant attorney general with the U.S. Department of Justice from 1995 to 1998. From 1998 to 2000, he was general counsel of the Department of the Navy. Stephen's practice is focused on controversy work for clients in the defense, aerospace, and related industries, as well as other matters involving national security. A substantial part of his practice is devoted to advice concerning U.S. foreign ownership restrictions and representation before the interagency Committee on Foreign Investment in the United States (CFIUS). Stephen has been nominated by President Obama to be general counsel of the Central Intelligence Agency (CIA), and his appointment is pending confirmation by the Senate.

Donald A. ("Andy") Purdy is a partner with the law firm of Allenbaugh Samini Gosheh, LLP (www.alsalaw.com), Costa Mesa, California, and Washington, D.C. He is also president of DRA Enterprises, Inc. (www.andypurdy.com), specializing in IT consulting, business development, and government relations, and co-director of the International Cyber Center at George Mason University. Andy was a member of the White House staff team that helped to draft the National Strategy to Secure Cyberspace (2003). He subsequently worked at the Department of Homeland Security for three and a half years helping to implement the national strategy, the last two heading the National Cyber Security Division and the U.S. Computer Emergency Readiness Team. Before joining the White House staff, Andy served as acting general counsel and chief deputy general counsel at the U.S. Sentencing Commission. He served as an assistant U.S. attorney for the Eastern District of Pennsylvania, senior staff counsel of the House Select Committee on Assassinations, special counsel to the House Committee on Standards of Official Conduct (Ethics), and counsel to the Senate Impeachment Trial Committee (on the articles against Judge Walter Nixon). Andy is a graduate of the College of William & Mary and the University of Virginia Law School.

Harvey Rishikof is a professor of law and former chair, Department of National Security Strategy, National War College. Harvey previously clerked for Judge Leonard I. Garth of the Third Circuit and was administrative assistant to Chief Justice William H. Rehnquist. He served as legal counsel to the deputy director of the FBI and as dean of Roger Williams School of Law.

Mark J. Robertson is a founding member of Klitenic Robertson PLLC and KR Security LLC in Washington, D.C. He represents clients in an array of government regulatory, enforcement, and public policy matters and counsels clients on transactions involving homeland security technology. Mark served with the U.S. Department of Homeland Security (DHS) as the associate general counsel for the Science & Technology Directorate. He also served as chief of staff to the general counsel, where he managed legal operations and provided legal and policy guidance on issues arising throughout the department. As the associate general counsel for Science & Technology, Mark provided legal and policy advice concerning the department's research and development efforts focused on countering chemical, biological, radiological, and nuclear threats, as well as the dangers of infectious disease. During his service with DHS, Mark also provided guidance on issues relating to immigration, international agreements, CFIUS transactions, transportation and cargo security, bio-defense, public health, incident management, procurement, infrastructure protection, intelligence sharing, and investigations. Prior to his public service, he practiced with national law firms representing emerging, privately held, and public companies with general corporate, commercial transactions, mergers and acquisitions, and finance matters. Mark received his J.D. from the University of Virginia School of Law and his B.A. from Hampden-Sydney College in Virginia.

Arianne Spaccarelli is a staff attorney at the University of Maryland Center for Health and Homeland Security (CHHS), where she has worked on the *Maryland Public Health Emergency Law Bench Book* and presented on issues related to the federal-state relationship in public health emergency law at the American Public Health Association. She has also worked with the Maryland legislature on legislation to protect healthcare providers from liability during emergencies and is currently serving as regional planner for the Montgomery County Office of Emergency

Management and Homeland Security. Prior to joining CHHS, she worked as a policy analyst and program administrator at the Baltimore City Health Department. Arianne is an honors graduate of Harvard University and University of Maryland Law School, where she earned a certificate in health law.

Colonel Lisa L. Turner is the Staff Judge Advocate (chief counsel) of North American Aerospace Defense Command and United States Northern Command. Following law school and admission to the Virginia State Bar, Lisa entered active duty in January 1990 as an Air Force judge advocate. She has served as a staff judge advocate for the 305th Air Mobility Wing, McGuire Air Force Base, and in Saudi Arabia in support of Operation SOUTHERN WATCH. She was an instructor in military justice and international and operations law at the Air Force Judge Advocate General's School. In addition to teaching lawyers from all military services, she taught members of the media prior to their embedded assignments in Operation IRAQI FREEDOM, and non-U.S. military and civilians in Tbilisi, Georgia, and Skopje, Macedonia. She has presented on a border security panel for the Harvard National Security and Law Association and co-taught CLE courses for Gratz College. Lisa has also served on the Air Staff as a legal advisor for the Air Force Drug Testing Program, a circuit trial counsel, and an area defense counsel. She has published in the *Aerospace Power Journal*, *Air Force Law Review*, and *Joint Forces Quarterly*. She was a senior editor for *I LEAD! Developing JAG Corps Leaders*. Lisa's awards include the Air Force Outstanding Young Attorney of the Year (Albert M. Kuhfeld Award). She holds degrees from Randolph-Macon Woman's College, Arizona State University College of Law, Air Command and Staff College, and National War College.

Jonathan Waldron is a partner at Blank Rome LLP in its Washington, D.C., office and concentrates his practice in maritime, international, and environmental law. Jonathan is ranked by Chambers USA as a leading shipping attorney. Jonathan counsels clients, both domestically and internationally, in areas such as citizenship and manning issues, including outer continental shelf exemptions; coastwise trade; criminal defense; environmental maritime compliance and pollution response; maritime security compliance; LNG licensing; and vessel/facility operations and legislative and regulatory affairs. He served in the U.S. Coast Guard for 20 years, attaining the rank of commander, and was senior counsel to the Marine Spill Response Corporation. He is a co-author with Andrew Dyer of the *Maritime Security Handbook*, a guide to understanding and complying with the new maritime-related security requirements. Jonathan is a visiting professor at the Massachusetts Maritime Academy, where he teaches on legal issues related to pollution response and spill management teams. He is a member of the Maritime Law Association and frequently speaks and writes on maritime issues.

Joel A. Webber is a practitioner with Couri & Couri law firm in Chicago, Illinois, and focuses on commercial and regulatory issues involved in the movement of freight. His legal career has also included corporate practice with the Wall Street firm of Cleary Gottlieb Steen & Hamilton and trial practice with the Major Offense Bureau of the Manhattan District Attorney under Robert Morgenthau. His management roles have included financing of aircraft, rail rolling stock, and truck fleets for Whirlpool Financial Corporation and GE Capital. He later invested in logistics software firms with GE Equity. Joel has a bachelor's degree from Wheaton College in Illinois and a J.D. from the University of Pennsylvania Law School. He is vice chair of the American Bar Association's Administrative Law Section's Homeland Security Committee. He is admitted to practice before the Illinois and New York bars.

Introduction

For many years the American Bar Association Section on Administrative Law and Regulatory Practice (AdLaw) has published books and other materials of interest to lawyers and non-lawyers focused on various aspects of government operations, such as rulemaking, and processes that affect government, such as lobbying. This new book on Homeland Security Law is a natural continuation of this established tradition.

By way of background, in recent years, the AdLaw Section has taken on a key role together with other Sections of the ABA in reviewing the new Homeland Security function of the government and in promoting Homeland Security Law as an expanding and growing area of legal practice that impacts both the private and public sectors. Beginning in 2006, the AdLaw Section, along with numerous ABA co-sponsors, has held a two-day program called the Homeland Security Law Institute with speakers who are experts in their aspects of Homeland Security Law and practice.

Out of this experience of building the Institute, at its meeting in the spring of 2008, the AdLaw Section Council and the Publications Committee of the council endorsed the concept of a book that would capture, for practitioners and the public alike, a number of areas critical to Homeland Security Law. The chapters that follow present, in an easy-to-use fashion, a select number of topics.

We hope you will enjoy this book and the iterations that the ABA AdLaw Section plans to publish in future years.

Thank you.

Administration of Homeland Security

CHAPTER 1

Homeland Security: An Inside Perspective of the Last Seven Years and a Look Ahead

Jessica R. Herrera-Flanigan[1]

Homeland security has gone from a concept to a critical mission of one of the largest federal agencies in less than eight years. As the Department of Homeland Security undergoes its first presidential transition since its creation, this chapter examines the processes leading to today's homeland security efforts. It evaluates the policy shifts and outcomes to date, as well as the challenges that exist for the Obama Administration.

In the past decade, the emergence of a "homeland security" concept has changed our nation's perceptions of what is needed to combat terrorists and—post-Katrina—natural disasters here at home. This concept evolved from a mostly academic military proposal that had gained little traction prior to September 11, 2001, into the biggest reorganization of the federal government since the creation of the Department of Defense in 1947. The process leading to the current homeland security structure has been neither perfect nor void of political influence. As a result, the outcomes of the government's efforts on this front have been mixed.

---

1. The author would like to thank Allison Seyferth, Gloria Eldridge, and P.J. Crowley for their comments and contributions to this chapter.

There have been several significant transitional periods since 2001 with regard to U.S. homeland security posture. The year 2009 began yet another transitional period as the United States saw the first presidential change since the creation of the Department of Homeland Security, the Homeland Security Council, and homeland security-oriented oversight committees in Congress. President Obama and Secretary Janet Napolitano face the challenge of objectively assessing existing homeland security strategies and structures to chart the future of homeland security. Part of the challenge will be determining the nation's actual homeland security mission. Making that determination requires an understanding of what has happened over the last eight years to bring us to our current posture. If not, to quote Edmund Burke, "Those who don't know history are destined to repeat it."

BEFORE SEPTEMBER 11, 2001: AN IDEA WITHOUT A MOTIVATION

When asked about homeland security, most Americans would probably say that our efforts began on September 11, 2001, when terrorists struck U.S. soil with a force not seen since the December 7, 1941, Pearl Harbor attacks. September 11 changed how government, the private sector, non-governmental organizations, academia, and individuals consider the day-to-day aspects of homeland security. Calls for a homeland security mission and organization, however, had been proposed before that date.

For example, in its February 2001 report, *The Road Map for National Security: Imperative for Change,* the U.S. Commission on National Security for the 21st Century (Hart-Rudman Commission) proposed creating a National Homeland Security Agency that would be responsible for planning, coordinating, and integrating the federal government's activities in homeland security.[2] Noting that a direct attack against American citizens *on American soil* was "likely over the next quarter century," the commission found that the United States was "very poorly organized to design and implement any comprehensive strategy to protect the homeland."[3]

---

2. U.S. Commission on National Security for the 21st Century, Road Map for National Security: Imperative for Change, The Phase III Report of the U.S. Commission on National Security/21st Century, Feb. 15, 2001.

3. *Id.* at viii, 10.

The Hart-Rudman Commission went on to propose a realignment of key assets and agencies to better help the U.S. government meet its "primary national security mission" of the 21st century: "the security of the American homeland."[4] Among other recommendations, the commission proposed consolidating the Federal Emergency Management Agency (FEMA), the Customs Service, the Border Patrol, and the Coast Guard within the new agency. The commission envisioned a regional approach to homeland security that would lead back to a federal agency consisting of three directorates:

- Directorate of Prevention to oversee border security;
- Directorate of Critical Infrastructure Protection to oversee cybersecurity and the implementation of Presidential Decision Directive 63;[5] and
- Directorate of Emergency Preparedness and Response, which would be a reconstituted FEMA.[6]

Under the plan, the agency also would have a National Crisis Action Center (NCAC), headed by a two-star National Guard general, which would act in a time of crisis or emergency and coordinate with state and local government as well as the private sector.[7]

Representative Mac Thornberry (R-TX) introduced legislation in early 2001 to fulfill the recommendations of the Hart-Rudman Commission and establish what was to be called the "National Homeland Security Agency." His legislation was not a priority, as homeland security simply wasn't on anyone's radar, including newly elected President George W. Bush, who had assumed office two months before, as both the president and the U.S. Congress were dealing with more immediate issues and priorities facing the new administration and the country.

THE 9/11 ATTACKS: MAKING A CASE FOR A HOMELAND SECURITY AGENCY

The attack predicted by the Hart-Rudman Commission did not wait a quarter of a century but occurred eight months later, on September 11, 2001. The unimaginable and horrifying attacks provided the motiva-

---

4. *Id.* at 10.
5. 63 Fed. Reg. 19,615.
6. *Id.* at 17.
7. *Id.*

tion to move forward with the creation of a dedicated homeland security agency.

The response was not to develop a comprehensive plan to protect the nation against attacks, but to respond and recover from the immediate threat facing the nation. On September 14, President Bush issued Proclamation 7463, Declaration of National Emergency by Reason of Certain Terrorist Attacks.[8] On that same day, both the House and the Senate unanimously passed the 2001 Emergency Supplemental Appropriations Act for Recovery from and Response to Terrorist Attacks on the United States. The bill dedicated $40 billion to disaster assistance; support for countering, investigating, and prosecuting terrorism; increased transportation security; repair of damaged public facilities and transportation systems; and support for national security.[9] On September 18, Congress passed a joint resolution authorizing the use of military force against those "responsible for the recent attacks launched against the United States."[10]

It was not until late September and early October 2001 that the federal government turned its attention to more long-term efforts of protection and prevention. Among the relevant legislation signed into law were the Aviation and Transportation Security Act (ATSA),[11] which created a Transportation Security Agency (TSA) within the Department of Transportation, and the Uniting and Strengthening America by Providing Appropriate Tools Required to Intercept and Obstruct Terrorism (USA PATRIOT ACT) Act of 2001, which provided investigative authority to law enforcement and intelligence agencies to combat terrorism.[12] Not passed but introduced were several additional bills that would create a U.S. counterterrorism agency called either the National Office for Combating Terrorism or the Department of National Homeland Security.[13]

President Bush countered calls for a new agency by creating two White House entities to address homeland security. On October 8, he issued Executive Order 13,228,[14] establishing the Office of Homeland

---

8. 66 Fed. Reg. 48,197–99.

9. Pub. L. No. 107-38: 115 Stat. 220.

10. Pub. L. No. 107-40: 115 Stat. 224.

11. Pub. L. No. 107-71: 115 Stat. 597.

12. Pub. L. 107-56, 115 Stat. 271.

13. *See, e.g.,* S. 1449 [introduced by Senator Bob Graham (D-FL), Sept. 21, 2001] and H.R. 3078, to create "the National Office for Combating Terrorism" [introduced by Representative Alcee Hastings (D-FL), Oct. 10, 2001], and S. 1534, to create the "Department of National Homeland Security" [introduced by Senator Joseph Lieberman (D-CT), Oct. 11, 2001].

14. 66 Fed. Reg. 51,812–17.

Security and the Homeland Security Council (HSC) to implement a "comprehensive national strategy to secure the United States from terrorist threats or attacks." The offices were tasked with "coordinating the executive branch's efforts to detect, prepare for, prevent, protect against, respond to, and recover from terrorist attacks within the United States."[15] President Bush appointed Tom Ridge, a former congressman and Pennsylvania governor, as Assistant to the President for Homeland Security, to direct the office.

A few weeks later, on October 29, the president issued his first two Homeland Security Presidential Directives detailing the organization and operation of the HSC and setting forth a national policy for combating terrorism through immigration policies.

The creation of these entities did not satisfy many in the government and in the private sector who believed that the nation was in dire need of a dedicated agency with the statutory authority and consolidated power to fulfill the mission assigned to the Office of Homeland Security. Those advocating this approach thought that Ridge's office was "little more than a symbolic attempt to confront the 21st-century threat that, as [the 9/11 attacks] demonstrated . . . confounded the nation."[16] In May 2002, both Representative Thornberry and Senator Joseph Lieberman (D-CT) introduced more detailed legislation to create a Department of National Homeland Security and the National Office for Combating Terrorism.[17] Under increasing political pressure from both parties, President Bush reversed course in early June 2002 and transmitted to Congress a proposal to create the Department of Homeland Security.[18]

The president's proposal had four major divisions: Border and Transportation Security; Emergency Preparedness and Response; Chemical, Biological, Radiological and Nuclear Countermeasures; and Information Analysis and Infrastructure Protection, and included the transfer of the Secret Service to the new department.[19] In addition to the Secret Service,

---

15. *Id.*

16. Susan Baer, *Ridge faces challenge as he takes counterterror post*, BALT. SUN, Oct. 8, 2001.

17. H.R. 4660 and S. 2452.

18. Susan Glasser & Michael Grunwald, *Department's Mission Was Undermined from Start*, WASH. POST, Dec. 22, 2005, at A01.

19. *Message to the Congress of the United States*, June 18, 2002, *available at* http://www.whitehouse.gov/news/releases/2002/06/20020618-5.html (accessed Sept. 15, 2008).

the proposed department would incorporate all or part of 22 agencies, including the Coast Guard, Border Patrol, Customs, Federal Emergency Management Agency, Animal and Plant Health Inspection Service, and Immigration and Naturalization Service; employ 170,000 individuals; and have a first-year budget of $38 billion. Representative Richard Armey (R-TX), at the president's request, introduced H.R. 5005 on June 24, 2002, to implement the president's goals.

At the same time, the House created a Select Committee on Homeland Security, with Representative Armey as chair and Representative Nancy Pelosi (D-CA) as ranking member, to assess the legislation.[20] As a harbinger of the congressional oversight problems that would hinder the new department and the future Homeland Security Committee, the proposed legislation was referred to 12 other committees in addition to the Select Committee.

The legislation faced uncertainty for several months due to controversy over a number of provisions, including collective-bargaining rights for more than 50,000 employees covered by existing union agreements.[21] The Homeland Security Act of 2002 finally cleared Congress on November 22, 2002, and was signed into law by President Bush on November 25.[22]

Thus, nearly two years after the Hart-Rudman Commission report and more than a year after the 9/11 attacks, the Department of Homeland Security (DHS) was born. Its daunting mission was defined as follows:

- prevent terrorist attacks within the United States;
- reduce the vulnerability of the United States to terrorism; and
- minimize the damage, and assist in the recovery, from terrorist attacks that do occur within the United States.

A simple yet broad mission for an agency tasked with preventing the next 9/11 from occurring.

---

20. The Select Committee was set up to expire once the legislation became law.

21. Nick Anderson, *Homeland Security bill wins House approval; could stall in the Senate*, SEATTLE TIMES, July 27, 2002.

22. Pub. L. No. 107-296, 116 Stat. 2135.

BUILDING BLOCKS: FOUNDATION OF A NEW SECURITY REGIME

In January 2003, President Bush nominated Governor Tom Ridge as the first Secretary of Homeland Security, and by the end of the month DHS was in business. Its creation, representing the biggest reorganization of the federal government since the National Security Act of 1947 created the Department of Defense, called for strong congressional oversight to ensure that the agency succeeded in fulfilling its mission. By March 1, the majority of the 22 agencies and 180,000-plus employees were officially merged into the new U.S. Department of Homeland Security, which was given a budget of $33.6 billion.

In these early days, the department faced three major challenges. First, it attempted to merge multiple management systems and processes from the 22 agencies into one without disrupting operations. The difficulty of this task led the Government Accountability Office (GAO) to designate the implementation and transformation of DHS as high risk.[23] Second, it had to assemble the multiple agencies and tasks according to the component structure laid out in the Homeland Security Act. With few exceptions, such as the Secret Service and the Coast Guard, many of the agencies found responsibilities taken from or added to their individual missions. Third, and most important, while undergoing the merger, DHS had to show progress in fulfilling its mission and keeping America secure.[24]

All these steps proved daunting and exhausting to the headquarters staff that either transferred or volunteered for the new agency. Just how exhausting was made apparent in congressional testimony given by the Assistant Secretary for Information Analysis, Paul Redmond, on June 30, 2003, on the $6 billion Project Bioshield. Redmond appeared before Congress without the expected opening or written statement. During questioning from members, he admitted he only had one staffer working on the bioterror threat and could not get the information he needed from the intelligence community because he did not have access to a secure net-

---

23. U.S Gov't Accountability Office, High-Risk Series: An Update, GAO-05-207 (January 2005).

24. *See, e.g.,* Siobhan Gorman, *Lawmaker decries 'disconnect' between intelligence, security,* Congress Daily, June 9, 2003, *quoting* ranking member Jim Turner, who said the department "has been mired down in the expected challenges of merging 22 agencies and has not come to grips with the core function of that department."

work.[25] In concluding his testimony, Redmond stated, "I'm trying to do my best at this point," a theme that would repeat itself throughout the agency's early days.[26] Less than four months after signing on with DHS and a few weeks after this appearance, Redmond resigned. He was not alone. The trend of staff departures and turnover would continue for the next six years.

Part of the agency's early challenges also emerged from its efforts to ensure that individual citizens were diligent and prepared, yet not fearful about their security. For example, the department was put in charge of the Homeland Security Advisory System (HSAS), a color-coded terrorism threat advisory scale that ranked the risk of terrorist attack. Red represented severe risk, while green meant low risk; in between were orange, yellow, and blue.

In early 2003, when the terror risk level was raised, it was suggested by some government officials that Americans stock up on emergency products such as duct tape and plastic sheeting to ready themselves for an attack.[27] In addition to being the center of late-night television commentary about duct tape, Secretary Ridge found himself having to reassure Americans that they were safe and that they did not need to rush to create "safe rooms" with duct tape and plastic sheeting.[28] Thus, the new agency and its leadership were learning that they could not operate in the same way as traditional federal bureaucracies. Its partners in preventing, preparing, and responding to terrorism and natural disasters were multiple, and its success depended on how it communicated with those partners, whether a citizen on the street, the cop on the beat, the CEO of a critical infrastructure company, or the Congress down the street.

CONGRESS: FIEFDOMS, POLITICS, AND OVERSIGHT

When House Leaders created a Select Committee during the 107th Congress to evaluate the president's homeland security proposal, they did so with the condition that it would cease to exist when the Homeland Security Act was passed. While there was support for reorganizing federal

---

25. *Bioterrorism project falls into intelligence gap*, NATIONAL JOURNAL, June 16, 2003.

26. *Id.*

27. Eric Lichtblau & Christopher Drew, *Ridge's Record: Color Alerts and Mixed Security Review*, N.Y. TIMES, Dec. 1, 2004.

28. *Ridge Tries to Calm America's Nerves: Government Official Cites Bad Tip on Terror*, cnn.com, Feb. 14, 2003.

agencies in the executive branch to secure our homeland, Congress did not have the same enthusiasm for self-realignment to oversee the agency it had created. As 9/11 Vice Chairman and former congressman Lee Hamilton (D-IN) would note on the jurisdictional issue, "What an enormous irony it would be if the Congress passed a bill, as we did, as you did, setting up a Department of Homeland Security for the executive branch and then didn't do anything itself to get their house in order to deal with homeland security."[29]

Unfortunately, that is essentially what happened. The Senate chose to delegate some responsibility for the management and organizational operations of the department to the Senate Committee on Governmental Affairs. Committees such as Senate Commerce and Judiciary, however, continued to have jurisdiction over specific agencies and functions that were merged into DHS.

The House, after much debate, took slightly bolder steps by creating a second Select Committee on Homeland Security. Representatives Christopher Cox (R-CA) and Jim Turner (D-TX) were chosen as chairman and ranking member, respectively, of this temporary committee, which had 27 Republican and 23 Democrat members.[30] Jurisdiction remained shared with numerous other committees. Indeed, jurisdiction over the department was shared among 88 committees and subcommittees, meaning that 412 congressional members and all 100 senators had some oversight responsibilities over the new fledging agency. Thus, the DHS leadership members soon found themselves spending as much time testifying as they did in performing their jobs.

In addition, Republican leadership appointed nine chairmen from a range of committees to serve on the Select Committee.[31] Most of these chairs stood to lose jurisdiction to the new committee if it was too effective or successful. The split jurisdiction, lack of interest from the chairmen members of the committee, and contempt for the temporary committee lead to Chairman Cox scrapping the first-ever attempt at a homeland security authorization bill in July 2004.[32]

---

29. Testimony of Lee Hamilton, House Select Committee on Homeland Security, Aug. 17, 2008.

30. Judy Schneider, *House Select Committee on Homeland Security: A Fact Sheet*, CRS Report for Congress, Oct. 4, 2004.

31. *Id.*

32. *See, e.g.,* Greta Wodele, *Partisan fissures appear over House Homeland Security bill*, CONGRESS DAILY, June 23, 2004; Greta Wodele, *Bipartisanship evaporates on Homeland Security authorization*, CONGRESS DAILY, July 22, 2004.

Congress's failure to realign itself prevented it from developing a cohesive yet comprehensive homeland security oversight function. In 2003 and for half of 2004, oversight was scattered. Democrats criticized the erratic nature of oversight and legislation through a series of reports issued by Congressman Turner and other Democratic members of the Homeland Security Committee.[33] There was bipartisan committee support for critical infrastructure protection, cybersecurity, and first-responder grant funding, but little influence and authority to move legislative ideas forward in these areas. Initially housed in borrowed Library of Congress space, the Select Committee's staff and members did what they could with limited resources to highlight problems and successes of DHS. In many ways, the committee was not that different from the agency it was overseeing. Both were new entities struggling to create cohesive and integrated organizations to better secure our nation.

THE 9/11 COMMISSION: WHY DID IT HAPPEN, HOW DID IT HAPPEN, AND WHAT DOES AMERICA DO NEXT?

Congress's struggle to further our nation's homeland security efforts changed in July 2004, but not because of an internal reorganization or anything that DHS accomplished. It changed because of the final report of the National Commission on Terrorist Attacks upon the United States (9/11 Commission). The commission was created by Congress and President Bush on November 27, 2002, to "make a full and complete accounting of the circumstances surrounding" the 9/11 attacks.[34] Chaired by former New Jersey Republican Governor Thomas Kean and vice-chaired by former Democratic Representative Lee Hamilton, it consisted of five Republicans and four Democrats. Its recommendations, released on July 22, 2004, established the basis for the next debate on homeland security.

The report chronicled what happened on September 11, the rise of "new terrorism" efforts, our evolving counterterrorism efforts, and failures that could have prevented or mitigated the attacks. It also contained 41 recommendations for protecting the nation against future attacks, covering such areas as emergency preparedness and response, transportation security, border security, intelligence community reform, civil liberties,

---

33. *See, e.g.,* JIM TURNER ET AL., WINNING THE WAR ON TERROR, July 2004, *available at* http://www.futurebrief.com/WinningtheWaronTerror.pdf (accessed on Sept. 30, 2008).

34. Pub. L. No. 107-306, 116 Stat. 2383.

executive power, congressional and administrative reform, non-proliferation, foreign policy, and public diplomacy.[35]

When members returned from their summer work period in September 2004, there was a flurry of legislative action in both the House and the Senate to implement the 9/11 Commission's recommendations. The emerging leaders on the issue included Senators Susan Collins (R-ME) and Joe Lieberman, and Representatives Chris Shays (R-CT) and Carolyn Maloney (D-NY). The 9/11 Commission's leaders endorsed their efforts.

Congressional action, however, was stymied over the next several months as fierce debate between the House and Senate ensued on what should be in a 9/11 Commission bill. An agreement tentatively reached in late November fell apart due to objections over military command and immigration issues raised by then Armed Services Chairman Duncan Hunter (R-CA) and Judiciary Chairman James Sensenbrenner (R-WI).[36] On December 7 and 8, the House and Senate passed a compromise bill, the Intelligence Reform and Terrorism Prevention Act of 2004 (IRTPA), which the president then signed into law on December 17. The law reformed the intelligence community by creating the National Counterterrorism Center (NCTC) and a Director of National Intelligence (DNI). It also addressed transportation security, border protection, security clearances, and several related matters. It did not, however, include Representative Sensenbrenner's proposed immigration language.

Since his immigration-related provisions did not make it into the final bill, Sensenbrenner continued to push for them to be enacted in other legislation. In 2005, he introduced the Real ID Act, which, among other things, implemented regulations for state driver's license and identification document security standards and authorized the building of a fence along the San Diego border with Mexico. In March 2005, the bill was attached as a rider to the Emergency Supplemental Appropriations Act for Defense, the Global War on Terror, and Tsunami Relief, which passed both the House and the Senate and was signed into law.

This would not end the debate over border security and immigration, as the issues continued to dominate a great deal of the homeland security debate over the next several years. There was, for example, the Secure Fence Act, introduced by Representative Peter King (R-NY), who

---

35. THE 9/11 COMMISSION REPORT, July 22, 2004, *available at* http://govinfo.library.unt.edu/911/report/911Report.pdf (accessed on Sept. 15, 2008).

36. Jamie Dettmer, *Lawmakers Seek President's Help to Pass 9/11 Bill*, N.Y. SUN, Nov. 22, 2004.

had replaced Chris Cox as the chairman of the Homeland Security Committee, which required a double-layer fence along hundreds of miles of border.[37] There were also failed attempts at comprehensive immigration reform. President Obama will have to decide how to address immigration, choosing between a "border security first," a piecemeal strategy, or a comprehensive-only approach. To date, the president has indicated that the last is his preference.

TRANSITION TO NEW LEADERS AND THE NATURAL DISASTER NO ONE EXPECTED

The passage of the Intelligence Reform Act at the end of the 108th Congress did not mean that the 9/11 Commission's recommendations had been fully implemented. Several of the 9/11 commissioners formed the 9/11 Public Discourse Project to continue the push for the recommendations' fulfillment. The project issued a report on December 5, 2005, grading the nation on fulfilling the recommendations. The report said, at best, that America's terrorist response was like a D student whose highest grade was one A- for tackling terrorist financing.[38]

While many of the 9/11 Commission recommendations remained unfulfilled, the passage of the Intelligence Reform Act did, in many ways, mark the end of the first phase of our nation's post-9/11 homeland security efforts. Just a few weeks before the legislation was finalized, Secretary Ridge announced he was resigning as DHS Secretary.[39] Also, at the close of the 108th Congress, the top Democrat on the House Select Committee, Representative Turner, retired from Congress due to a Texas redistricting effort that left him without a district.[40] In addition, it was not clear whether the Select Committee, whose charter expired at the end of the session, would continue during the 109th Congress. Homeland security, as envisioned in the days after 9/11, faced new challenges and its first major change in leadership.

Despite objections from many chairmen, the House voted on January 4, 2005, to make the temporary House Committee on Homeland

---

37. Pub. L. No. 109-367; 120 Stat. 2638.

38. *Final Report on 9/11 Commission Recommendations,* 9/11 Public Discourse Project, Dec. 5, 2005, *available at* http://www.gpoaccess.gov/911/pdf/fullreport.pdf (accessed on October 2, 2008).

39. John Mintz & Mike Allen, *Ridge Leaving Cabinet: Homeland Security Changes Predicted,* WASH. POST, Dec. 1, 2004, at A01.

40. *Democrat Turner to Retire from House,* UPI, Jan. 9, 2004.

Security a permanent committee. Representative Cox was chosen as its first chairman. Representative Bennie G. Thompson (D-MS) was chosen to serve as the ranking Democratic member. The committee, under H.R. 5, was given jurisdiction on "overall homeland security policy," as well as on border and port security (except immigration policy and non-border enforcement); customs (except customs revenue); integration, analysis, and dissemination of homeland security information; domestic preparedness for and collective response to terrorism; homeland security research and development; and transportation security. This defined jurisdiction, however, was not exclusive in many of these areas. The Senate did not take a similar approach but did acknowledge the need for some focus on homeland security. It replaced the Committee on Governmental Affairs with a Committee on Homeland Security and Governmental Affairs. Jurisdiction, as in the House, remained spread across various Senate committees.

In early 2005, President Bush announced the nomination of, and the Senate confirmed, former Third Circuit Court of Appeals Judge Michael Chertoff as the second Secretary of DHS. Moving quickly, during one of his first appearances before Congress, Secretary Chertoff announced that he was "initiating a comprehensive review of the Department's organization, operations, and policies."[41] This "Second Stage Review," which became known as 2SR, focused on a six-point agenda:

1. Increased preparedness, with particular focus on catastrophic events.
2. Strengthened border security and interior enforcement and reform immigration processes.
3. Hardened transportation security without sacrificing mobility.
4. Enhanced information-sharing with our partners, particularly with state, local, and tribal governments and the private sector.
5. Improved DHS stewardship, particularly with stronger financial, human resource, procurement and information technology management.
6. Re-alignment of the DHS organization to maximize mission performance.[42]

---

41. *Department of Homeland Security Reorganization: the 2SR Initiative,* CRS Report for Congress, Aug. 19, 2005.
42. *Id.*

Thus, less than two years after its creation, the department already was engaging in a reorganization effort. Many of the foundational changes recommended by the new secretary came from a December 2004 think-tank report, which evaluated how well DHS had fulfilled its mission as detailed by the Homeland Security Act of 2002.[43] The report offered more than 40 recommendations and argued that DHS needed to be significantly reorganized if it were to succeed.

The realignment focused on a handful of ideas. For example, Secretary Chertoff proposed creating a DHS Policy Office, Operations Directorate, Chief Intelligence Officer, Chief Medical Officer, and an Assistant Secretary for Cybersecurity. The secretary created a Preparedness Directorate that would include Grants & Training, Infrastructure Protection, Cybersecurity, the U.S. Fire Administration, the National Capital Region, and the Chief Medical Officer.[44] In addition, other initiatives such as the Secure Freight Initiative and the Secure Borders and Open Doors initiative were included in the 2SR plan.

The 2SR effort was met with both praise and criticism from congressional and outside experts. In the House, Representative Thompson raised concerns with the secretary's efforts to "flatten" the department by increasing the number of direct reports to his office.[45] Representative Cox, who in short order would be nominated as the chairman of the Securities and Exchange Commission, held a series of hearings examining the proposals. 2SR proceeded to be examined by Congress for most of the summer of 2005 but found its completion disrupted in late August, when the nation faced the first of two of the most intense hurricanes in recent history.

On August 29, 2005, Hurricane Katrina struck the U.S. Gulf Coast. Captured on television, the government's failures were stark: America watched as thousands were left stranded with little food or water in downtown New Orleans. America saw an uncoordinated response, with federal, state, and local agencies lacking the capability or ability to share critical information. President Bush's praise of FEMA Director Michael Brown in

---

43. David Heyman & James Jay Carafano, *DHS 2.0: Rethinking the Department of Homeland Security*, HERITAGE FOUND., Dec. 13, 2004.

44. *See* Statement of Secretary Michael Chertoff, U.S. Dep't of Homeland Security, Senate Comm. on Commerce, Science & Transp., July 19, 2005.

45. *See* http://www.sec.gov/about/commissioner/cox.htm (accessed on Sept. 15, 2008).

the days after the hurricane quickly went from "Brownie, you're doing a heck of a job" to an acceptance of the controversial director's resignation.

The department had no time to recover and regroup from Katrina before Hurricane Rita made landfall on September 24 near Sabine Pass, Texas. Between the two hurricanes, more than 800,000 citizens were displaced from their homes. Not since the Dust Bowl had so many Americans found themselves homeless. Rather than building the leaner and more efficient DHS that he envisioned, Secretary Chertoff found himself defending its capabilities and even its existence. America placed most of the blame for the disarray caused by the disasters on the new DHS and FEMA.

Everyday Americans were not the only ones to blame the department. The Senate, the House, and the White House all initiated their own investigations into the government's response to Katrina.[46] All three investigations found shortcomings at all levels of government. In response, Senators Collins, Lieberman, and Ken Salazar (D-CO) introduced the Post-Katrina Emergency Management Act of 2006 on July 25, 2006, to address many of the report's recommendations.[47] The legislation, among other things, laid out specific qualifications for the head of FEMA and streamlined reporting chains to the secretary, Homeland Security Council, and the president. The legislation also codified a number of the 2SR recommendations. Much of the legislation was attached as an amendment to the Department of Homeland Security Fiscal Year 2007 Appropriations bill, which was signed into law on October 4, 2006.

DUBAI PORTS: THE GLOBAL ECONOMY MEETS HOMELAND SECURITY

Hurricane response was not the only issue complicating DHS's efforts at success. In February 2006, the "Dubai Ports" controversy arose. Dubai Ports World, a United Arab Emirates (UAE) government-owned company, was in the midst of purchasing Peninsular and Oriental Steam Navigation Company, a British company that held the leases of port facilities in New York, New Jersey, Pennsylvania, Maryland, Louisiana, and

---

46. *See*
47. *See* S. 3721, *available at* http://thomas.loc.gov/cgi-bin/bdquery/z?d109:SN03721:@@@D&summ2=m& (accessed on Sept. 20, 2008).
48. *See Key questions about the Dubai port deal,* http://www.cnn.com/2006/POLITICS/03/06/dubai.ports.qa/index.html (accessed on Sept. 26, 2008).

Florida.[48] There was an outcry from a number of lawmakers who claimed that allowing a foreign-owned company to manage operations at six major U.S. seaports undermined national security. Some of the criticism, including that of Chairman King, dealt specifically with the UAE and its perceived role with terrorist organizations.[49] There were demands that the Committee on Foreign Investment in the United States (CFIUS) investigate any and all terrorist ties that Dubai Ports World might have.[50] The attention surrounding Dubai Ports also focused some attention on port security and the need to strengthen maritime security. As a result, Congress passed the Security and Accountability For Every (SAFE) Port Act, which the president signed into law on October 13, 2006.[51]

REMEMBERING THE 9/11 COMMISSION'S UNIMPLEMENTED RECOMMENDATIONS

The beginning of the 110th Congress in 2007 started yet another chapter in DHS's history. The previous November, the Democrats were elected into the majority in both the House and Senate. Representative Thompson became Chairman Thompson, and Senator Lieberman became Chairman Lieberman. Speaker Nancy Pelosi and Senate Majority Leader Harry Reid (D-NV) announced an aggressive legislation plan for the first 100 hours of the new Congress. First on the agenda was H.R. 1, Implementing Recommendations of the 9/11 Commission Act of 2007, introduced by Chairman Thompson on January 5, 2007.[52] The bill, which went straight to the House floor, passed 299-128.[53] The Senate's companion bill, S. 4, passed by a vote of 60-38 on March 13, 2008.

The legislation, divided into 24 titles, covered numerous homeland security and related international security issues. Most significantly, it contained language adjusting the allocation of homeland security grants to reflect a more risk-based approach. It also mandated a Quadrennial Homeland Security Review (QHSR) and tackled such issues as interoperability; information sharing and intelligence sharing with state, local, and tribal governments; critical infrastructure security; weapons of mass destruction;

---

49. *Id.*
50. *Id.*
51. Pub. L. No. 109-347; 120 Stat. 1884.
52. *See* http://www.govtrack.us/congress/bill.xpd?bill=h110-1&tab=summary (accessed on Sept. 28, 2008).
53. *See* http://www.govtrack.us/congress/bill.xpd?bill=h110-1#votes (accessed on Sept. 28, 2008).

transportation security; rail security; surface transportation; and terrorist travel.

The legislation was stalled for nearly four months because of a White House veto threat. While the White House and DHS disagreed with a number of provisions, the veto threat mostly focused on language giving collective-bargaining rights to aviation screeners. That language ultimately was dropped, and on July 26 and 27 the legislation passed the Senate and House. The president signed the legislation on August 3, 2007.

Criticism about the legislation focused mostly on what it did *not* contain. Specifically, many argued that the legislation failed to enact one of the key recommendations of the 9/11 Commission—the streamlining of oversight of DHS.[54] The department continued to report to 86 different congressional committees. Between 2003 and 2007, agency officials had testified "761 times, provided roughly 7,800 written reports and answered more than 13,000 questions for the record."[55] The jurisdictional challenges facing DHS and Congress likely will remain an issue in the Obama administration, unless Congress changes its rules to address the issue.

LOOKING BEYOND 2008—THE FUTURE OF HOMELAND SECURITY

In 2009, the Department of Homeland Security may face its most significant challenge to date. During the first year of the past two administrations, terrorists have struck on U.S. soil.[56] There is much concern that terrorists will strike again in 2009, during a critical transitional time.[57]

The appointment of Arizona Governor Janet Napolitano as secretary of the Department of Homeland Security has largely been viewed positively. The Secretary's handling of the swine flu epidemic, as well as her tackling of border security, has received praise. Like her predecessors, however, she has not escaped scrutiny. Her first few months were marred

---

54. *See* Remarks by Homeland Security Secretary Michael Chertoff on 2007 Achievements and 2008 Priorities, Dec. 12, 2007, *available at* http:// www.dhs.gov/xnews/speeches/sp_1197513975365.shtm (accessed on Sept. 28, 2008).

55. *Id.*

56. Terrorists struck the World Trade Center in February 2003, less than two months after President Clinton's inauguration. The 9/11 attacks occurred nine months into President Bush's administration.

57. *See* Robert Pear, *Behind the Scenes, Teams for Both Candidates Plan for a Presidential Transition*, N.Y. Times, Sept. 20, 2008.

by the release of an intelligence report on right-wing extremists prepared by career DHS analysts. The report created a political firestorm and resulted in passage of a Resolution of Inquiry by the Homeland Security Committee. The new department, it appears, continues its education and growing process.

In articulating the homeland security policy of the future, the Obama administration will have a lot of questions it must answer—in particular, what is the mission of the Department of Homeland Security? Answering that question does not necessarily require a revamping or reshuffling of DHS's components and agencies. Rather, it requires a refocusing on how America and the new president envision our security efforts. In many ways, it requires a reexamination of the recommendations of the Hart-Rudman Commission. For example, have we made homeland security a necessary priority in our overall national security strategy? Have we adequately prepared the American people for potential threats? Do we have effective partnerships with international, state, local, and tribal governments? Have we effectively eliminated government overlap and duplication?

Again, Congress eventually must make decisions, particularly on congressional jurisdiction and oversight. There is little question that congressional oversight must be streamlined to assure that a new administration is not bogged down with hundreds of duplicative and overlapping hearings, briefings, and requests. If an incident did occur, there must be a clear chain of command and oversight to avoid chaos. What Congress decides to do on this front could very well be a critical factor in the success of our nation's future homeland security efforts.

America has been fortunate to have avoided attack during the past eight years. Our homeland security efforts during this time have been a mixed bag of challenges, missteps, and successes. No one party or branch of government should get credit or blamed for the success or failures of our efforts to date. What comes next for homeland security will largely be decided by what we have learned since 9/11.

CHAPTER 2

State and Federal Emergency Powers

by Michael Greenberger and Arianne Spaccarelli

As the federal and state response to Hurricane Katrina demonstrated, a failure to understand and utilize legal authorities properly during a disaster can slow response efforts, destroy trust in government, and exacerbate chaos and civil unrest. This chapter will provide an overview of the statutory and constitutional authority for state and federal response to emergencies, including a description of typical state emergency management statutes, a summary of the major federal statutes related to public health emergency response, and a discussion of the constitutional limits on federal actions during a public health emergency.

Public health emergencies have unpredictable and far-reaching impacts, which rarely confine themselves to local, state, or even national borders and require officials at all levels of government to respond quickly and flexibly. Almost a century ago, what at first appeared to be a localized cluster of a few particularly serious cases of a garden-variety influenza in March 1918[1] had sickened 25 million and killed 675,000 Americans (out

---

1. The report of 18 severe cases of influenza, three of them fatal, in Haskell, Kansas, was among the first reports of the Spanish influenza that would later be recognized as the cause of the pandemic that reached its peak in the fall of 1918 and winter of 1918–1919. ALFRED W. CROSBY, AMERICA'S FORGOTTEN PANDEMIC 18 (Cambridge Univ. Press, 1989); U.S. Dep't of Health & Human Servs., "The Great Pandemic: the United States in 1918–1919," Web page, http://1918.pandemicflu.gov/the_pandemic/01.htm (last viewed Sept. 29, 2008).

of a population of 105 million) a year later.[2] Doctors were in short supply; nurses were in even shorter supply.[3] Phone service was hobbled by
high absenteeism.[4] Some local governments sought to remedy the dire
shortage of coffins by making coffins themselves and seizing shipments
meant for other cities.[5] More recently, Hurricane Katrina battered the
Gulf Coast, displacing 770,000,[6] stranding tens of thousands in New
Orleans[7] after levee and flood-wall breaches flooded 80 percent of the
city,[8] and ultimately killing over 1,400 people in Louisiana alone.[9] Total
property damage was close to $100 billion, making it the costliest disas-
ter in U.S. history.[10] Almost four years later, the Gulf Coast is still re-
building; New Orleans has recovered only 72 percent of the population it
had, and 36 percent of its housing remains vacant.[11]

The need for quick, decisive action in response to a rapidly evolving
crisis can make legal concerns seem almost trivial. Health-care workers,
engineers, police officers, sanitary workers, medicine, and sandbags are
needed to deliver services and maintain critical infrastructure; lawyers
and laws, some might say, just get in the way. However, while emergencies may require some legal niceties to be overlooked, a clear understanding of applicable legal authorities and safeguards is vital to an effective
response effort. Failure to utilize legal authorities properly can slow re-

---

2. CROSBY, *supra* note 1, at 205–06; U.S. Dep't of Health & Human
Servs., *supra* note 1. The pandemic would eventually kill about 20 million
people worldwide.

3. CROSBY, *supra* note 1, at 51.

4. *Id.* at 75 (describing the problem in Philadelphia), 97–98 (describing
the problem in San Francisco).

5. *Id.* at 1, 83.

6. FRANCES FRAGOS TOWNSEND, OFFICE OF THE PRESIDENT, THE FEDERAL RESPONSE
TO HURRICANE KATRINA: LESSONS LEARNED 69 (2006), *available at* http://
www.whitehouse.gov/reports/katrina-lessons-learned.pdf (last viewed Sept.
29, 2008).

7. *Id.* at 39.

8. AM. SOC'Y OF CIVIL ENGINEERS, THE NEW ORLEANS HURRICANE PROTECTION
SYSTEM: WHAT WENT WRONG AND WHY 1 (2007), *available at* http://www.asce.org/
files/pdf/ERPreport.pdf (last viewed Sept. 29, 2008).

9. Louisiana Dep't of Health and Hospitals, Reports of Missing and
Deceased (Aug. 2, 2006), *available at* http://www.dhh.louisiana.gov/offices/
page.asp?ID=192&Detail=5248 (last viewed Sept. 29, 2008).

10. *Id.*

11. Adam Nossiter, *After Fanfare, Hurricane Grants Leave Little Mark*,
N.Y. TIMES, Aug. 30, 2008, at A23.

sponse efforts, destroy trust in government during a time of crisis, and create further chaos and civil unrest. For instance, Hurricane Katrina response efforts were hampered by a dispute over the federal government's role in leading response efforts and by its belief that it did not have the authority to deploy troops to restore order in Louisiana without the governor's permission.[12] The resulting delay in full deployment of federal resources contributed to the lawlessness that plagued New Orleans in the immediate aftermath of the hurricane and extended the period of time during which evacuees were forced to endure the "barbaric and subhuman conditions" at the New Orleans Superdome and Convention Center.[13]

This chapter will provide an overview of the statutory and constitutional authority for state and federal response to emergencies, including a description of typical state emergency management statutes, a summary of the major federal statutes related to public health emergency response, and a discussion of the constitutional limits on federal actions during a public health emergency.

STATE AUTHORITY DURING PUBLIC HEALTH EMERGENCIES

The authority to respond to public health emergencies is primarily vested with the states and is derived from the police powers reserved to them by the Tenth Amendment. The police power is the "power inherent in the state to prescribe within the limits of the federal and state constitutions reasonable regulations necessary to preserve the public order, health, safety or morals."[14] For both constitutional and practical reasons, the U.S. Department of Homeland Security's National Response Framework (NRF) reiterates the importance of the states in emergency response, emphasiz-

---

12. *See* Michael Greenberger, *Did the Founding Fathers Do "A Heckuva Job"? Constitutional Authorization for the Use of Federal Troops to Prevent the Loss of a Major American City*, 87 B.U. L. REV. 397 (2007); Eric Lipton, et al., *Political Issues Snarled Plans for Troop Aid*, N.Y. TIMES, Sept. 9, 2005, at A1; Susan B. Glasser & Michael Grunwald, *The Steady Buildup to a City's Chaos: Confusion Reigned at Every Level of Government*, WASH. POST, Sept. 11, 2005, at A1.

13. Greenberger, *supra* note 12, at 403–04.

14. Tighe v. Osborne, 149 Md. 349, 356 (1925).

ing that emergencies should be managed at the lowest jurisdictional level possible.[15]

In the exercise of their police powers, states generally grant governors, state health officers, boards of health, and other state and local officials and agencies broad powers to prepare for and respond to public health emergencies. Powers utilized during public health emergencies are most often granted by emergency management and civil defense statutes, and public health statutes relating to communicable disease control.[16] While the exercise of these powers during an emergency is rarely challenged in court, it is usually upheld, both because of judicial reluctance to interfere with actions taken to respond to the exigencies of an emergency and because of the traditional latitude that states are given in the exercise of their police powers.[17]

Emergency Management and Civil Defense Statutes

Although emergencies are rare events in the popular imagination, they are actually declared quite often. In 2007, the Federal Emergency Management Agency (FEMA) declared 63 major disasters at the request of state governors for events ranging from floods to wildfires,[18] a figure that does not include any local or state emergencies that did not reach the level of major disasters. State and local officials respond to those emergencies using the authorities and structures created by laws that are variously referred to as "emergency management," "civil defense," or "emergency

---

15. U.S. Dep't of Homeland Sec., National Response Framework 10 (January 2008), *available at* http://www.fema.gov/pdf/emergency/nrf/nrf-core.pdf (last viewed Sept. 29, 2008).

16. State constitutions also generally designate their respective governors as commanders-in-chief of their state militias (*see, e.g.,* Md. Const. art. 2, § 8; Cal. Const. art. 5, § 7). This power is not discussed in this chapter because the commander-in-chief power is virtually indistinguishable from the various statutory powers granted to the governor, which include the authority to use the state militia for public health emergency response activities.

17. *See* United Haulers Ass'n, Inc. v. Oneida-Herkimer Solid Waste Mgmt. Auth., 127 S. Ct. 1786, 1795 (2007) (noting that "[t]he States traditionally have had great latitude under their police powers to legislate as to the protection of the lives, limbs, health, comfort, and quiet of all persons.")) (internal citations omitted).

18. Fed. Emergency Mgmt. Agency (FEMA), Disaster Information Web site, http://www.fema.gov/news/disasters.fema?year=2007 (last viewed Sept. 29, 2008).

powers" statutes. These laws authorize various state and local officials, usually the governor and the chief executive officers of localities, to declare states of emergency, deploy resources, and expend funds for emergency response efforts, order evacuations, and take a variety of other extraordinary actions (including, in some states, suspending the effect of statutes) as necessary to effectively respond to and terminate the emergency. The details vary from state to state, but Maryland's laws are representative of national norms.

Similar to other states, the Maryland Emergency Management Agency (MEMA) Act[19] defines emergencies broadly as the threat or occurrence of:

> (1) a hurricane, tornado, storm, flood, high water, wind-driven water, tidal wave, earthquake, landslide, mudslide, snowstorm, drought, fire, explosion, and any other disaster in any part of the State that requires State assistance to supplement local efforts in order to save lives and protect public health and safety; or (2) an enemy attack, act of terrorism, or public health catastrophe.[20]

The scope of the governor's power after declaring a state of emergency is similarly broad. Under the MEMA Act, the governor may, "in order to protect the public health, welfare, or safety":

- Suspend any statute, rule, or regulation of a state agency or of a political subdivision;
- Compel and control the evacuation of an affected area;
- Control entry to and exit from an emergency area;
- Control movement of people and occupancy of buildings in an affected area;
- Authorize the use of private property for emergency response efforts;

---

19. MD. CODE ANN., PUB. SAFETY §§ 14-101 through 14-115 (West 2003 & Supp. 2006).

20. *Id.* § 14-101(c) (West 2003 & Supp. 2006). For a similarly broad definition, see N.Y. McKINNEY'S EXEC. LAW § 20(2)(a) (defining a disaster as the "occurrence or imminent threat of widespread or severe damage, injury, or loss of life or property resulting from any natural or man-made causes, including, but not limited to, fire, flood, earthquake, hurricane, tornado, high water, landslide, mudslide, wind, storm, wave action, volcanic activity, epidemic, air contamination, blight, drought, infestation, explosion, radiological accident, water contamination, bridge failure or bridge collapse.").

- Provide for temporary housing; and
- Authorize the clearance and removal of debris and wreckage.[21]

The Governor's Emergency Powers subtitle, which predates the MEMA Act, grants the governor additional authority to "promulgate reasonable orders, rules, or regulations that the Governor considers necessary to protect life and property or calculated effectively to control and terminate the public emergency . . ." including, but not limited to, orders that:

- Control places of public assembly and amusement;
- Establish curfews;
- Control the sale, transportation and use of alcohol; and
- Control the possession, sale, carrying, and use of dangerous weapons and explosives.[22]

The breadth of powers granted by such statutes is what makes them so useful for state officials facing unpredictable crises. For instance, the authority to control public gatherings and movement in an affected area is particularly useful to deter transmission of infectious disease during an epidemic or to control civil unrest and looting.

The power to suspend statutes or regulations is one of the most sweeping powers that states can grant. This power can be used to create temporary ad hoc emergency exceptions to statutes that, for instance, impose strict deadlines for court proceedings, limit the scope of practice of healthcare professionals, or bar out-of-state professionals from providing services. Although several states grant this power to their governors,[23] it has rarely been challenged in court.[24]

---

21. MD. CODE ANN., PUB. SAFETY § 14-107(d)(1)(i)–(vii).

22. ID. § 14-303(b). The statute requires that the governor declare a state of emergency, but it is not clear whether the declaration must be made under the subtitle (which provides for declarations of "public emergencies" and "energy emergencies") or can be made under any of the statutes authorizing declarations of emergency. A "public emergency" under the subtitle is defined with similar breadth as an "emergency" under the MEMA Act. See MD. CODE ANN., PUB. SAFETY § 14-301(c) (defining public emergency as, among other things, "a crisis, disaster, riot, or catastrophe").

23. See, e.g., N.Y. MCKINNEY'S EXEC. LAW § 29-a.

24. Although a smattering of cases mention the power, there are very few that make a holding as to its validity. Those that exist tend to be trial court cases. See, e.g., People v. Haneiph, 191 Misc. 2d 738, 745 N.Y.S.2d 405 (N.Y.C. Crim. Ct., 2002) (upholding the validity of an order suspending the effect of the "speedy trial" statute, pursuant to the governor's statutory authority to

Procedural requirements for issuing orders and declaration under emergency management statutes are typically minimal. Many statutes impose time limits on orders and declarations but permit renewal for successive periods for as long as the emergency continues.[25] Some require presentation of orders and declarations to the state legislature, which can be given a legislative veto.[26] For the most part, however, there are few checks on the executive's power during a state of emergency, which, while it allows quick and decisive action, does pose a legitimate concern for civil liberties advocates.

Public Health Emergency Statutes

Emergency management and civil defense statutes are designed to be broad and flexible. However, they do not provide sufficient authority for the measures needed to prepare for and respond to public health emergencies caused by communicable diseases and conditions. Surveillance, compelled medical testing and treatment, quarantine and isolation, and testing and decontamination of contaminated property are traditional tools used to control infectious disease. Power to mandate these and other public health tactics derives both from long-standing public health laws and regulations and from more recently enacted legislation based on the Model State Emergency Health Powers Act.[27]

State and local health officers and boards of health have long used the aforementioned techniques to control infectious disease. In addition to quarantine (the separation of healthy individuals suspected of expo-

---

"temporarily suspend the specific provisions of any statute" if compliance with the provision would "prevent, hinder, or delay action necessary to cope with the disaster.").

25. *See, e.g.*, MD. CODE ANN., PUB. SAFETY § 14-107(a)(3) (describing the 30-day time limit for declarations of states of emergency, with successive 30-day extensions permitted); N.Y. MCKINNEY'S EXEC. LAW § 29a(2)(a) (limiting the duration of an order suspending a law to 30 days, with successive 30-day extensions permitted).

26. *See, e.g.*, MD. CODE ANN., PUB. SAFETY § 14-107(a)(4) (permitting the General Assembly to cancel a declaration of state of emergency by joint resolution).

27. The Model State Emergency Health Powers Act (*available at* http://www.publichealthlaw.net/MSEHPA/MSEHPA.pdf (last viewed Sept. 30, 2008)) has become integrated into the Turning Point Model State Public Health Act (*available at* http://www.turningpointprogram.org/Pages/pdfs/statute_mod/MSPHAfinal.pdf (last viewed Sept. 30, 2008)).

sure to infectious disease from unexposed individuals) and isolation (the separation of infected individuals from those unexposed), authorities sought to prevent and mitigate outbreaks of disease by, for example, requiring immunization for smallpox,[28] the wearing of masks in public during the Spanish flu pandemic,[29] and destruction of tubercular cattle.[30] The laws authorizing these actions remain on the books in many states, but they often fail to take into account either the scientific advances of the last century or the contemporary legal norms for protection of individual rights.[31]

To correct this deficiency and help states improve their preparedness to respond to emerging public health threats, the Model State Emergency Health Powers Act (MSEHPA) was developed in the wake of September 11 and the anthrax attacks.[32] Since then, at least 38 states have adopted the MSEHPA in whole or in part.[33] Because most have adopted only partial or modified versions of the act, it is most useful to use the Maryland law enacted based on the Model Act as an exemplar of a modernized statute for responding to public health emergencies.

The Maryland Catastrophic Health Emergencies (CHE) Act grants the governor, the secretary of health and mental hygiene (Maryland's state health officer), and their designees several powers to detect, prepare for, and respond to a catastrophic health emergency, defined as "a situation in which extensive loss of life or serious disability is threatened imminently because of exposure to a deadly agent."[34] The powers granted by the CHE Act can be exercised only with respect to conditions caused by "deadly agents," defined as any chemical agent, level of radiation, or

---

28. Jacobson v. Commonwealth of Mass., 197 U.S. 11 (1905) (upholding compulsory smallpox vaccination).

29. CROSBY, *supra* note 1, at 102.

30. Kroplin v. Truax, 119 Ohio St. 610 (1929).

31. Lawrence O. Gostin, et al., *The Model State Emergency Health Powers Act: Planning for and Response to Bioterrorism and Naturally Occurring Infectious Diseases*, 288:5 JAMA 622, 623 (August 2002).

32. JAMES G. HODGE, JR. & LAWRENCE O. GOSTIN, THE MODEL STATE EMERGENCY HEALTH POWERS ACT—A BRIEF COMMENTARY (January 2002), *available at* http://www.publichealthlaw.net/MSEHPA/Center%20MSEHPA%20Commentary.pdf (last viewed Sept. 30, 2008).

33. The Center for Law and the Public Health, Model State Emergency Health Powers Act Web site, http://www.publichealthlaw.net/ModelLaws/MSEHPA.php (last viewed Sept. 30, 2008).

34. MD. CODE ANN., PUB. SAFETY § 14-3A-02(a).

biological toxin or agent capable of causing extensive loss of life or serious disability.[35] Some states, following the definition of public health emergency found in the Model Act,[36] apply different limits; Minnesota, for instance, limits the applicability of many statutory provisions to diseases caused by bioterrorism or new, novel, or previously controlled or eradicated communicable diseases.[37]

Power to Seize and Control Property

The declaration of a CHE triggers sweeping powers to control property and persons. To ensure that the state possesses and can efficiently allocate resources and supplies needed to control the disease or outbreak, the governor may order the secretary or other official to:

- seize anything needed to respond to the medical consequences of the emergency;
- designate and gain access to a facility needed to respond to the emergency, after working collaboratively with health-care providers to the extent feasible; and
- regulate the use, sale, dispensing, and transportation of anything needed to respond to the medical consequences of the emergency, including using:

---

35. *Id.* § 14-3A-02(c).

36. Model State Public Health Act § 1-102 (45) (see *supra* note 27):

Public health emergency means an occurrence or imminent threat of an illness or health condition that: (a) is believed to be caused by any of the following: (i) bioterrorism; (ii) the appearance of a novel or previously controlled or eradicated infectious agent or biological toxin; or (iii) a natural disaster, a chemical attack or accidental release, or a nuclear attack or accident; and (b) poses a high probability of any of the following harms: (i) a large number of deaths in the affected population; (ii) a large number of serious or long-term disabilities in the affected population; or (iii) widespread exposure to an infectious or toxic agent that poses a significant risk of substantial future harm to a large number of people in the affected population.

37. MINN. STAT. ANN. § 144.419. The statute limits the definition of communicable disease to diseases "caused by a living organism or virus and believed to be caused by bioterrorism or a new or novel or previously controlled or eradicated infectious agent or biological toxin that can be transmitted person to person and for which isolation or quarantine is an effective control strategy . . . ." *Id.* at § 144.419(1)(a)(2).

- rationing;
- stockpiles;
- shipment prohibitions;
- price controls; and
- any other appropriate action.[38]

These provisions are less expansive than those in the Model Act dealing with control of property during an emergency. The Model Act does not, for instance, require collaboration with health-care providers before using their facilities.[39] These powers would be useful during, for instance, an influenza pandemic, when medical supplies would likely be in short supply and health-care facilities overwhelmed with both the sick and the worried well. Rationing and otherwise controlling distribution of medicines and other supplies could prevent hoarding and price gouging. Designating ambulatory care centers as medical "surge" sites would allow state officials to ease the pressure on hospitals and emergency rooms.

Power to Control and Utilize Health-Care Providers

To complement the power to commandeer supplies and facilities for the purpose of managing the medical consequences of an emergency, the Maryland CHE Act also authorizes the governor to "order any health care provider, who does not voluntarily participate, to participate in disease surveillance, treatment, and suppression efforts or otherwise comply with the directives of the Secretary or other designated official" during a declared CHE.[40] Whether or not a CHE has been declared, the secretary has the authority to require health-care providers to develop and implement emergency plans[41] and to assist in surveillance and investigations related to deadly agents by providing information, making regular reports, and providing the secretary access to facilities that may have been exposed to deadly agents.[42] The statute defines "health care provider" to include both individual health-care practitioners and health-care facilities.[43]

---

38. MD. CODE ANN., PUB. SAFETY § 14-3A-03(b)(1)&(2).
39. Model State Public Health Act § 6-103(a)(3) (*see supra* note 27).
40. MD. CODE ANN., PUB. SAFETY § 14-3A-03(c).
41. MD. CODE ANN., HEALTH-GEN. § 18-903.
42. *ID.* § 18-904(b).
43. MD. CODE ANN., PUB. SAFETY § 14-3A-01(e); MD. CODE ANN., HEALTH-GEN. § 18-901(g).

In addition to being subject to conviction of a misdemeanor for violating an order under the statute,[44] an individual health practitioner who defies an order issued by the secretary may face punishment by his licensing board, including suspension or revocation of his license and a civil fine.[45] The Model Act grants state and local health officials even greater authority over health-care providers during a public health emergency, allowing the officials to require providers to "assist in the performance of vaccination, treatment, examination, testing, decontamination, quarantine, or isolation of any individual as a condition of licensure . . . ."[46] The "stick" of mandatory participation in response efforts is accompanied by an important "carrot" in both the Maryland statute and the Model Act: health-care providers are immune from civil liability for acts done in good faith or without gross negligence or willful misconduct when attempting to comply with orders promulgated pursuant to the statute.[47]

Quarantine, Isolation, and Compelled Medical Testing and Treatment

Finally, both the Model Act and the Maryland CHE Act authorize compelled medical testing and treatment, immunizations, and quarantine and isolation. The Maryland Act generally requires that these steps be "medically necessary and reasonable to treat, prevent, or reduce the spread" of a disease caused by a "deadly agent,"[48] although the secretary may order an individual to undergo "appropriate and necessary" medical evaluation and treatment if he has "reason to believe" that the individual has been

---

44. MD. CODE ANN., PUB. SAFETY § 14-3A-08 (violations of governor's orders); MD. CODE ANN., HEALTH-GEN. § 18-907(a) (violations of secretary's orders).

45. MD. CODE ANN., HEALTH-GEN. § 18-907(c).

46. Model State Public Health Act § 6-104(d)(1) (*see supra* note 27).

47. MD. CODE ANN., PUB. SAFETY § 14-3A-06 (civil and criminal immunity for acts in good faith under a CHE proclamation); MD. CODE ANN., HEALTH-GEN. § 18-907(d) (immunity for acts in good faith while attempting to comply with the CHE Act, so long as there is no willful misconduct); Model State Public Health Act § 6-105(b) (*see supra* note 27) (immunity for actions under the direction of the state during a public health emergency, so long as there is no gross negligence or willful misconduct).

48. MD. CODE ANN., PUB. SAFETY § 14-3A-03(b)(3) (governor's power to order the secretary to issue orders during a CHE); MD. CODE ANN., HEALTH-GEN. § 18-905(a)(1)(ii) (secretary's power to order quarantine on his own initiative).

exposed to a deadly agent.[49] In Maryland, these powers may be utilized by the secretary even when there has been no CHE declaration if the secretary determines that the disease can be medically contained without a declaration.[50] The Model Act grants even greater power, permitting state and local public health agencies to compel medical examination, treatment, quarantine, and isolation of individuals who have been or may have been exposed to a contagious disease that poses a "significant risk or danger to others or the public's health[,]"[51] although the action must be the least restrictive means of protecting the public health and safety.[52]

The Model Act and state statutes based upon it took modern, post–*Goldberg v. Kelly*[53] due process jurisprudence into account when drafting the provisions relating to quarantine and isolation orders. Under both the Maryland CHE Act and the Model Act, individuals are entitled to appointed counsel and expedited review of the validity of a quarantine order.[54] The acts also allow hearings to be conducted without the personal presence of affected individuals who are unable to appear, as long as either their authorized representative can appear or the hearing is conducted by a means (such as videoconferencing) that allows the individual to fully participate.[55]

---

49. MD. CODE ANN., HEALTH-GEN. § 18-905(a)(1)(i).

50. *Id.* § 18-905(b)(1).

51. Model State Public Health Act § 5-101(b)(4) (see *supra* note 27). The breadth of this authority has been criticized because it could, according to some interpretations, include mandatory testing, treatment, quarantine, and isolation for such diseases as seasonal influenza or HIV (*see., e.g.*, George Annas, *Blinded by Terrorism: Public Health and Liberty in the 21st Century*, 87 HEALTH MATRIX 33, 51–52 (2003).

52. Model State Public Health Act § 5-106 (c) (referring to mandatory testing and examination) (*see supra* note 27). *See also* Model State Public Health Act § 5-107(b) (referring to mandatory treatment) and § 5-108 (referring to quarantine and isolation).

53. 397 U.S. 254 (1970).

54. MD. CODE ANN., PUB. SAFETY § 14-3A-05(c)(3) (requiring that a hearing be held within 3 days of the individual filing a request) and (f)(2) (requiring the court to appoint counsel for individuals not represented by counsel); Model State Public Health Act § 5-108(f)(1) (requiring courts to rule on applications for relief within 48 hours and to hold hearings related to breaches of conditions of quarantine within 5 days) and (4) (requiring courts to appoint counsel at government expense).

55. MD. CODE ANN., PUB. SAFETY § 14-3A-05(e); Model State Public Health Act § 5-108(f)(3).

The Maryland Act and the Model Act differ in one important respect: the Maryland Act does not contemplate a role for the courts unless an affected individual chooses to exercise her right to appeal the quarantine order,[56] while the Model Act requires that quarantine orders either be issued by a court or, if a temporary order is permitted, be confirmed by a court within 10 days of issuance after notice and opportunity for the affected individuals to participate.[57] Although a detailed discussion of the constitutional due process requirements that might apply to quarantine and isolation is outside the scope of this chapter, it should be noted that the nineteenth- and early twentieth-century cases addressing the constitutionality of quarantines do not require such a pre-quarantine process.[58] However, as previously mentioned, these decisions predate contemporary due process jurisprudence, and several states have chosen to adopt the Model Act framework for quarantine orders.[59]

FEDERAL AUTHORITY DURING PUBLIC HEALTH EMERGENCIES

Congress has enacted several statutes authorizing the federal government to assist with, and sometimes assume operational control over, emergency response and prevention efforts. These include:

- The Robert T. Stafford Disaster Relief and Emergency Assistance Act of 1974 (the Stafford Act), which authorizes the federal government to provide assistance to states and individuals

---

56. *See* MD. CODE ANN., PUB. SAFETY § 14-3A-05(a) & (b); MD. CODE ANN., HEALTH-GEN. § 18-905 & § 18906(a). The Maryland Act provides that the secretary (or other official) issue a quarantine directive and does not require the state to seek court approval either before or after the order is issued.

57. Model State Public Health Act § 5-108(d) (temporary orders may be issued by the public health agency if "delay in imposing the isolation or quarantine would significantly jeopardize the agency's ability to prevent or limit the transmission of a contagious or possibly contagious disease to others[']," but a court must authorize continued quarantine or isolation within 10 days) & (e) (requiring the public health agency to petition the court for a quarantine or isolation order in all other circumstances).

58. *See, e.g.*, Compagnie Francaise de Navigation a Vapeur v. Bd. of Health of State of Louisiana, 186 U.S. 380 (1902).

59. *See, e.g.*, 20 DEL. CODE REGS. § 3136(5).

during emergencies after a governor declares a state of emergency and requests assistance from the federal government;[60]

- The Homeland Security Act of 2002, vesting the Department of Homeland Security with authority over most federal disaster preparedness and response activities;[61]
- The Insurrection Act, authorizing deployment of active military for domestic law enforcement purposes to suppress insurrections and enforce federal laws;[62]
- The Pandemic and All Hazards Preparedness Act of 2006, vesting the Department of Health and Human Services with authority over public health emergency preparedness and response activities;[63]
- The Public Health Act, authorizing the Secretary of Health and Human Services to declare, prepare for, and provide assistance in responding to and preparing for public health emergencies (including disease outbreaks and bioterrorism);[64] and
- 42 U.S.C.A. § 264, authorizing the Surgeon General to make and enforce regulations, including quarantines, necessary to prevent the introduction or spread of transmission of communicable disease from foreign countries into the United States or between the states.

Despite the variety of statutes that authorize federal emergency response activities, the scope of the federal government's public health emergency powers is less expansive than that of the states. The federal government does have authority under the statutes listed above to provide virtually any type of assistance, including deploying military personnel for law enforcement purposes, to a state upon request by the state's governor. However, the federal power to deploy resources or assume operational control of response efforts is circumscribed by statute and the Constitution.

---

60. Pub. L. No. 93-288, 88 Stat. 143 (1974).
61. Pub. L. No. 107-296, 116 Stat. 2135 (2002).
62. 18 U.S.C.A. § 1385.
63. Pub. L. No. 109-417, § 101; 120 Stat. 2831, 2832 (2006).
64. 42 U.S.C.A. §§ 243(c) & 247d.

Posse Comitatus Act, the Insurrection Act, and the Use of Active Duty Military

Because public health emergencies often lead to civil unrest, military resources are sometimes needed to supplement or replace state and local law enforcement. If federal troops are deployed domestically to respond to such an emergency, the United States Northern Command (NORTHCOM) has operational control.[65] NORTHCOM provides command and control of Department of Defense (DoD) efforts and coordinates defense support of civil authorities. As DoD assistance is normally required only during emergencies that exceed the capabilities of local, state, and federal agencies, once the lead responder agency can resume full control of the incident without military assistance, NORTHCOM will relinquish operational control.[66]

The use of military to restore order and enforce the law is among the most controversial steps the government can take during an emergency. The Posse Comitatus Act (PCA), enacted in 1878 in the wake of Reconstruction, prohibits use of the military to enforce domestic law "except in cases and under circumstances expressly authorized by the Constitution or Act of Congress."[67] The PCA's prohibition covers active-duty military, including reservists, and the federalized National Guard,[68] but not the Coast Guard[69] or National Guard units acting under state control.

There are several statutory exceptions to the PCA's general prohibition. First, the Insurrection Act allows the president, even in the absence of a state request, to direct the armed forces and federalized militia to suppress an "insurrection, domestic violence, unlawful combination, or conspiracy" if state or local law enforcement is incapable of protecting individuals or if the problem activity "opposes or obstructs the execution of the laws of the United States or impedes the course of justice under those laws."[70] President George H.W. Bush used the authority to deploy troops at a state's request to suppress domestic violence to respond to the

---

65. U.S. Northern Command, About USNORTHCOM, http://www. northcom.mil/About/index.html (last visited Sept. 14, 2007).

66. *Id.*

67. 18 U.S.C.A. § 1385.

68. *Id.*

69. The Coast Guard is under the control of the Department of Homeland Security, not the Department of Defense. 14 U.S.C.A. § 1.

70. 10 U.S.C.A. § 333 (a)(1)(B)–(a)(2)(A).

1992 Los Angeles riots.[71] President Washington used an early version of the act to suppress the Whiskey Rebellion in 1795, despite the reluctance of Pennsylvania's governor.[72] Finally, President Eisenhower used this authority to deploy federal troops to enforce a desegregation order in Little Rock in 1957.[73]

The Stafford Act also permits deployment of the military for law enforcement purposes during a disaster at the request of an affected state's governor or on the president's own initiative if the disaster affects a subject area over which "the United States exercises exclusive or preeminent responsibility and authority."[74] Additionally, during an emergency involving chemical or biological weapons of mass destruction, the U.S. Attorney General may request direct law enforcement assistance from the Department of Defense when it is "considered necessary for the immediate protection of human life and civilian law enforcement officials are not capable of taking action."[75] These and other statutory exceptions are in addition to the constitutional powers outlined below, which, to the extent they permit the president to deploy military for law enforcement purposes without congressional authorization, are also exceptions to the PCA.

Constitutional Authority for Federal Action during Emergencies

Statutes authorizing the federal government to provide emergency assistance at an affected state's request fall squarely within Congress's Spending Clause authority to tax and spend for the general welfare.[76] However, the unilateral deployment of military or other resources to an affected

---

71. *See* Nicholas Lemann, *Insurrection*, NEW YORKER, Sept. 26, 2005, at 67–68.

72. *See* Papers of George Washington: The Whiskey Insurrection, http://gwpapers.virginia.edu/documents/whiskey/index.html (last visited Apr. 1, 2007) (discussing George Washington's diary entries related to the Whiskey Rebellion). Pennsylvania Governor Thomas Mifflin told President Washington that he "was reluctant to use military forces," but "pledged to cooperate with any action the President decided to take." Jason Mazzone, *The Security Constitution*, 53 UCLA L. REV. 29, 110 (2005).

73. *See* Lemann, *supra* note 71, at 68.

74. 42 U.S.C.A. § 5191(b).

75. 10 U.S.C.A. § 302(d)(2)(B)(i).

76. U.S. CONST. art. I, § 8, cl. 1.

area, imposition of quarantines by the Surgeon General,[77] or conditions placed on the assistance provided may invite challenges to the federal government's constitutional authority to assume control of matters traditionally left to the states. Authority for such potentially controversial federal actions is based primarily on the Commerce Clause, the Insurrection Clause, the Guarantee Clause, the Necessary and Proper Clause, and the Spending Clause.

Commerce Clause

The Commerce Clause affords Congress the power "[t]o regulate Commerce with foreign Nations, and among the several States, and with Indian Tribes."[78] The Supreme Court has long held that the Commerce Clause permits Congress to "regulate and protect the instrumentalities of interstate commerce or persons or things in interstate commerce[.]"[79] The Commerce Clause thus provides the primary authority for federal quarantine regulations, which permit the Surgeon General to detain individuals to prevent the spread of communicable disease from foreign countries into the United States or among the states,[80] and other statutes authorizing the federal government to directly control channels of interstate commerce or persons or things in interstate commerce during a disaster.

The Commerce Clause justifies unilateral federal intervention even when an event is not so directly tied to commerce. Some public health law scholars have argued that recent jurisprudence has significantly limited Congress's power to intrude on the state's traditional police powers.[81] It is true that since the Supreme Court held in *United States v. Lopez* that Congress only had the power to regulate "those activities that substantially affect interstate commerce,"[82] courts have evaluated legisla-

---

77. *See* 42 U.S.C.A. § 264 (granting the Surgeon General authority to apprehend, detain, or conditionally release individuals to prevent the spread of communicable disease from foreign countries into the U.S. or from one state or U.S. possession to another).

78. U.S. CONST. art. I, § 8, cl. 3.

79. Pierce County, Wash. v. Guillen, 537 U.S. 129, 147 (2003) (quoting United States v. Lopez, 524 U.S. 549, 558 (1995)). *See also Shreveport Rate Cases*, 234 U.S. 342 (1914) and Southern Ry. Co. v. United States, 222 U.S. 20 (1911).

80. 42 U.S.C.A. § 264.

81. *See, e.g.*, Lawrence O. Gostin, *Public Health Theory and Practice in the Constitutional Design*, 11 HEALTH MATRIX 265, 289–90 (2001).

82. United States v. Lopez, 514 U.S. 549, 559 (1995).

tion touching on areas within the states' traditional police powers more rigorously.[83] However, the devastating economic impact of public health emergencies is almost never limited to the affected state. For example, the terrorist attacks of September 11 cost the nation's businesses, including airlines, insurers, and others, billions of dollars and cost tens of thousands of workers their jobs.[84] More recently, Hurricane Katrina caused $100 billion of property damage in several states, sent thousands of victims across state borders, and seriously disrupted oil production and refining.[85] Even under the stricter Commerce Clause jurisprudence that has emerged in recent years, statutes authorizing unilateral federal action during catastrophic emergencies easily meet the standard of regulating activities that "substantially affect" interstate commerce.

Moreover, *Gonzales v. Raich*[86] strongly suggests that major public health emergencies would be deemed to affect interstate commerce substantially enough to justify unilateral federal intervention even if the immediate emergency itself was confined to one state. In *Raich*, the Supreme Court ruled that Congress, through the Controlled Substance Act,[87] could regulate intrastate commerce in the growth, distribution, and sale of marijuana for medicinal purposes and preempt state legislation supporting such commerce, because the production in question affected interstate commerce by endangering the nation's public health.[88] In so ruling, the majority rejected the argument that this exercise of Commerce Clause authority "encroached on the States' traditional police powers to . . . protect the health, safety, and welfare of their citizens."[89] Considering *Raich*'s confirmation of federal authority over state regulation of even purely local activities if they could have a substantial effect on interstate commerce by endangering public health, unilateral federal response to any major emergency is likely to be considered a proper exercise of Congress's authority.

---

83. *See, e.g.*, United States v. Morrison, 529 U.S. 598 (2000). *See also* ERWIN CHEMERINSKY, CONSTITUTIONAL LAW: PRINCIPLES AND POLICIES § 3.3.5 (3d ed. 2006).

84. GAIL MAKINEN, CONGRESSIONAL RESEARCH SERVICE, THE ECONOMIC EFFECTS OF 9/11: A RETROSPECTIVE ASSESSMENT (2002), http://www/fas/org/irp/crs/RL31617.pdf (last viewed Oct. 2, 2008).

85. Greenberger, *supra* note 12, at 402 (2007).

86. Gonzales v. Raich, 545 U.S. 1 (2005).

87. 21 U.S.C.A. §§ 801–802, 811–814, 821–830, 841–844(a), 846–853, 854–865, 871–881, 882–887, 889–904.

88. *Raich*, 545 U.S. at 29–32.

89. *Id.* at 66 (Thomas, J., dissenting).

Insurrection Clause

The Insurrection Clause authorizes Congress "[t]o provide for calling forth the Militia to execute the Laws of the Union, to suppress Insurrections, and repel Invasions."[90] As the name suggests, this is a primary source of authority for the Insurrection Act. Along with the Guarantee Clause (discussed *infra*), the Insurrection Clause has its roots in the Founding Fathers' concern with the safety and democratic stability of state governments.[91] Shays Rebellion in 1787, an insurrection against Massachusetts's high taxes, stoked this concern and exposed the flaws in the Articles of Confederation that prevented Massachusetts from being able to rely on either a federal government or its fellow states for support.[92] A few years after the Constitution was ratified, Congress used its authority under the Insurrection Clause to enact the Insurrection Act of 1792. As has been discussed, various versions of the act have been used to suppress insurrection and riots, enforce federal laws, and protect citizens' civil rights, both with and without states' consent. A public health emergency that causes widespread lawlessness, as occurred in New Orleans during Hurricane Katrina,[93] means that state and local governments are unable to protect the basic civil rights of their citizens or enforce federal law. Even without the affected state's consent, congressionally authorized unilateral federal action would be permissible under the Insurrection Clause to enforce federal law.

Guarantee of a Republican Form of Government Clause

The Guarantee Clause provides that "[t]he United States shall guarantee to every State in this Union a Republican Form of Government, and shall protect each of them against invasion; and on Application of the Legislature, or of the Executive (when the Legislature cannot be convened) against domestic Violence."[94] Along with the Insurrection Clause, it is a primary source of authority for the Insurrection Act. Like the Insurrection Clause, the Guarantee Clause has its roots in the turbulent post-

---

90. U.S. CONST. art. I, § 8, cl. 15.
91. Greenberger, *supra* note 12, at 417 (2007).
92. For discussion of Shays Rebellion and the restive political environment before and after ratification of the Constitution, see Greenberger, *supra* note 12, at 417 (2007) and Jason Mazzone, *The Security Constitution*, 53 UCLA L. REV. 29, 47–50 (2005).
93. Greenberger, *supra* note 12, at 403–04 (2007).
94. U.S. CONST. art. IV, § 4.

Revolutionary environment.[95] However, unlike the Insurrection Clause, the Guarantee Clause imposes an affirmative duty on the federal government to act. Neither the duty nor the power it creates is confined to a particular branch of government, indicating that it confers authority on both Congress and the president.

The scope of the Guarantee Clause authority is untested, but it is noteworthy that President Lincoln based his authority for taking military action against the South during the Civil War on the Guarantee Clause rather than on his war powers.[96] The complete breakdown of orderly government services within a state during a public health emergency may trigger the Guarantee Clause, because such a breakdown deprives citizens of the benefits and protection of a republican form of government. Even in the absence of express congressional authorization, the president may be within his constitutional powers to unilaterally deploy troops and authorize other federal action to restore a republican form of government.

Necessary and Proper Clause

The Necessary and Proper Clause provides Congress the power "[t]o make all Laws which shall be necessary and proper for carrying into Execution the foregoing Powers [in Article I], and all other Powers vested by the Constitution in the Government of the United States, or in any Department or Officer thereof."[97] This power is important to regulation of local, non-economic activity incidental to Congress's power under the Commerce Clause. For instance, the majority opinion in *Raich* rested in part on the Necessary and Proper Clause.[98] Justice Scalia's concurrence stressed this, stating that "Congress's regulatory authority over intrastate activities that are not themselves part of interstate commerce (including activities that have a substantial effect on interstate commerce) derives from the Necessary and Proper Clause."[99] According to Justice Scalia, inasmuch as local production, sale, and use of marijuana could undermine the prohibition on interstate commerce in marijuana, Congress had the power to regulate it.[100]

---

95. *See* Jonathon Toren, *Protecting Republican Government from Itself: The Guarantee Clause of Article IV, Section 4*, 2 N.Y.U. J. L. & LIBERTY 371, 374–92 (2007).

96. RONALD D. ROTUNDA & JOHN E. NOWAK, TREATISE ON CONSTITUTIONAL LAW: SUBSTANCE AND PROCEDURE (FOURTH) § 3.4(d) (2007).

97. U.S. CONST. art. I, § 8, cl. 18.

98. *Raich*, 545 U.S. at 24.

99. *Id.* at 34 (Scalia, J., concurring).

100. *Id.* at 42 (Scalia, J., concurring).

The reasoning in both the majority and concurring opinions in *Raich* indicate that the Necessary and Proper Clause is a proper basis to legislate on matters that, while not squarely within a subject matter covered by its other constitutional authorities, are nevertheless necessary to exercise the federal government's constitutional powers effectively.

Spending Clause

The Spending Clause authorizes Congress to tax and spend for the general welfare.[101] As mentioned above, many of the statutes authorizing disaster relief to the states are exercises of this power. These statutes generally require a state request in order to trigger federal action, thereby avoiding some of the constitutional challenges associated with unilateral federal actions. However, statutes enacted pursuant to Congress's Spending Clause authority often require states to meet certain standards or take certain actions to be eligible for aid. States may challenge such conditions as congressional overreaching, but they are generally upheld as long as they meet the standard set forth in *South Dakota v. Dole*.[102] Conditions on the provision of funds are a valid exercise of Congress's spending power as long as the conditions (1) are stated clearly; (2) serve the general welfare; (3) are reasonably related to the purpose for which federal funds are being allocated; and (4) do not induce states to violate an independent constitutional bar.[103] Even statutory requirements that states accept increased federal authority over disaster relief efforts in exchange for receiving aid would likely be permissible under this standard.

CONCLUSION

Throughout history, public health emergencies have required swift and flexible responses from all levels of government. State and local governments will continue to take the lead in response, but the federal government has an important constitutional and statutory role in preparing for and responding to emergencies. It is important to understand the range of legal powers and authorities at all levels of government to ensure that these powers are effectively and efficiently utilized during a catastrophic event.

---

101. U.S. Const. art. I, § 8, cl. 1.
102. 483 U.S. 203 (1987).
103. South Dakota v. Dole, 483 U.S. 203, 207–08 (1987).

CHAPTER 3

Understanding the Role of Northern Command in the Defense of the Homeland: The Emerging Legal Framework—Authorities and Challenges

by Lisa L. Turner, Jeanne Meyer, and Harvey Rishikof

United States Northern Command (USNORTHCOM), the first unified geographic combatant command dedicated to protecting and supporting the homeland, has two primary missions: defense of the homeland and support of civil authorities. Following a broad overview of USNORTHCOM's missions and its position within the Department of Defense structure, this chapter briefly examines USNORTHCOM's collaborative work with a broad spectrum of entities in order to fulfill its missions. The chapter then examines in depth some of the particular functional areas in which USNORTHCOM operates, such as support to the Department of Homeland Security and the Federal Emergency Management Agency after a man-made or natural disaster, and support to law enforcement.

The 21st century poses a broad range of threats to, and challenges for, national security that include not only traditional military aggression but also terrorist attacks and natural disasters. In 2002, in recognition of these challenges, the Department of Defense (DoD) established United States Northern Command (USNORTHCOM), the first unified geographic combatant command[1] dedicated to protecting and supporting the homeland. USNORTHCOM has two primary missions: defense of the homeland and support of civil authorities. Although consolidation of these two missions under one unified command is new, the missions themselves, and the legal authorities supporting the missions, are not. Rather, the authorities trace their roots back to the birth of our nation. The challenge for USNORTHCOM is how to accomplish its assigned missions in accordance with an extremely complex and ever-changing political and legal environment. This chapter provides a broad overview of USNORTHCOM's missions and its position within the larger unified combatant command structure. It will then take a brief look at USNORTHCOM's work with a broad spectrum of entities to fulfill its missions. Finally, it will examine some particular functional areas in which USNORTHCOM operates.

UNIFIED COMBATANT COMMANDS AND USNORTHCOM

USNORTHCOM is one of 10 unified combatant commands within the United States military. Unified combatant commands were created through 10 U.S. Code section 161, "Combatant commands; establishment," which directs the president, with the advice of the chairman of the joint chiefs of staff, to establish unified combatant commands and prescribe the forces of those commands. That statute defines a unified combatant command as a "military command which has broad, continuing missions and which is composed of forces from two or more military departments." Unified

---

1. A "unified command," also called a "unified combatant command," is a command with a broad continuing mission under a single commander and composed of significant assigned components of two or more military departments that is established and so designated by the president, through the secretary of defense, with the advice and assistance of the chairman of the joint chiefs of staff. Some of the commands, such as USNORTHCOM, are oriented along geographic lines. Other unified commands are oriented along functional lines, such as U.S. Transportation Command. JOINT PUBLICATION 1-02, DOD DICTIONARY FOR MILITARY AND ASSOCIATED TERMS.

combatant commands conduct U.S. military operations while the military services organize, train, and equip the force.

Unified combatant commands are governed by the Unified Command Plan (UCP), a regularly revised and updated document produced by the DoD for presidential approval. The UCP provides unified combatant commanders with basic guidance and establishes unified combatant command missions, responsibilities, and force structure. For geographic commands, the UCP delineates the area of responsibility (AOR); for functional commands, it specifies functional responsibilities.[2] The first UCP was approved by the president of the United States on December 14, 1946, and has been repeatedly updated and changed since that time.[3]

USNORTHCOM was established on April 25, 2002, when President Bush approved a revised UCP.[4] As a geographic unified command, USNORTHCOM's AOR includes the continental United States, Alaska, Canada, Mexico, and the surrounding water out to approximately 500 nautical miles. The Gulf of Mexico and Straits of Florida are included as well. The December 2008 UCP expanded the AOR to include the U.S. Virgin Islands, Puerto Rico (VI/PR), the Bahamas, and the Turks and Caicos. The U.S. Pacific Command has responsibility for the defense of, and civil support to, Hawaii and U.S. territories and possessions in the Pacific. USNORTHCOM is also responsible for U.S. theater security cooperation with the AOR countries.

Unless otherwise directed by the president, the chain of command to the combatant command runs from the president to the secretary of defense to the commander of the combatant command.[5] Thus, the commander, USNORTHCOM (CDRUSNORTHCOM) is responsible to the

---

2. JOINT PUBLICATION 1-02, DOD DICTIONARY FOR MILITARY AND ASSOCIATED TERMS.

3. *See generally* OFFICE OF THE CHAIRMAN OF THE JOINT CHIEFS OF STAFF, JOINT HISTORY OFFICE, HISTORY OF THE UNIFIED COMMAND PLAN, 1946–1993.

4. USNORTHCOM began operations on Oct. 1, 2002. The headquarters is located at Peterson Air Force Base in Colorado Springs and is co-located with a bi-national command commonly known as NORAD (North American Aerospace Defense Command). CDRUSNORTHCOM also commands NORAD. NORAD grew out of the Cold War era but remains vitally relevant today. In 2008, NORAD celebrated its 50th anniversary of providing aerospace warning and aerospace control for North America. In 2006, the NORAD Agreement was renewed and the mission of maritime warning was added to its responsibilities.

5. 10 U.S.C. §§ 162(b) & 164(b).

president and to the secretary of defense for the performance of USNORTHCOM assigned missions.[6] On behalf of the secretary of defense, policy direction and oversight are primarily provided by the assistant secretary of defense for homeland security and America's security affairs (ASD (HD & ASA)).[7] The president and the secretary of defense normally communicate with the commander of the combatant commands through the chairman of the joint chiefs of staff, who also oversees the activities of the combatant commands.[8]

Unlike other geographic commands, few forces are permanently assigned to USNORTHCOM. Recognizing the sensitivity to a standing military force in the homeland, most forces employed under the command and control of USNORTHCOM are permanently assigned, by the UCP, to Joint Forces Command, a functional unified command. Command and control of those forces are then provided to USNORTHCOM for particular identified missions.[9]

USNORTHCOM's organizational structure consists of a variety of component and subordinate commands. For example, Joint Forces Headquarters National Capital Region (JFHQ-NCR) is responsible for land-based homeland defense, defense support of civil authorities, and incident management in the National Capital Region. Joint Task Force–Civil Support (JTF-CS) provides planning and integration of DoD support to a lead federal agency in the event of domestic chemical, biological, radiological, nuclear, or high-yield explosive (CBRNE) consequence management operations. Joint Task Force–North supports federal law enforcement agencies in their counter-drug, counter-narcoterrorism, and associated threat operations within and along the approaches to the continental United States.

---

6. 10 U.S.C. § 164.

7. A position created by Congress in 2002 in the Bob Stump National Defense Authorization Act for Fiscal Year 2003 (Pub. L. No. 107-314). The assistant secretary of defense (Special Operations and Low-Intensity Conflict & Interdependent Capabilities (ASD (SO/LIC & IC))) has policy oversight for combating terrorism activities and civil support for domestic CBRNE events.

8. 10 U.S.C. § 163.

9. As of Jan. 1, 2009, USNORTHCOM's component and subordinate commands include Joint Forces Headquarters National Capital Region (JFHQ-NCR); Joint Task Force Alaska (JTF-Alaska); Joint Task Force Civil Support (JTF-CS); Joint Task Force North (JTF North); Army North (ARNORTH); Marine Forces North (MARFORNORTH); and Air Force North (AFNORTH). JTF-CS and JTF North were recently realigned under ARNORTH.

USNORTHCOM executes its traditional military defense mission of homeland defense (HD) on behalf of the DoD as lead federal agency on order of the president as commander-in-chief. DoD is rarely, if ever, in the lead for USNORTHCOM's other mission, civil support. A key form of civil support, USNORTHCOM largely provides the specialized military skills and capacity to support a comprehensive national response to a catastrophic event. CDRUSNORTHCOM's civil support vision is to "respond not a minute too soon, or a second too late. In providing defense support of civil authorities, we respond to natural and manmade disasters, save lives, prevent loss and mitigate suffering."[10]

CDRUSNORTHCOM is normally also the commander of NORAD, a bi-national U.S. and Canadian command whose mission is to provide aerospace control and aerospace and maritime warning for North America.[11] The resulting synergies created by bringing USNORTHCOM and NORAD under one commander are readily apparent when one considers the critical homeland defense role played by NORAD. Because of the aerospace warning mission and through agreements with other commands, NORAD monitors the aerospace domain and detects, validates, and alerts the command of actual or potential attacks conducted by aircraft, missiles, or space vehicles. NORAD's aerospace control mission ensures air sovereignty and air defense of Canadian and U.S. airspace. Post-September 11, 2001, NORAD expanded its focus from an outward-looking threat to also include one originating inside North America. Operation Noble Eagle (ONE) provides air sovereignty and defense, including response to terrorist threats of hijacked airliners and threats of attacks from commercial and general aviation. Together, USNORTHCOM and NORAD provide an active, layered defense for America.

UNITY OF EFFORT THROUGH INTERAGENCY AND INTERGOVERNMENTAL COORDINATION

There is much discussion inside the beltway these days about the need for interagency reform. Many current and retired departmental secretaries, ambassadors, four-star generals, and senior civilians have gone on record with their support, in concept, of legislative efforts to enable U.S. federal agencies to work together more effectively for "unity of effort."

---

10. N. Am. Aerospace Defense Command & U.S. Northern Command, Vision 2020, Oct. 1, 2007.

11. *See* note 2.

Because of the nature of the civil support mission, USNORTHCOM was created with a strong interagency structure, processes, and culture. As USNORTHCOM works to anticipate needs and send requests for support from state and local entities, it cultivates relationships through the National Guard Bureau (NGB) with state National Guards to learn the authorities and response plans of the states. USNORTHCOM also has worked diligently to collaborate with interagency partners to create a unity of effort in responding to domestic crises. USNORTHCOM's key operational link to the federal and state response is through a defense coordinating officer (DCO). A DCO is a senior field-grade officer assigned to one of the 10 designated Federal Emergency Management Agency (FEMA) regions. The DCO is the DoD's single point of contact with federal and state agencies responding to the crisis. Among the DCO's primary responsibilities are coordinating, processing, and forwarding requests for military assistance to the appropriate military organizations.

USNORTHCOM's Commander's Joint Interagency Coordination Group (JIACG) serves to integrate and synchronize information regarding the activities and capabilities of numerous military, federal, state, non-governmental, and private-sector organizations. Nearly 40 departments and agencies are represented in this group, including the Department of Homeland Security (DHS), FEMA, Environmental Protection Agency, Customs and Border Protection, Federal Bureau of Investigation, Federal Aviation Administration, and the Department of Health and Human Services (HHS). The legal environment involves a vast array of federal and state agencies and their particular rules and regulations, and can become quite complex.

USNORTHCOM also reaches beyond governmental organizations to the private sector. The JIACG also includes the American Red Cross and various volunteer organizations and commercial entities. The extensive daily coordination and interaction among USNORTHCOM's various partners enables pre-planning and anticipation of potential needs during a crisis. For example, a lesson learned from the Hurricane Katrina response was the value of understanding where major private-donor organizations such as faith-based groups were delivering a particular form of support. Federal authorities can then better determine where remaining needs can be filled. A common saying at USNORTHCOM is that if you are exchanging business cards with your colleagues at a disaster site, it's too late. Valuable time is lost if pre-coordination is not occurring on a continuing basis, before any crisis occurs. Legal issues involve the administrative law arena—for example, ensuring that the government does not provide unfair competitive advantage to one public-sector company, which also contracts with the government, over another company that may want to contract with the government. Acceptance and transportation of gifts from the private sector to the stricken area or to troops supporting relief efforts is another closely regulated area that is often relevant.

FUNCTIONAL AREAS

Homeland Defense. USNORTHCOM and NORAD anticipate, prepare for, plan, and address a variety of homeland defense issues. Much of that analysis and planning is conducted in classified settings. While geography largely protects the United States from kinetic attacks, recent technological developments challenge USNORTHCOM, particularly with regard to weapons of mass destruction and associated delivery systems. An attack by a rogue or hostile nation-state is squarely an HD mission. Although the Department of Homeland Security has a mission focus on asymmetric terrorist threats to the homeland, the president can exercise his authority as commander-in-chief to respond to a terrorist attack in such circumstances as a threat to the existence of the nation. Should this situation arise, DoD could be in the lead, providing command and control of operations through USNORTHCOM. Likewise, the NORAD Operation NOBLE EAGLE mission defending against terrorism in the sky was added to the conventional NORAD mission defending against an outward attack by a nation-state. Since the addition of maritime warning to the NORAD mission in 2006, NORAD and USNORTHCOM have been working to further develop the maritime warning and maritime defense aspects of their respective missions.

   Chemical, Biological, Radiological, Nuclear, and High-Yield Explosives (CBRNE). CBRNE is one area where HD and civil support (CS) missions intersect and overlap. HD would include defense of a nuclear attack from a rogue state—for example, ballistic missile defense. Much of the defense against nuclear weapons is conducted through the U.S. government's foreign affairs strategy, often in the form of the non-proliferation regime. If, on the other hand, a terrorist were to smuggle a weapon of mass destruction into the United States, the DoD could be in a supporting role to the attorney general, specifically the Federal Bureau of Investigation.[12] Efforts to mitigate the consequences of an attack would also be CS, but in support of DHS. Congress directed the creation of a

Civil Support DoD CBRNE response team capable of "detection, neutralization, containment, dismantlement, and disposal of weapons of mass destruction containing [CBRNE]."[13] That legislation was operationalized under USNORTHCOM on October 1, 2008, when the CBRNE Consequence Management Response Force (CCMRF, pronounced "sea-smurf") became assigned to USNORTHCOM. The team provides a range of options for commanders to support civilian authorities, including logistics, medical, and evacuation.

In mid-September 2008, USNORTHCOM, its components, and a CCMRF team participated in an exercise in how it would respond to assist civilian authorities if a 10-kiloton nuclear device were detonated in America's heartland. Military lawyers assisted in training the CCMRF unit prior to the exercise and then participated in the exercise itself. Issues addressed ranged from arming troops to respond in self-defense to determining who has authority to move remains of deceased persons, working with civil authorities in the event civilians refuse decontamination, and identifying the authority of troops to enter buildings in search of injured civilians.

Critical Infrastructure. Critical infrastructure can be both an HD and a CS mission. Critical infrastructure is defined under statute as "systems and assets, whether physical or virtual, so vital to the United States that the incapacity or destruction of such systems and assets would have a debilitating impact on security, national economic security, national public health or safety, or any combination of those matters."[14] Title 6, sections 101, 121–123, and 131–134 also guide critical infrastructure protection (CIP). The *National Strategy for Homeland Security* and *National Strategy for the Physical Protection of Critical Infrastructures and Key Assets*, as well as HSPD-7 and DoD directives, establish CIP policy and direction.

The vast majority of critical infrastructure is owned by the private sector. CIP, particularly of DoD-owned assets, is pertinent to the USNORTHCOM force protection mission. Were the president to designate critical infrastructure for DoD purposes, military forces under the command of USNORTHCOM could be used to protect those assets as an HD mission. The legal point here is that as an HD mission, it would be under the president's commander-in-chief direction, not law enforce-

---

12. 18 U.S.C. § 831.
13. 50 U.S.C. § 2314.
14. 42 U.S.C. § 5195c.

ment, and therefore not restricted by the Posse Comitatus Act (discussed in more detail below). No assets are currently designated as critical infrastructure for defense purposes. However, critical infrastructure is identified for CS mission. USNORTHCOM may be called upon to provide supplies, materials, services, and equipment to mitigate the damage caused by a natural or man-made disaster. For example, when commercial communication systems are disabled, FEMA may request that USNORTHCOM provide communication support such as a closed-loop system, which provides capability for emergency responders and the military to communicate.

Maritime Defense, Security, and Support. As with CIP, the maritime mission can be HD, CS, or homeland security. As the USSR discovered in the 1980s, the foundation of a nation-state's strength lies in its economic might. In the globalized economic world, some 95 percent of trade with North America is conducted through the shipping industry. Interruption of this commerce route, even for a short period of time, can have devastating economic impacts. Additionally, not all of the millions of shipping containers that enter U.S. ports each year can be searched. For that reason, maritime threats must be addressed and thwarted at the earliest opportunity—again, largely offshore. As mentioned, NORAD has a maritime warning mission for North America, although it does not exclusively perform this role. The sea approaches are also within USNORTHCOM's AOR. DHS, U.S. Coast Guard, is the lead for maritime security, including maritime law enforcement, but other departments and agencies may play a significant role, such as the Department of Energy. USNORTHCOM, through Fleet Forces Command (FFC), executes the maritime HD mission. FFC can also provide civil support, such as that provided under the Stafford Act[15] by the USS *Nassau* post–Hurricane Ike in Galveston, Texas, in 2008. In addition to previously mentioned legal framework, customary international law also applies—for example, 12-mile territorial sea. Specific maritime legislation includes the Maritime Transportation Security Act and the Safety of Life at Sea Convention, among others.

Public Health Emergencies. "Perhaps no area of homeland security law is as complex for the national security lawyer as that pertaining to public health preparedness and emergency response," asserted Judge James

---

15. Robert T. Stafford Disaster Relief Act of 1979 (Stafford Act), 42 U.S.C. § 5121 *et seq.* as amended.

E. Baker, a former National Security Counsel attorney and current military appeals court judge.[16] Much of this area of law and associated organizational structure developed starting in the 1990s. Although the president may use the Public Health Service as "a branch of the land and naval forces of the United States"[17] in time of war or presidential-declared emergency, almost all DoD work in this area is civil support. Under statute and the National Response Framework (NRF), USNORTHCOM supports other federal agencies, such as HHS. Issues include restrictions on movements (e.g., quarantine), logistic preparedness and response (e.g., use of military hospitals), medical support (e.g., military providers caring for disaster victims), patient evacuation, animal and plant disease eradication (in support of U.S. Department of Agriculture), and vector control. USNORTHCOM participates in interagency bioterrorism exercises. Additionally, the UCP makes USNORTHCOM the DoD lead unified commander to synchronize DoD global planning efforts and U.S. military response to a pandemic influenza outbreak.

Law Enforcement and Law Enforcement Support. DoD also provides civil support to various law enforcement agencies. At the USNORTHCOM level, two primary types of support are for counterdrug missions and national special security events. Authorities and limitations on supporting law enforcement are also long-standing, but not fully restrictive.

One of the most important limitations on use of the armed forces for law enforcement is the Posse Comitatus Act (PCA), 18 U.S.C. § 1385. The PCA was enacted in 1878 in response to a series of military activities during the Reconstruction era. Congress passed the PCA after President Grant allowed U.S. marshals to use federal troops at polling places in Florida, arguably influencing the vote toward President Hayes. The act states:

> Whoever, except in cases and under circumstances expressly authorized by the Constitution or Act of Congress, willfully uses any part of the Army or the Air Force as a posse comitatus or otherwise to execute the laws shall be fined under this title or imprisoned not more than two years, or both.

Subsequent case law and DoD regulations have clarified the PCA to result in two basic prohibitions: active-duty military personnel are

---

16. JAMES E. BAKER, IN THE COMMON DEFENSE: NATIONAL SECURITY LAW FOR PERILOUS TIMES 285 (N.Y.: Cambridge Univ. Pr., 2007).

17. 42 U.S.C. § 217.

generally prohibited from engaging in law enforcement activity and from directly and actively supporting law enforcement authorities. Examples of prohibited activities include arrests, interrogations, searches, seizures, and surveillance.

As stated in the PCA itself, there can be exceptions to the prohibition "in cases and in circumstances expressly authorized by the Constitution or Act of Congress." Perhaps one of the most interesting exceptions is the president's ability to call out Title 10 military forces to suppress a rebellion or insurrection in a state. In this case, Title 10 forces would be performing a direct law enforcement mission by helping to restore order to a community.

Arguably, this exception to the PCA is grounded in both the Constitution and an Act of Congress. Article IV, section 4 of the Constitution states that "the United States shall . . . on Application of the Legislature, or of the Executive (when the Legislature cannot be convened) [protect the state] against domestic Violence." This authority is also reflected in Title 10, Chapter 15 of the U.S. Code, titled "Insurrection," which allows for the use of federal military forces to restore order during times of civil disturbance.[18] Under the Insurrection Act, federal forces may be used under three specific circumstances. First, under section 331, the president may use federal forces to suppress an insurrection within a state at the request of the state governor. Arguably, President George H.W. Bush relied on this section of the Insurrection Act in May of 1992, when he responded to California Governor Wilson's request for assistance in responding to the riots in Los Angeles.[19] The president may also act on his own authority under section 332 to call federal forces to respond when he believes that a state cannot or will not enforce federal laws within the state. Presidents Eisenhower and Kennedy relied on this authority when ordering federal troops to enforce public school desegregation in Arkansas and Alabama and control civil rights protests in Alabama and Mississippi. Finally, section 333 authorizes the president to use federal forces to respond to any "insurrection, domestic violence, unlawful combination, or conspiracy" if the state cannot maintain public order and the violence hinders the execution of the state and federal laws, resulting

---

18. 10 U.S.C. §§ 331–335.

19. Most commentators cite the Los Angeles riots as an example of section 331 support. However, although the governor did ask for assistance, it is debatable under which provision the assistance was provided given the section 331 requirement for an "insurrection." The presidential proclamation cited the entire act.

in deprivation of citizens' constitutional rights. Under this authority, President Kennedy sent federal forces to Alabama in 1963 during the civil rights marches.

Prior to sending federal forces under the Insurrection Act, the president is required to first issue a proclamation ordering the insurgents to cease and desist all violence and disperse within a limited time.[20] If the disturbance does not end, the president will issue an executive order to the secretary of defense directing him to use the armed forces as necessary to restore order.[21] In reality, these two documents normally come very close in time. When federal forces are employed, their response is coordinated by the Department of Justice as the primary federal agency responsible for the federal response to restore law and order.[22]

Congress amended the Insurrection Act in 2006, arguably expanding the president's authority to use federal forces in a state without the state's request. In 2007, the 2006 changes were reversed in response to significant political pressure from state governors. These legislative changes and reversals are largely reflective of the U.S. governmental structure, which dissipates power and built-in inherent tensions between state and federal authorities.

A series of statutes provide the authority for the DoD to support law enforcement authorities in various ways, including provision of information and expert advice, operation and maintenance of equipment, use of equipment and facilities, and training.[23] These statutes addressed overall support to law enforcement authorities. For example, the DC sniper murders, in which 14 people were killed and three others critically injured, began in October 2002, the same month that USNORTHCOM became operational. The DoD, through USNORTHCOM, provided a military reconnaissance airplane platform as civil support to the FBI. This platform employed unique aerial surveillance and night vision capabilities. Military pilots flew the airplane and operated onboard systems but the FBI directed the surveillance, flight plan, and follow-on law enforce-

---

20. 10 U.S.C. § 334.

21. Examples include Exec. Order No. 10,703, 22 Fed. Reg. 7628 (Sept. 24, 1957) (order authorizing use of military forces for desegregation in Arkansas); Exec. Order No. 11,118, 28 Fed. Reg. 9863 (Sept. 10, 1963) (order authorizing use of military forces for desegregation in Alabama); Exec. Order No. 12,804, 57 Fed. Reg. 19,361 (May 5, 1992) (order authorizing use of military forces in response to rioting in California).

22. Exec. Order No. 12,656, 53 Fed. Reg. 47,491 (Nov. 18, 1988).

23. 10 U.S.C. §§ 371–381.

ment. Thus, the military was simply operating equipment rather than engaging in or actively supporting law enforcement activities. Other provisions include emergency situations involving chemical or biological weapons of mass destruction;[24] assistance in the case of crimes against members of Congress;[25] protection of the president, vice president, and other designated dignitaries;[26] and removal of persons unlawfully present on Indian lands.[27]

When providing support to law enforcement personnel, military forces act under a specific set of rules regarding the use of force. Military forces performing CS missions, including support of law enforcement, use the Standing Rules for Use of Force (SRUF).[28] There are clear legal limitations on the use of force by military forces conducting HD or CS land operations within the homeland, requiring different rules from those used in overseas combat. USNORTHCOM trains its staff to be particularly careful not to use the term "Rules of Engagement (ROE)" when discussing homeland military peacetime operations. Rather, because of limitations on the use of the Armed Forces inside the United States against its citizens, the SRUF apply. The legal and operational differences and distinctions between ROE and RUF are critical. ROE presumes an enemy facing our military forces in a battle space, with whom we may need to engage. The premise of RUF in a CS mission is that forces are conducting mission on friendly territory, interacting with U.S. citizens, and presumably will not have to engage personnel. If any level of force is required, normally for self-defense, the lowest level of force is usually required, and only to the point of allowing civilian law enforcement to engage and address the threat. RUF for a particular mission can be tailored, for example, to reflect state law addressing under what circumstances someone can enter private property during a declared emergency.

Counterdrug Mission. Support to LE counterdrug (CD) activities is a significant and ongoing mission for USNORTHCOM. USNORTHCOM provides support primarily through JTF-North. In 1989, Congress passed legislation specifically addressing DoD support to CD law enforcement

---

24. 10 U.S.C. § 382.

25. 18 U.S.C. § 351.

26. 18 U.S.C. § 1751; and the Presidential Protection Assistance Act of 1976.

27. 25 U.S.C. § 180.

28. CJSCI 3121.01B, *Standing Rules of Engagement and Standing Rules for the Use of Force for U.S. Forces.*

authorities. Since then, Congress has annually given the DoD authority and funding to support federal, state, local, and foreign CD agencies.[29]

In accordance with these statutes, USNORTHCOM provides significant CD support to law enforcement authorities in the United States, particularly along the Mexican border. Similar to assistance provided during a disaster, there must first be a request for assistance from an appropriate agency, and then the military acts in a supporting role to the lead federal agency. For CD support, the lead federal agency is normally elements within the U.S. Customs and Border Protection. A requirement for provision of military support is that the support provided be a capability that is unique to the military. Normally, this constitutes high-end equipment or capabilities that are not commonly resident in federal or state agencies. For example, key categories of support include linguist and analyst services, detection and monitoring of movement near the border, and aerial and ground reconnaissance, all of which involve specialized equipment and personnel. Another key requirement is that the military unit providing the support gain training benefits from the mission. Units normally volunteer to provide the requested support and integrate the CD missions into their training plans for future DoD missions. Since September 11, 2001, CD missions have provided benefits beyond the reduction of drug smuggling into the United States. The same capabilities used during a CD mission, such as detection and monitoring of drug traffickers across the border, can also detect movement of illegal weapons and personnel. JTF-North can share this information with law enforcement authorities to potentially tighten and protect our borders against terrorist infiltration and attack.

Federal Level Security. USNORTHCOM also provides significant support to law enforcement for national special security events (NSSEs). The secretary of the Department of Homeland Security has the authority to declare an event an NSSE, and when that happens, the U.S. Secret Service (USSS) becomes the lead federal agency responsible for security design, planning, and implementation.[30] For example, USNORTHCOM provided military support to the USSS for the Republican and Democratic national conventions in 2008. Interestingly, USNORTHCOM provided support for these events at two levels. First, as directed by the

---

29. Nat'l Defense Auth. Act of 1991, Pub. L. No. 101-510, § 1004, as amended.

30. 18 U.S.C. § 3056.

secretary of defense, USNORTHCOM provided command and control of assets directed to support the USSS, such as explosive-detecting dog teams and chemical response teams. At the same time, USNORTHCOM provided the personnel to augment and support the Minnesota and Colorado National Guards, who were the governors' primary military response force. PCA issues came to the fore in providing support for these events. As noted above, the PCA applies to active duty personnel. Therefore military forces provided by USNORTHCOM could only *support* law enforcement authorities and were careful not to engage directly in law enforcement activity. National Guard forces, however, are not restricted by PCA. Therefore, they were able to respond with forces to both assist local law enforcement in keeping order as well as engage directly in law enforcement activities, such as crowd control. Again demonstrating close links between NORAD and USNORTHCOM, NORAD typically provides temporary flight restrictions and other airspace control measures enforcement for NSSEs upon request from the USSS.

CONCLUSION

This chapter has provided a broad overview of USNORTHCOM's missions. Yet the American people and culture tend to be very cautious about the use of Title 10, Active Duty military personnel in the homeland. A 2002 Congressional Research Service (CRS) report identified civil-military relations as a key issue for Congress upon the formation of USNORTHCOM.[31] The CRS asserted that "[t]he mission of NORTHCOM also raises questions about the impact the command might have on civil-military relations, including legal, political, and cultural boundaries on the role of the military in American society."[32]

The CRS also identified concerns regarding the more than 100-year-old constraints on the use of military for law enforcement purposes. The small standing force, the significant limitations on the use of force, and the subordination to civil authorities constrain USNORTHCOM while enabling it to defend and assist as required. Legislative changes will continue to be made as the political system shifts authorities vertically and horizontally across and among local, state, tribal, and federal gov-

---

31. CHRISTOPHER BOLKCOM, LLOYD DESERISY & LAWRENCE KAPP, CONGRESSIONAL RESEARCH SERVICE REPORT, HOMELAND SECURITY: ESTABLISHMENT AND IMPLEMENTATION OF NORTHERN COMMAND, Oct. 1, 2002.

32. BOLKCOM, ET AL., *id.* at 5.

ernments. Other legislative changes will either broaden or further constrain the role of the DoD in the homeland as the public gains confidence in the value of USNORTHCOM or expresses concern about the danger of a portion of the armed forces focused inwardly. Coordination between civilian and military authority in a crisis will be the critical test of the USNORTHCOM framework. Policymakers and commanders alike must continue to be sensitive to the strategic implications of their decisions as they execute missions in a way that preserves the U.S. Constitution and heritage of civilian control of the military.

Commerce and Commercial Transactions

CHAPTER 4

The USA PATRIOT Act and the Federal Anti-Money-Laundering Regime

by Mark J. Biros[1]

Compliance with the federal anti-money-laundering laws in a post-September 11, 2001, world is the topic of this chapter. A summary of federal anti-money-laundering laws is presented along with an evaluation of the impact of the USA PATRIOT Act on the federal anti-money-laundering regime. Regulatory guidance, enforcement trends, and practical advice to ensure compliance with the USA PATRIOT Act are highlighted.

INTRODUCTION

After the September 11, 2001, terrorist attacks, the United States government increased its focus significantly on fighting terrorist financing as part of the global war on terror. The Bush administration made it a top priority to pursue the money being used to finance the attacks to forestall future attacks. As then-Treasury Secretary Paul O'Neil stated, the administration was intent on "starving the terrorists of funding and shutting down the institutions that support or facilitate terrorism."[2]

---

1. The author wishes to gratefully acknowledge the substantial contribution of Scott Carpenter, an associate at Proskauer Rose LLP.

2. Paul O'Neill, Secretary of the Treasury, Statement on Signing of Executive Order Authorizing the Treasury Department to Block Funds of Terrorists and Their Associates (Sept. 24, 2001).

In connection with these efforts to disrupt the financial vitality of terrorists and other criminal organizations, Congress passed, and the president signed, the Uniting and Strengthening America by Providing Appropriate Tools Required to Intercept and Obstruct Terrorism Act of 2001 (the PATRIOT Act).[3] The PATRIOT Act modifies financial institutions' obligations to monitor and report potential money-laundering activities. In short, financial institutions were conscripted to help the government combat terrorism. Serving as so-called "gatekeepers" of financial transactions, the information institutions provide to law enforcement has proven to be of considerable importance in combating money laundering.[4] If, however, a company fails to provide law enforcement with pertinent information regarding money laundering or terrorist financing, it puts itself, other companies, and the whole financial system at risk.

As Section II of this chapter illustrates, the PATRIOT Act extends preexisting requirements under the federal anti-money-laundering statutes, criminal statutes addressed to money laundering, and other regulatory prohibitions. Section III describes the role of regulators in interpreting the PATRIOT Act and analyzes emerging trends in regulatory enforcement. Lastly, Section IV provides practical pointers and outlines steps that businesses should to take to comply with the PATRIOT Act.

LEGAL BACKGROUND

The Federal Anti-Money-Laundering Statutes Prior to Enactment of the PATRIOT Act

The central goal of the federal anti-money-laundering statutes is to detect when businesses in the United States may be used to facilitate money laundering or other illegal financing activities. In general, money laundering is an activity through which criminals take advantage of the United States' open financial system to launder criminal proceeds by changing the identity of such illicit funds to make them appear to have a legitimate source.

The Bank Secrecy Act of 1970 (BSA), also known as the Currency and Foreign Transactions Reporting Act, was the first major anti-money-laundering legislation.[5] The BSA established recordkeeping and report-

---

3. Pub. L. No. 107-56, 115 Stat. 272 (2001).

4. *See* Hutman & Herrington, *Money Laundering Enforcement & Policy*, 39 INT'L L. 649 (2005).

5. 31 U.S.C. § 5311 *et seq.*

ing requirements applicable to U.S. banks, such as mandatory reporting of cash payments over $10,000 in Currency Transaction Reports (CTRs).[6] In addition, the Money Laundering Control Act of 1986 (MLCA), another statute amended by the PATRIOT Act, improved the BSA by criminalizing the acts of money laundering and structuring of transactions to evade BSA reporting requirements.[7] The MLCA also directed banks to develop procedures reasonably designed to ensure and monitor compliance with the reporting and recordkeeping requirements of the BSA. In addition, Congress has passed other statutes to update the federal anti-money-laundering scheme to meet new challenges.[8] Before September 11, the typical targets of these laws were drug traffickers and members of organized crime. Since then, the range of targets has expanded greatly.

The anti-money-laundering provisions of the PATRIOT Act amended these older laws to meet the challenges of combating terrorism.[9] Over time, legislators learned that although "terrorist financing includes the use of both clandestine and legitimate sources of financing . . . terrorists and their support organizations have been found to use the same methods as other criminal groups to launder funds."[10] Accordingly, the PATRIOT Act built upon the BSA's requirements by adding new obligations and expanding the scope of the statute.

Terrorist financing, however, poses greater challenges to law enforcement because it is "more difficult for banking organizations to identify. Funding for terrorist attacks does not always require large sums of money, and the associated transactions may not be complex. The movement of small sums of money for laundering or terrorist purposes can be

---

6. *Id.*

7. 18 U.S.C. §§ 1956 & 1957.

8. *See, e.g.*, The Annunzio-Wylie Anti-Money Laundering Act of 1992, Pub. L. No. 102-550, 106 Stat. 4044 (toughening penalties for financial institutions found guilty of money laundering); The Money Laundering Suppression Act of 1994, Pub. L. No. 103-325, 108 Stat. 2243 (improving regulatory examination procedures to better detect money-laundering schemes in financial institutions).

9. *See generally* Daryl Shetterly, *Starving the Terrorists of Funding: How the United States Treasury is Fighting the War on Terror*, 18 REGENT U. L. REV. 327 (2006).

10. Testimony of Herbert A. Biern, The Bank Secrecy Act and the USA PATRIOT Act, Nov. 17, 2004, *at* http://www.federalreserve.gov/boarddocs/testimony/2004/20041117/default.htm.

a challenge for a banking organization to identify with no other information."[11] Thus, the expansion of anti-money-laundering laws and regulations to fight terrorism altered the complexity of the anti-money-laundering regime. The PATRIOT Act subjected financial institutions, which had existing obligations under federal money-laundering statutes, to heightened compliance and reporting requirements. It also expanded the scope of money-laundering rules to businesses that originally were not covered by the money-laundering statutes.

Overview of Title III of the PATRIOT Act Regarding Financial Transactions

Title III of the PATRIOT Act, also known as the International Money Laundering Abatement and Anti-Terrorist Financing Act of 2001, sets forth the post-September 11 anti-money-laundering obligations.[12] These provisions apply to all "financial institutions," a term defined under the BSA as including banks, thrift institutions, and credit unions, as well as certain entities not typically thought of as financial businesses.[13] Among other things, the PATRIOT Act requires:

- Anti-money-laundering programs across the financial services industry;

---

11. *Id.*

12. *See generally* Michael Shapiro, *The USA PATRIOT Act and Money Laundering*, 123 BANKING L. J. 629 (2006); Taft & Poulon, *Compliance Obligations and Enforcement Actions under the USA PATRIOT Act*, 60 CONSUMER FIN. L.Q. REP. 316 (2005).

13. "The definition of 'financial institution' includes the following entities: (1) an insured bank; (2) a commercial bank or trust company; (3) a private banker; (4) an agency or branch of a foreign bank in the United States; (5) any credit union; (6) a thrift institution; (7) a broker or dealer registered with the SEC; (8) a broker or dealer in securities or commodities; (9) an investment banker or investment company; (10) a currency exchange; (11) an issuer, redeemer, or cashier of travelers' checks, checks, money orders, or similar instruments; (12) an operator of a credit card system; (13) an insurance company; (14) a dealer in precious metals, stones, or jewels; (15) a pawnbroker; (16) a loan or finance company; (17) a travel agency; (18) a licensed sender of money or any other person who engages as a business in the transmission of funds, including any person who engages as a business in an informal money transfer system or any network of people who engage as a business in facilitating the transfer of money domestically or internationally outside of the conventional finance institutions system . . . ." *See* Taft & Poulon, *supra* note 12, at 317.

- Customer identity verification programs; and
- Information sharing between the government and institutions, as well as voluntary information sharing among financial institutions.

Anti-Money-Laundering Programs

Section 352 of the PATRIOT Act requires all financial institutions to establish anti-money-laundering programs (AML Programs), and grants the Treasury Department the authority to promulgate basic standards for such programs. AML Programs generally must include (i) the development of internal policies, procedures, and controls; (ii) the designation of a compliance officer; (iii) an ongoing employee training program; and (iv) an independent audit function to test the program.[14]

The PATRIOT Act also aims to curb terrorist financing and other financial crimes by requiring financial institutions, through their AML Programs, to report potential money laundering. For example, banks subject to the BSA must file Suspicious Activity Reports (SARs) to inform the government of suspected money-laundering violations or other suspicious activities.[15] SARs help law enforcement to initiate money-laundering investigations, sharpen the focus of investigations already under way, and furnish information with which investors can identify emerging patterns related to money laundering. Since the enactment of the PATRIOT Act, the filing of timely, accurate, and complete SARs has become of significant importance to federal agencies. And, as illustrated in its enforcement actions, the government has made SAR compliance a top enforcement priority.

Customer Identity Verification

Pursuant to Section 326 of the PATRIOT Act, federal regulators have issued rules requiring financial institutions to implement risk-based Customer Identification Programs (CIPs). A CIP should be tailored to an institution's size and type of business and should be integrated into its AML Program. Under these rules, financial institutions must implement procedures to verify the identity of a customer who opens an account by obtaining identifying information and confirming its accuracy. Although

---

14. *Id.*

15. *See* 12 C.F.R. § 21.1. For the PATRIOT Act's amendments relating to SARs, see section 351 of the PATRIOT Act.

the compliance requirements are significant, banks need only verify the identity of a customer who opens a new account to the "extent reasonable and practicable."[16]

A CIP also must include procedures for preserving records of information used to verify a person's identity during the CIP's implementation.[17] Certain identifying information, such as a customer's name, address, and date of birth, must be preserved. Furthermore, the institution must determine whether a customer appears on any government-issued list of known or suspected terrorist organizations. As described in more detail below, in the immediate aftermath of the September 11 attacks, the government published, and continues to publish, lists of known or suspected terrorists or terrorist organizations, which institutions must consult to ensure that they are not servicing such individuals or entities.

Information Sharing

The Treasury Department has enacted regulations to promote information sharing regarding individuals or entities that are suspected of participating in money laundering or terrorist financing.[18] Section 314 of the PATRIOT Act seeks to encourage greater information sharing and cooperation between financial institutions to better assist them in detecting and reporting money laundering and financial activities of terrorist groups. An institution that shares information must provide notice to the secretary of the treasury of its plans to do so. Any institution that shares information under this provision will be afforded protection from liability for sharing information or from failing to notify the suspect party that such sharing has taken place.

---

16. *See, e.g.,* 31 C.F.R. § 103.122(b).

17. *See generally* Taft & Harrell, *Customer Identification, Money Laundering Compliance, and Safeguarding of Customer Information under the GLB Act, the USA PATRIOT Act, and OFAC Rules,* 58 Consumer Fin. L.Q. Rep. 286 (2004).

18. 31 C.F.R. § 103.100.

REGULATORY GUIDANCE

Agency Regulations

The Financial Crimes Enforcement Network

The U.S. Department of the Treasury established the Financial Crimes Enforcement Network (FinCEN) in the 1990s as part of the government's increased efforts to combat money laundering. FinCEN is charged with enforcing the requirements of the BSA and other money-laundering laws. In 2004, FinCEN was integrated into the Treasury Department's Office of Terrorism and Financial Intelligence to help fight the financial war on terror and curb other financial crimes.

FinCEN is a key source of information and guidance regarding compliance with the federal anti-money-laundering statutes and regulations. For example, FinCEN recently released regulations governing enhanced due diligence of correspondent accounts maintained by certain foreign banks.[19] Under Section 312 of the PATRIOT Act, U.S. financial institutions are required to apply "enhanced due diligence" when establishing or maintaining a correspondent account for a foreign bank that is operating (1) under an offshore license; (2) in a jurisdiction found to be uncooperative with international anti-money-laundering principles; or (3) in a jurisdiction found to be of primary money-laundering concern under Section 311 of the USA PATRIOT Act. Under the final rules, covered financial institutions have flexibility to apply the enhanced due diligence procedures according to the institution's risk profile.[20]

In general, FinCEN focuses upon six categories of financial institutions: (1) depository institutions, (2) insurance companies, (3) casinos, (4) securities and futures businesses, (5) precious metals and jewelry businesses, and (6) money service businesses (MSBs). FinCEN has issued several pronouncements clarifying compliance requirements specific to the different industries covered under the PATRIOT Act.[21] Companies should note that FinCEN also has provided industry-specific examples of suspicious activity "red flags," patterns that are indicative of

---

19. 31 C.F.R. § 103.176.
20. *Id.*
21. *See* FinCEN Guidance, *at* http://www.fincen.gov/statutes_regs/guidance/.

money laundering.[22] As described below, companies should incorporate and build upon such guidance when meeting the AML compliance requirements.

The Office of Foreign Assets Control

The Office of Foreign Assets Control (OFAC) of the Department of the Treasury administers and enforces economic and trade sanctions based on U.S. foreign policy and national security goals against targeted foreign countries, terrorists, international narcotics traffickers, and those engaged in activities related to the proliferation of weapons of mass destruction. With certain exceptions authorized by the secretary of the treasury, 31 C.F.R. § 500.201 prohibits transactions involving property in which any designated foreign country or any national has, at any time on or since the effective date, had any direct or indirect interest. The most recent example of these prohibitions occurred when the Iranian Transactions Regulations (ITR) were amended to rescind authorization that permitted financial institutions to participate in "U-turn" transactions with Iran.[23]

Moreover, OFAC regularly publishes a list of Specially Designated Nationals (SDNs)—individuals and entities with which U.S. persons[24]

---

22. *See, e.g.*, FinCEN, *Recognizing Suspicious Activity—Red Flags for Casinos and Card Clubs*, Aug. 1, 2008, *at* http://www.fincen.gov/statutes_regs/guidance/html/fin-2008-g007.html; FinCEN, *Anti-Money Laundering Program and Suspicious Activity Reporting Requirements for Insurance Companies*, Mar. 20, 2008, *at* http://www.fincen.gov/statutes_regs/guidance/pdf/fin-2008-g004.pdf.

23. *See* Press Release, Treasury Revokes Iran's U-Turn License, Nov. 6, 2008, *at* http://www.treas.gov/press/releases/hp1257.htm (Previously, "U.S. financial institutions were authorized to process certain funds transfers for the direct or indirect benefit of Iranian banks, other persons in Iran or the Government of Iran, provided such payments were initiated offshore by a non-Iranian, non-U.S. financial institution and only passed through the U.S. financial system en route to another offshore, non-Iranian, non-U.S. financial institution.").

24. "The term person means an individual, partnership, association, corporation, or other organization." 31 C.F.R. § 500.308. A person subject to the jurisdiction of the United States includes: (1) any citizen or resident of the United States wherever located; (2) a person within the United States as set forth in 31 C.F.R. § 500.330; (3) a corporation organized under the laws of the United States or any territory, possession or district of the United States; and (4) any corporation, partnership or association wherever organized or doing business that is owned or controlled by persons specified in (1) and (3) above. 31 C.F.R. § 329.

are barred from conducting transactions.[25] U.S. persons should compare their entire customer database to the updated SDN list. According to OFAC, financial institutions have a duty to "block" transactions involving persons on the SDN list by freezing the funds in their possession. Banks also have a duty to "reject" transactions that do not involve a person listed on the SDN, but otherwise violate OFAC rules. Blocked transactions should be reported to FinCEN as suspicious transactions requiring the filing of an SAR. OFAC also provides industry-specific guidance to assist compliance with the PATRIOT Act.[26]

Additional Resources

The Office of the Comptroller of the Currency (OCC) has undertaken a number of anti-money-laundering initiatives, including forming the National Anti-Money Laundering Group (NAMLG), which targets banks for examinations regarding compliance with money-laundering laws examinations. In addition, the OCC works with FinCEN to enhance its ability to identify banks with money-laundering risk. Similar to FinCEN or OFAC, the OCC provides guidance, bulletins, and FAQs regarding money laundering and may serve as an additional resource to financial institutions seeking to comply with the PATRIOT Act's anti-money-laundering provisions.[27]

Furthermore, several federal agencies, known as the Federal Financial Institutions Examination Council (FFIEC), jointly released a *Bank Secrecy Act/Anti-Money Laundering Examination Manual*[28] (FFIEC Manual). In publishing the FFIEC Manual, the agencies sought to ensure consistent enforcement of the federal anti-money-laundering statutes and regulations and to provide additional guidance to financial institutions on compliance. The FFIEC Manual highlights each institution's obligation to develop and implement risk-based policies, procedures, and processes to combat money laundering and terrorist financing. Although the

---

25. *See* OFAC Specially Designated Nationals and Blocked Persons, *at* http://www.ustreas.gov/offices/enforcement/ofac/sdn/t11sdn.pdf.

26. *See* OFAC Information for Industry Groups, *at* http://www.ustreas.gov/offices/enforcement/ofac/regulations/index.shtml.

27. *See* OCC, COMBATING MONEY LAUNDERING AND TERRORIST FINANCING: BSA GUIDANCE FOR BANKERS AND EXAMINERS, *at* http://www.occ.treas.gov/BSA/BSAGuidance.htm.

28. FFIEC *Bank Secrecy Act/Anti-Money Laundering Examination Manual*, June 23, 2005, *at* http://www.occ.treas.gov/handbook/1-BSA-AMLwhole.pdf.

FFIEC Manual was published to guide regulators through their examination of AML Programs, companies can use it as a resource regarding BSA requirements and the expectations of federal regulators.

Recently, FinCEN and the Internal Revenue Service (IRS) published a similar manual to aid examiners of MSBs (*FinCEN/IRS Manual*).[29] According to FinCEN, the *FinCEN/IRS Manual* seeks "to enhance BSA examiners' ability to perform risk-based examinations of MSBs, provide a resource to enhance the consistency of BSA examination procedures, and provide a summary of BSA compliance requirements and exam procedures to the MSB industry."[30] The publication of the *FinCEN/IRS Manual* "underscores the government's ongoing initiatives to promote consistent, efficient, and effective AML efforts across all sectors of the financial industry subject to BSA regulations."[31]

Enforcement Actions

The federal anti-money-laundering laws and regulations authorize federal regulators, such as FinCEN, OFAC, and the OCC, to bring civil enforcement actions against violators and to seek remedies including civil monetary penalties. The Department of Justice (DOJ) also may bring charges for violations constituting criminal offenses. Often, civil and criminal cases are instituted simultaneously and subject defendants to increased penalties. Detailed below are examples of important enforcement actions brought by federal regulators for violations of money-laundering laws and regulations.

In one significant 2004 enforcement action, the Birmingham, Alabama–based AmSouth Bank agreed to pay civil and criminal fines totaling $50 million for violations of the BSA.[32] According to regulators, AmSouth maintained accounts in furtherance of a Ponzi scheme implemented by two individuals, but failed to detect and report the scheme despite red flags that should have alerted AmSouth to suspicious con-

---

29. BANK SECRECY ACT/ANTI-MONEY LAUNDERING EXAMINATION MANUAL FOR MONEY SERVICES BUSINESSES, Dec. 9, 2008, *at* http://www.fincen.gov/news_room/rp/files/MSB_Exam_Manual.pdf.

30. Press Release, FinCEN Announces Release of Manual to Aid Examiners of Money Services Businesses, Dec. 9, 2008, *at* http://www.fincen.gov/news_room/nr/pdf/20081209.pdf.

31. *Id.*

32. DOJ Press Release, AmSouth Bank Agrees to Forfeit $40 Million, Oct. 12, 2004, *at* http://www.usdoj.gov/usao/mss/documents/pressreleases/october2004/amprsrels.htm.

duct. In particular, regulators charged that "AmSouth failed to conduct a risk assessment of its customer base" and failed to "monitor customers with cash-intensive activity to determine if the activity was suspicious."[33] FinCEN and the DOJ brought parallel civil and criminal enforcement actions against AmSouth in which it agreed to pay a $10 million civil penalty and a $40 million criminal fine.

Another major enforcement action was brought against Riggs Bank by FinCEN. Riggs had certain high-risk customers, including former Chilean leader Augusto Pinochet, as well as countries such as Equatorial Guinea and the Kingdom of Saudi Arabia.[34] FinCEN claimed that Riggs failed to (i) tailor an AML Program to the risks of its business, (ii) implement its existing policies and procedures, and (iii) respond to detected incidents of suspicious activity.[35]

As to tailoring its program to the risks of its business, FinCEN stated that "Riggs' internal controls were not designed to take into account the exposure posed by the customers, products, services, and accounts from high-risk international geographic locations that are commonly viewed as high-risk for money laundering."[36] These deficiencies led to failures to follow CIP and due diligence procedures. Riggs also failed to monitor compliance especially with regard to its high-risk transactions.

Moreover, Riggs violated SAR requirements by failing to detect "the most basic situations that an effective SAR program should be designed to detect and report."[37] Not only did Riggs not have adequate procedures to detect suspicious conduct, Riggs also failed to file timely SARs. In fact, in some instances Riggs issued reports with respect to activity that had occurred three years earlier. On May 13, 2004, Riggs agreed to pay a $25 million civil penalty. Then, on January 27, 2005, Riggs settled criminal charges with the DOJ for its inability to file proper SARs by pleading guilty to a single-count indictment, paying a $16 million fine, and consenting to a period of five years' corporate probation.

One OCC enforcement action also highlights the need for institutions to tailor their programs to the risks involved in their businesses. In *In re Federal Branch of Arab Bank PLC*, the OCC stated that the branch

---

33. *In re* AmSouth Bank, FinCEN Assessment of Civil Money Penalty, 2004-02 (Oct. 12, 2004).

34. *In re* Riggs Bank, N.A., FinCEN Assessment of Civil Money Penalty, 2004-01 (May 13, 2004).

35. *Id.*

36. *Id.* at 2.

37. *Id.* at 5.

"engaged in substantial funds transfer operations, including a significant number of transactions for participants who did not and do not have accounts at the Branch but whose transactions were originated by or received by other offices of Arab Bank and its affiliates or by other third-party correspondent banks."[38] Due to the "inadequacy of the Branch's Bank Secrecy Act controls over its funds transfer operations" and "in light of the high risk characteristics of many of the transactions," the OCC imposed a civil monetary penalty of $24 million.[39]

Recently, in *In re Sigue Corporation*, FinCEN and the DOJ alleged that Sigue, which provided money transmission services from the United States to Mexico and Latin America, "assisted customers in the structuring of transactions represented to be drug-trafficking proceeds to avoid the currency transaction reporting requirements of the Bank Secrecy Act."[40] In particular, Sigue did not tailor its transaction monitoring system to address risks associated with its volume of business, the geographical reach of the transactions processed, or the hefty dollar amounts they involved. And, although Sigue implemented an automated monitoring system, it failed to implement adequate supplemental review of transactions. Sigue also did not adequately train its staff. According to FinCEN, "[i]n some cases, training was neither completed nor documented, and was generally inadequate considering the scope, volume and nature of Sigue's activity."[41] As a result, on January 24, 2005, Sigue agreed to pay approximately $15 million in penalties. Sigue also agreed to commit an additional $9.7 million to improve its AML Program.

Even large, well-known institutions are not immune from enforcement actions. Notably, in 2007, American Express Bank International and American Express Travel Related Services Company had to disgorge $55 million and pay approximately $25 million in fines.[42] The government claimed that American Express "operated in certain high-risk jurisdictions and business lines without commensurate systems and controls

---

38. *In re* Federal Branch of Arab Bank PLC, OCC Consent Order, 2005-101 (Aug. 17, 2005).

39. *Id.* at 2.

40. *In re* Sigue Corp. and Sigue LLC, FinCEN Assessment of Civil Money Penalty, 2008-01 (Jan. 28, 2008).

41. *Id.* at 3.

42. DOJ Press Release, *American Express Bank International Enters into Deferred Prosecution Agreement and Forfeits $55 Million to Resolve Bank Secrecy Act Violations*, Aug. 6, 2007, *at* http://www.usdoj.gov/opa/pr/2007/August/07_crm_584.html.

to detect and report money laundering and other suspicious activity in a timely manner, as well as manage the risks of money laundering, including the potential for illicit drug trafficking-based Black Market Peso Exchange transactions."[43]

Specifically, American Express's monitoring parameters were not "risk focused" and were set too high, "thereby substantially reducing the likelihood that suspicious activity would be detected."[44]

Enforcement Trends

In its enforcement cases, the government provides useful insight into what it may consider to be industry "worst practices." The government has demonstrated little patience for noncompliance, and consequently it has used its enforcement actions to make examples of entities with seriously deficient policies and procedures. Indeed, as indicated by a former director of FinCEN, enforcement actions were brought "against institutions [found] to have significant programmatic failures," and "the orders implementing these actions were written as a 'road map' for other institutions to follow. . . ."[45] In general, regulators have identified certain common deficiencies in AML Programs, such as (1) the development of anti-money-laundering programs, (2) the proper implementation of internal controls, and (3) the submission of suspicious activity reports.

The main focus of regulators has been on the development of adequate policies and procedures to ensure compliance with anti-money-laundering laws and regulations. Regulators examine the sufficiency of internal controls to see if they meet the nature of the business. Failure to tailor an AML Program to the risks posed by an institution's business likely will lead to enforcement proceedings and sanctions.

Another lesson of recent enforcement actions is that regulators look to see if financial institutions are implementing their internal controls adequately. In many of the enforcement cases noted above, companies failed to train employees properly and direct them on how to monitor suspicious activity. In some cases, such as *Sigue*, financial institutions

---

43. *In re* American Express Bank Int'l, American Express Travel Related Services, Inc., FinCEN Assessment of Civil Money Penalty, 2007-01 (Aug. 6, 2007).

44. *Id.* at 3.

45. William J. Fox, Director of FinCEN, Remarks at the American Bankers Association/American Bar Association Money-Laundering Enforcement Seminar (Oct. 25, 2004).

failed to monitor suspicious activity by ineffectively using automated systems. Moreover, regulators have penalized institutions that do not provide for management or the board of directors to conduct appropriate oversight of an AML Program, or otherwise fail to designate a sufficient number of individuals to ensure day-to-day compliance.

Finally, the regulatory agencies have put great emphasis on violations of SAR obligations. Since SARs help law enforcement determine the extent of any possible criminal activity, failure to comply with SAR requirements may lead to criminal charges. Indeed, the criminal charges in the *AmSouth* and *Riggs* cases were based in large part on the institutions' failure to submit compliant SARs.[46] Tardy, incomplete, and inaccurate SARs were at the heart of the problem. But regulators also will look to the proper maintenance of books and records regarding SARs.

HOW TO AVOID NONCOMPLIANCE

Full compliance with the anti-money-laundering provisions of the PATRIOT Act is imperative. Although meeting those obligations can be costly, the dangers of noncompliance can be much greater. As illustrated by the government's enforcement actions, noncompliance can result in severe penalties. Moreover, companies involved in criminal transactions stand to lose goodwill and reputation.

Regulators expect that U.S. entities will review the regulations, develop appropriate risk-based policies, implement these policies, and monitor compliance on a regular basis. As stated above, these AML policies and procedures are designed to prevent a company's involvement in money laundering and to provide the types of information that the law enforcement agencies need to investigate suspicious transactions.

Since the risks of noncompliance are evident, businesses must be willing to conduct proper due diligence and commit the resources necessary to achieve compliance. All financial institutions, plus those that operate in commercial enterprises where money laundering may occur, must incorporate new and heightened procedures into their existing compliance programs. Once a financial institution knows its obligations under the PATRIOT Act, it can fulfill its compliance obligations by assessing the risks posed by money laundering and then establishing written procedures to address those risks.

---

46. *See* Hutman & Herrington, *supra* note 3, at 653–54.

Identify Risk Factors

In developing a written AML Program, one size does not fit all.[47] Federal agencies have warned, as they did in *AmSouth* and *Riggs*, that companies must tailor their programs to their own specific business practices and client bases. Merely applying existing practices or copying another company's "homework" will not suffice. A company's program must be specifically tailored to the types of money-laundering risks posed by virtue of its customers or the products or services it offers. The anti-money-laundering rules, though, provide companies with the flexibility to determine the risks they face and adopt policies and procedures that fit those risks. As the director of FinCEN recently stated, "We [FinCEN] recognize that financial crime is insidious, and that there are finite compliance resources to devote to the problem. To be effective and efficient, these finite resources should be focused first and foremost on the greatest risks."[48]

To that end, a financial institution must first conduct a risk assessment to determine what factors related to its business augment the risk of money laundering. Conducting a thorough risk assessment is one of the most important steps to establishing a sound and compliant AML Program. A deficient risk assessment could well lead to a deficient and ineffective program and, consequently, enforcement actions and the imposition of substantial monetary penalties.

Because an AML Program must reflect the size and complexity of the financial institution and the nature and scope of its activities, companies should look to five categories of risk factors: (1) types of customers, (2) types of products and services, (3) types of transactions, (4) types of accounts, and (5) geographic locations involved.[49] By reviewing the certain types of customers, accounts, or transactions that pose heightened money-laundering risks, companies can better determine the extent of their risk exposure. For example, companies that maintain accounts related to foreign customers, overseas accounts, cash-based businesses, or money services businesses have an increased potential for money laundering.

---

47. James H. Freis, Director of FinCEN, Remarks at SIFMA Anti–Money Laundering Compliance Conference (Mar. 5, 2008).

48. *Id.*

49. *See* Timothy White, *How to Implement Risk-Based OFAC Monitoring Practices*, ABA Bank Compliance, Sept. 2007, *at* http://www.aba.com/NR/rdonlyres/CC139B64-7199-4568-BAD5-3EFFE9F7BDA3/49045/OFACCoverStoryWhite.pdf.

Some federal agencies provide guidance for conducting risk assessments and identifying risk factors. For example, OFAC issues risk matrices for different industries, which an institution can use to gauge the extent of its own risk.[50] Under an OFAC risk matrix, banks that have a high number of international transactions and a high number of customer fund transfers are at greater risk of being used as a vehicle to launder money or finance terrorism. On the other hand, banks that have no overseas branches and do not provide customers with electronic banking services fall on the "low risk" end of the spectrum. Additionally, as stated above, FinCEN provides some industry-specific lists of "red flags" of suspicious activity.[51] Companies, however, should not merely replicate general regulatory guidance. Rather, a risk assessment needs to be detailed, comprehensive, and fact-specific.

After a company has identified its risk factors, it should evaluate the level of risk involved for each factor (high, moderate, or low risk). To do this evaluation, companies should use regulatory guidance, such as the OFAC risk matrices, as a comparison. Companies also should document and preserve their risk assessments, as well as the determinations made while conducting them.

Develop and Implement AML Procedures

After a U.S. entity has conducted a thorough risk assessment and identified its risk factors, it must put together policies and procedures aimed to detect, investigate, and remedy noncompliance. Although companies, especially large ones, are not expected to monitor every transaction and customer, they should concentrate AML Programs to monitor those areas identified as the highest risk.

Generally speaking, the detection aspect of an AML Program is a fundamental due diligence requirement calling for a business to utilize sound controls that will ensure that it recognizes and addresses red flags of money laundering or other suspicious activity. For instance, the *FinCEN/ IRS Manual* states:

---

50. *See, e.g.*, *Risk Factors for OFAC Compliance in the Securities Industry*, Nov. 2008, *at* http://www.ustreas.gov/offices/enforcement/ofac/policy/ securities_risk_11052008.pdf; *OFAC Risk Matrices for Financial Institutions*, June 2005, *at* http://www.treas.gov/offices/enforcement/ofac/faq/ matrix.pdf; *Risk Matrix for the Charitable Sector*, *at* http://www.treas.gov/ offices/enforcement/ofac/policy/charity_risk_matrix.pdf.

51. *See supra* note 20.

Monitoring systems typically include some combination of employee identification, manual systems, and automated systems. The MSB should ensure adequate staff is assigned to the identification, research, and reporting of suspicious activities, taking into account the MSB's overall risk profile and the volume of transactions. After thorough research and analysis, decisions to file or not to file an SAR-MSB should be documented.[52]

Federal regulations are broad enough to provide companies the flexibility to tailor policies to the specific risks they face. Companies should have systems and procedures in place to distinguish routine transactions from ones that rise to the level of suspicious activity.

Financial institutions also should look to established methods and emerging trends in money-laundering activities, such as:

- disproportionate wire transfer activities;
- frequent transfers to unrelated third parties;
- attempts to hide the source or destination of funds or assets;
- transfers to countries with reputations for banking secrecy;
- transactions involving offshore holding companies; and
- customer unwillingness or inability to provide information regarding its identity, occupation, or assets.

To help prevent and remedy possible money laundering or terrorist financing, a company's AML Program must set forth procedures to investigate and respond appropriately to indications of criminal activity. When a threat is detected, a business must evaluate the risks involved to determine if a transaction is in fact suspicious and, if so, how to respond. The *FinCEN/IRS Manual* states that "[u]pon identification of unusual activity, additional research is typically conducted. The MSB will generally have to make two decisions once it becomes aware of unusual activity related to a transaction: Whether to file an SAR-MSB; and regardless of whether an SAR-MSB is filed, whether to monitor the customer going forward."[53] Moreover, untimely and inaccurate SARs affect law enforcement's ability to examine whether a crime has been or is being committed. As a matter of

---

52. BANK SECRECY ACT/ANTI-MONEY LAUNDERING EXAMINATION MANUAL FOR MONEY SERVICES BUSINESSES, Dec. 9, 2008, *at* http://www.fincen.gov/news_room/rp/files/MSB_Exam_Manual.pdf.

53. *Id.*

best practices, an SAR should be filed whenever a transaction appears to be suspicious.[54] Although this may lead to "defensive" filings, it may be beneficial in order to avoid the appearance of inattentiveness, or worse, an unintended violation of the PATRIOT Act.

To implement an AML Program, companies must involve officers, directors, and senior and other levels of management in the development and oversight of the program to ensure that appropriate personnel and financial resources are devoted on a continuing basis. Complacency is not an option for businesses that want to ensure compliance with the PATRIOT Act. And as is evidenced in the enforcement actions, companies have been penalized for failing to assign sufficient staff and resources to implement AML procedures. Moreover, companies should maintain records that demonstrate compliance with the anti-money-laundering laws and regulations. For instance, companies should keep a detailed log documenting reviews of OFAC's SDN list, as well as measures taken to block funds or transactions.

Lastly, adequate staff training is a vital and often overlooked step to achieving proper compliance. Even the most robust AML Program will fall short if it is not adequately communicated to those required to implement it. Training should be conducted periodically. Certain staff members who are assigned to high-risk areas may need to receive additional training. Additional training also should be provided when an AML Program is revised or updated to address new and unanticipated risks or technological advances. In addition, these staff members may need to receive more frequent training to keep them informed about emerging risks. Likewise, staff members that are required to perform complex or sensitive AML Program functions may require more advanced or more frequent training.

CONCLUSION

President Bush famously stated that the United States would "starve the terrorists of funding, turn them against each other, rout them out of their safe hiding places and bring them to justice."[55] The administration bol-

---

54. *See, e.g.*, *id.* ("A SAR must be filed no later than 30 calendar days from the date of the initial detection of facts that may constitute a basis for filing a SAR-MSB.")

55. President George W. Bush, Remarks on United States Financial Sanctions against Foreign Terrorists and Their Supporters and an Exchange with Reporters (Sept. 24, 2001).

stered the anti-money-laundering measures to curb terrorist financing following the September 11, 2001 terrorist attacks. And pursuant to the PATRIOT Act, financial institutions play a vital role in this counter-terrorism scheme.

Consequently, financial institutions must have systems in place to monitor transactions and report information to law enforcement. No "one-size-fits-all" procedure or decision-making process can or should be devised. Although certain decisions, such as how to monitor transactions and whether to submit an SAR, will be largely subjective, companies will need to be aware of their risk factors and knowledgeable about their customers' status and activities. Companies then must develop AML Programs implementing procedures designed to detect, investigate, and remedy any identified risks. Ultimately, financial institutions will be held accountable by federal regulators based upon the efficacy of these AML Programs.

CHAPTER 5

Compliance Is Not Enough: What It Really Takes to Maintain Responsible Information Security

by Donald A. Purdy, Jr.[1]

Private and governmental organizations must recognize that cyber intrusions and attacks, insider threats, and other virtual disruptions pose a real threat to their mission and reputations. Accordingly, organizations should proactively build information risk and other data risk into their risk-management planning and infrastructure. That risk approach should address confidentiality, integrity, and availability of data, and, although it should meet compliance requirements, it should be focused on managing risk and should incorporate a risk-management culture into the business processes of the organization, including IT operations, security, business continuity, and disaster recovery.

On May 29, 2009, President Obama highlighted the dependency of the United States on cyberspace for the nation's economic well-being, public safety and law enforcement, national security, and personal privacy. He said real-world attacks on, and intrusions into, key government and private networks demonstrate the significant risk the nation faces. The president announced that he was creating the post of cybersecurity coordinator to oversee "a new comprehensive approach to securing America's digital infrastructure." Private and governmental organiza-

---

1. The author is grateful for the excellent assistance of Jon Sherman, an associate in WilmerHale's Washington, D.C., office.

tions across the country have significant challenges of their own in helping to address the risks to the digital infrastructure on which government and the private sector depend.

The last decade has seen an alarming increase in highly publicized cyber security and data breach incidents that cause direct economic damage and undermine confidence in information technology-dependent business and government processes.[2] These blows to the economic and social infrastructure have justifiably raised concerns among corporate and government leaders and given them reason to ask what actions are necessary to reverse this trend. The TJX fiasco of 2007[3] and the Department of Veterans Affairs' data breach[4] are prime examples of socially damaging information security disasters.

Legitimate concerns about data-processing risk—at least the data breach component—have resulted in the proliferation of regulatory provisions, best practices guidance, and private-sector standards, such as those contained in the Sarbanes-Oxley Act, the Health Insurance Portability and Accountability Act (HIPAA), the Federal Information Security Management Act (FISMA), the North American Electric Reliability Corporation (NERC) reliability standards, the Payment Card Industry Data Security Standard (PCI), and state and local measures, with more in the pipeline at the federal and state levels. As hackers and more sophisticated malicious actors, terrorists, and organized criminals rapidly innovate new kinds of threats, Congress and state legislatures are promulgating new statutes and contemplating more, and adding provisions, each of which imposes additional costs, administrative burdens, and/or liability risks on private and public organizations alike. Ultimately, government officials must partner with private commercial entities to understand and neutralize risks to data security.

---

2. Rita Tehan, Congressional Research Service, Data Security Breaches: Context and Incident Summaries (2007), http://www.fas.org/sgp/crs/misc/RL33199.pdf.

3. *TJX Says Theft of Credit Data Involved 45.7 Million Cards*, N.Y. Times, Mar. 30, 2007, at C2.

4. *U.S. Says Personal Data on Millions of Veterans Stolen*, Wash. Post, May 22, 2006, *available at* http://www.washingtonpost.com/wp-dyn/content/article/2006/05/22/AR2006052200690.html; David Stout & Tom Zeller, Jr., *Agency Delayed Reporting of Theft of Veterans' Data*, N.Y. Times, May 24, 2006, at A24.

FEDERAL AND STATE REGULATION OF INFORMATION SECURITY

Over the last decade, federal and state government officials have come to recognize the vulnerability of electronic data and the threats to personal and national security posed by computer and network breaches. Compromised personal information can facilitate identity theft, credit card or check fraud, or the evasion of law enforcement authorities.[5] Federal and state legislatures and agencies, as well as private organizations, have responded with a variety of legal requirements, risk-mitigation guidelines, and other measures to protect sensitive information about critical infrastructure and to safeguard the privacy of personal data. While this field is constantly evolving, the past decade or so has seen some notable advances in governmental regulation and private self-regulation, and proactive, strategic approaches to information risk management.

Enacted in 2002 as part of the E-Government Act, the Federal Information Security Management Act (FISMA) governs computer and network security for all federal agencies. The law requires each federal agency to develop and implement safeguards against data breaches and other cyber-attacks. These programs are required to protect the agency's operations and assets, in addition to those of private contractors. More specifically, FISMA requires agencies to assess the risk of "unauthorized access, use, disclosure, disruption, modification, or destruction of information and information systems"; to "cost-effectively" mitigate such threats; to ensure that all personnel (including contractors) are adequately trained and informed; to test the efficacy of security measures in place, at least once annually; to detect, analyze, and remedy any shortfalls in the security policies and procedures; and to establish adequate procedures for responding to breaches, while maintaining the continuity of operations. The act also requires each federal agency to undergo an annual independent security audit. The National Institute of Standards and Technology within the U.S. Department of Commerce is working to help implement FISMA.[6]

---

5. GINA MARIE STEVENS, CONGRESSIONAL RESEARCH SERVICE, DATA SECURITY: FEDERAL AND STATE LAWS (2006), *available at* http://assets.opencrs.com/rpts/RS22374_20060203.pdf.

6. 44 U.S.C. §§ 3541 *et seq.*; *see also* National Institute of Standards and Technology, Computer Security Resource Center, Federal Information Security Management Act (FISMA) Implementation Project, *available at* http://csrc.nist.gov/groups/SMA/fisma/overview.html#background.

The Sarbanes-Oxley Act of 2002 (SOX) contains provisions requiring companies to maintain adequate internal controls over their financial disclosure mechanisms and procedures. Two provisions in particular relate to information security. Section 302 requires the CEO and CFO of a filing company to certify that they have reviewed the report and believe that it is accurate and complete as to all material facts, including omissions that would be misleading, and that all financial information accurately reflects the company's actual condition. The CEO and CFO must also certify that they "are responsible for establishing and maintaining internal controls"; have established such internal controls to ensure that material information is made known to them; periodically evaluate these controls; report any defects in the internal controls to the auditors; and disclose any remedial measures taken.[7] Section 404 requires the company to file an internal control report evaluating the security of reporting structures.[8] Under Section 404, the Securities and Exchange Commission's (SEC's) final rule requires the report to contain: "management's assessment of the effectiveness of the company's internal control over financial reporting . . . ; a statement identifying the framework used by management to evaluate the effectiveness of the company's internal control over financial reporting; and a statement that the [auditors] . . . issued an attestation report on management's assessment." The company must also report any material changes to the internal management of financial disclosure.[9]

The Health Insurance Portability and Accountability Act of 1996 (HIPAA) regulates the use and disclosure of individuals' health information. The Department of Health and Human Services (HHS) Office of Civil Rights is charged with implementing this legislation to protect the privacy of patient health information. All "individually identifiable health information," including medical records, treatment, and all payments, is protected.[10] The detailed specifications of the Privacy Rule outline permissible uses and disclosures of protected health information, including: (1) to the individual; (2) pursuant to treatment, payment, and health-care

---

7. Sarbanes-Oxley Act (2002) § 302, 15 U.S.C. § 7241.

8. Sarbanes-Oxley Act (2002) § 404, 15 U.S.C. § 7262.

9. U.S. Securities & Exchange Commission, Final Rule: Management's Report on Internal Control Over Financial Reporting and Certification of Disclosure in Exchange Act Periodic Reports, *available at* http://www.sec.gov/rules/final/33-8238.htm

10. Pub. L. 104-191, 42 U.S.C. § 1301 *et seq.*; *see also* U.S. Dep't of Health & Human Services, OCR Privacy Brief: Summary of the HIPAA Privacy Rule, *available at* http://www.hhs.gov/ocr/privacysummary.pdf.

operations; (3) opportunity to agree or object to disclosures; (4) disclosures incidental to an otherwise permissible use and disclosure; (5) public interest disclosures (e.g., for law enforcement); and (6) limited disclosures for research, public health, or health-care operations.[11] The Privacy Rule contains data security requirements, compelling companies to maintain administrative procedures, training programs, and policies to prevent intentional or unintentional use or disclosure of protected data.[12] HHS notes that "such safeguards might include shredding documents containing protected health information before discarding them, securing medical records with lock and key or pass code, and limiting access to keys or pass codes."[13] The HIPAA Security Rule sets forth a more detailed list of administrative, technical, and physical safeguards. These target workforce security, information access management, security incident procedures, facility access controls, device and media controls, person or entity authentication, and transmission security.[14]

The Gramm-Leach-Bliley Act of 1999 (GLBA)[15] followed in HIPAA's footsteps, requiring financial institutions to systematically implement administrative, physical, and technical safeguards "to insure the security and confidentiality of customer records and information"; "to protect against any anticipated threats or hazards to the security or integrity of such records"; and "to protect against unauthorized access to or use of such records or information which could result in substantial harm or inconvenience to any customer."[16] In addition to mandating procedural safeguards, GLBA contains consumer notice and informed consent provisions similar to those contained in HIPAA. A consumer may opt out and request nondisclosure of private information to a third party.[17]

The North American Electric Regulatory Corporation (NERC), a non-governmental, self-regulatory organization which is overseen by the U.S. Federal Energy Regulatory Commission (FERC) and Canadian authorities, has promulgated standards designed to ensure the reliable op-

---

11. 45 C.F.R. § 164.502(a)(1).

12. 45 C.F.R. § 164.530(c).

13. U.S. Dep't of Health & Human Services, OCR Privacy Brief: Summary of the HIPAA Privacy Rule, *available at* http://www.hhs.gov/ocr/privacysummary.pdf.

14. HIPAA Security Standards for the Protection of Electronic Personal Health Information , 45 C.F.R. § 164.

15. 15 U.S.C. § 6801 *et seq.*

16. *Id.*

17. 15 U.S.C. § 6802.

eration of bulk power systems. Following the 2003 power blackout in the northeastern United States and parts of Canada, pursuant to new federal law, FERC authorized NERC to enforce these mandatory standards and impose fines for noncompliance. Among these reliability standards is a set of guidelines for Critical Infrastructure Protection that includes (1) mandatory sabotage reporting; (2) critical cyber asset identification associated with the operation of bulk electric power; (3) security management controls; (4) physical protection of critical cyber assets; (5) systems security management; (6) incident reporting and response planning; and (7) recovery plans for critical cyber assets.[18]

In similar fashion, an association of credit card companies established a set of payment account security standards known as the Payment Card Industry Data Security Standard (PCI DSS). The PCI DSS contains 12 requirements organized by six fundamental principles: (1) build and maintain a secure network; (2) protect cardholder data; (3) maintain a vulnerability management program; (4) implement strong access control measures; (5) regularly monitor and test networks; and (6) maintain an information security policy.[19]

State legislatures have enacted data security measures as well, which have typically focused on breach notification requirements (i.e., requiring persons, business entities, and in some cases state agencies to notify victims of data breach incidents) rather than systemic prevention or information management guidelines. While some state laws do mandate the implementation of data security programs and procedures in addition to post-breach notification,[20] most simply designate federal information security requirements as an exemption to the notification rule. In many state data security statutes, entities subject to, and in compliance with, federal regulations under HIPAA, the GLBA, or the Federal Interagency Guidance on Response Programs for Unauthorized Access to Customer Information and Customer Notice are exempt from the state requirements.[21] In some of

---

18. North American Electric Regulatory Corp. (NERC), Reliability Standards, *available at* http://www.nerc.com.

19. The PCI Security Standards Council, Payment Card Industry (PCI) Data Security Standard Ver. 1.1 (2006), https://www.pcisecuritystandards.org/security_standards/pci_dss.shtml.

20. MINN. STAT. § 325E.61, § 609.891.

21. *See, e.g.,* ARIZ. REV. STAT. ANN. § 44-7501 (exemptions for GLBA- and HIPAA-compliant entities); LA. REV. STAT. ANN. § 51:307 *et seq.* (exemption for financial institutions in compliance with the Federal Interagency Guidance on Response Programs for Unauthorized Access to Customer Information and Customer Notice); Michigan.

these laws, the mere fact of federal regulation in the area preempts the state law, as in Minnesota, where financial institutions and entities covered by HIPAA are per se exempt. Almost all of the state laws create a safe harbor for encrypted data. The statute is inapplicable if the lost, stolen, or accessed data was encrypted, redacted, or secured in another manner.

The state statutes vary in their definitions of covered entities and the scope of protected personal information. Almost all of the statutes cover private individuals and commercial entities that possess, own, or license data containing personal information. Some of the laws refer to the broad category of "information brokers"[22] or "data collectors."[23] A significant number of states apply their law to state agencies as well,[24] and several include biometric data in the definition of nonpublic, personal information.[25] Most of the statutes require that notice be given to victims of a data security breach, unless either (1) disclosure would impede a law enforcement investigation[26] or (2) the breach has not compromised personal data, or identity theft, fraud, or other harm to the victim is unlikely to result.[27] Above a certain state-specific threshold number of victims, the state is usually required to inform consumer-reporting agencies.[28] Nine of the 50 states have given their residents a private right of action to recover damages.[29]

Finally, there is another wave of legislation under consideration in Congress that addresses both data breach and identity theft, as well as cybercrime and cybersecurity. One of the most comprehensive bills introduced on the subject was the Personal Data Privacy and Security Act of

---

22. GA. CODE ANN. § 10-1-910 *et seq.*

23. 815 ILL. COMP. STAT. 530/1 *et seq.*

24. *See, e.g.,* ARK. CODE ANN. § 4-110-101 *et seq.*; CAL. CIV. CODE § 1798.29, 1798.82; 815 ILL. COMP. STAT. 530/1 *et seq.*; N.Y. STATE TECH. LAW § 208.

25. *See, e.g.,* NEV. REV. STAT. §§ 205.461-4675; TEX. BUS. & COM. CODE ANN. § 48.001 *et seq.*

26. *See, e.g.,* IND. CODE § 1.IC 4-1-10.

27. *See, e.g.,* WIS. STAT. § 895. 507; 73 PA. CONS. STAT. § 2302; N.C. GEN. STAT. § 75-65.

28. *See, e.g.,* FLA. STAT. ANN. § 817.5681 (more than 1,000 individuals); GA. CODE ANN. § 10-1-910 *et seq.* (more than 10,000 individuals).

29. *See* CAL. CIV. CODE § 1798.29, 1798.82; DEL. CODE ANN. tit. 6, Ch. 12B §§ 101–104 (treble damages and reasonable attorney fees); LA. REV. STAT. ANN. § 51:307 *et seq.*; MINN. STAT. § 325E.61, § 609.891; N.H. REV. STAT. ANN. § 359-C; N.C. GEN. STAT. § 75-65 (only if actual injury results from the statutory violation); R.I. GEN. LAWS § 11-49.2-1 *et seq.*; TENN. CODE ANN. § 4-48-101 *et seq.*, § 4-48-201 *et seq.*; WASH. REV. CODE § 19.255.010.

2007, co-sponsored by Senators Patrick Leahy and Arlen Specter.[30] The bill makes intentionally accessing a computer without authorization a racketeering activity under the RICO statute; imposes a fine or prison term of up to five years for concealing a security breach; preempts all state regulation of data brokers, defined as commercial entities engaged in collecting, transmitting, or providing access to sensitive, personally identifiable information on more than 5,000 individuals; requires brokers to disclose personal data to the requesting individual and correct inaccuracies; requires the maintenance of a data privacy and security program with risk control policies, regular testing, and procedures to prevent unauthorized access by any business keeping electronic data on more than 10,000 U.S. persons (exempts certain financial institutions and HIPAA-covered entities); and lastly, requires security breach notification to any U.S. resident victim, unless such disclosure would jeopardize a criminal investigation or undermine national security.[31] Some of the pending bills amend FISMA and vest authority to establish data breach prevention and response plans, encryption requirements, and breach notification guidelines for the federal agencies in the Office of Management and Budget (OMB).[32] With respect to private data brokers, one House bill gives the Federal Trade Commission (FTC) exclusive authority to establish security and breach notification guidelines.[33] The flurry of legislation signals, if nothing else, that the threats to information security are both real and unresolved.

DANGERS OF COMPARTMENTALIZED COMPLIANCE

New waves of compliance requirements have been promulgated so quickly, many organizations have come to focus on tactically—and nominally—meeting the requirements rather than adopting a more systematic, risk-management approach to address underlying vulnerabilities and new threats.

Not infrequently, so-called standards and compliance requirements exacerbate the workload of cyber-security professionals and can lead them to a narrow focus on internal processes rather than achieving objec-

---

30. The Personal Data Privacy and Security Act, S. 495, 110th Cong. (2007).

31. *Id.*

32. *See* The Federal Agency Data Breach Protection Act, H.R. 2124, 110th Cong. (2007); The Federal Agency Data Protection Act, H.R. 4791, 110th Cong. (2007).

33. The Data Accountability and Trust Act, H.R. 958, 110th Cong. (2007).

tive results. It can become too easy for overworked and often under-resourced managers to obsess about meeting formal requirements, benchmarks, and service-level agreements and lose sight of the purpose of IT and IT security and assurance: securing business processes against disruption.[34]

The tactical approach to compliance has several drawbacks. First, compliance requirements and best practices invariably strive to foil known threats. In many respects, explicit compliance requirements represent an outmoded perspective on guarding against yesterday's threats. Even if such requirements successfully close a widely shared vulnerability, hackers and sophisticated attackers will invariably soon move on to exploit new and previously unknown weaknesses. Human nature and Murphy's Law work to ensure that new kinds of unforced errors will eventually bloom into embarrassing and/or dangerous realities. Already, security professionals have been surprised at the risks presented by USB thumb drives and other portable storage devices, wireless Internet access, and laptop computers (and, soon, Blackberrys) that go missing. Who can guess which new technologies will reveal security downsides?

Too often, data security professionals work in silos insulated from mainstream business processes. Some of the silos are conceptual. Security professionals are there to protect data, assets, and occasionally people, but not always business processes. Other silos can result as a matter of policy. Many mainstream business managers and IT system managers simply do not want to grant security people authority that might impact business operations or, from their perspective, interfere with achieving service-level agreements.

Many top executives and senior managers—in the private sector and in government—are also uncomfortable with their ability to understand and manage IT security. They prefer to de facto delegate what they perceive as technical matters to technical people. Some still do not recognize IT as a mission-critical process on par with traditional management

---

34. "An effective, enterprise-wide compliance–risk management program is flexible to respond to change, and it is tailored to an organization's corporate strategies, business activities, and external environment. In addition, an effective, enterprise-wide compliance–risk management program requires strong board and senior management oversight." Speech by Mark W. Olsen, Governor, Federal Reserve Board, before the Fiduciary and Investment Risk Management Association's 20th Anniversary Training Conference, April 10, 2006.

disciplines such as finance, production, marketing, distribution, human resources, etc. This can result in an overdelegation of responsibility for security to technical leads, further isolating security decision making from existing business risk-management processes.

The mirror image of this problematic separation of authority is that all too often the only people who assess the success or failure of security programs (and their own job performance) are security practitioners, whether on staff or outsourced. They view the world in technical terms and too frequently have no insight into the business impact of their activities.

All of these factors can lead organizations to treat cyber security as a narrowly focused compliance, or check-off, exercise. Organizations will comply with the letter of laws, regulations, and standards but fail to fully take into account their impact on business operations. As noted earlier, it is not that anyone—management, security professionals, legislators, lawyers—is deliberately trying to do harm, but a compliance culture has arisen that can reward all classes of actors for tunnel vision. What we really need to do is rethink the role of standards compliance—to no longer treat it as a goal in and of itself, but as an activity integrated into a more holistic view of overall business results optimization.

FROM COMPLIANCE TO RISK MANAGEMENT

The first step in closing the compliance and business effectiveness gap is for executives and senior managers to treat security as any other management discipline. Security and resilience should be addressed as part of a risk-management approach that integrates security, disaster recovery, business continuity, resilience, and IT operations.

This is as important as other organizational risk issues and, accordingly, is too important to be left to technologists to treat as an entirely technical tactical issue. Accordingly, C-level executives and senior managers must have an expertise in technology that is equivalent to their knowledge and understanding of other business administration fundamentals: accounting, finance, production, marketing, human resources, and the like.

They should ensure that the focus on cyber security and information risk is on effective risk management that is fully cognizant of the responsibilities to internal and external stakeholders and business drivers, rather than only to compliance with externally prescribed standards. Although the need to comply with external requirements means that it is essential that the enterprise be aware of whether the risk-management activities "will get us through the next SOX audit," that should not be the overarching standard for success. Rather, the ongoing question should be: "Are we taking actions that are in the best interests of the business, shareholders, and other owners and investors, and customers?" Put another way, the organizational leadership should cultivate a culture of responsibility and accountability, not just compliance.

The best organizations strategically manage the risks they face relative to the mission and goals of the organization. It is essential that cyber security and information risk and assurance be managed consistently with risk management of the organization generally, so that it is part of the responsibility of the board of directors, the CEO, corporate executives, and senior management.

Among the questions inherent in a risk-management framework and corporate culture are the following:

1. Relative to the mission of the organization and the critical functions necessary to advance that mission, what risks should most concern us?
2. What actions are necessary to mitigate that risk?
3. When and how do we track that risk and our efforts to mitigate it?
4. How do we facilitate periodic, independent assessment? Put another way, what are the risk-adjusted costs and benefits of mitigation and avoidance actions?

Even non-technical, C-level executives and senior managers must communicate with their technical leads as they do with anyone else who reports to them. The communication is critical to developing and enhancing over time the mutual understanding of what the superior or supervisor needs to focus on to assess and audit status, goals, direction, and milestones. Supervisors can and should ask tough questions as they exercise their responsibilities to provide strategic guidance and oversight.

Even a layman superior or supervisor should know what the capability of the technical team is to dynamically assess in real time the state of the information system and the devices connected to it, and whether the system and its component devices are in compliance with policy. In defense and homeland security parlance, that is sometimes referred to as situational awareness. In addition to the state of the internal systems, situational awareness refers to the status of external activities that could impact the organization's information system. Although there are technical aspects to these questions, a layman can understand the essentials, expect action to be taken to correct deficiencies, and ultimately ensure that there is a process in place for independent audit.

Surprisingly, many organizations lack fundamental information about what devices are connected to their network and the status of those devices from a vulnerability perspective, and they lack the ability to remedy those vulnerabilities in real time. Many that have some technical knowledge still cannot assess whether the status information is accurate or the risks have in fact been mitigated. Many of those lack any capability to remediate known risks in real time. Meaningful risk assessment and effective risk mitigation, which are essential to a risk-management program, require that those administering the enterprise know, in near real time, what devices are connected to the network and whether each device is in compliance with the organization's security policies, and have the ability to bring each noncompliant device into compliance or bar it from the network. At a minimum, an organization's security programs, processes, and actions should be developed and implemented from a position of real-time situational awareness and response.

In many ways, it is shocking how little many managers know about what happens in their information infrastructures, particularly when it comes to information security problems. From a corporate responsibility and governance perspective, it is equally amazing that many C-level executives and senior managers do not know this reality about their organizations. In other areas of their management duties, they would never countenance this reality. To do their jobs, they must demand more.

An additional reality of information systems and networks is that many security incidents (sometimes referred to as "blowouts") will not be detected until weeks or even months after they occur, if ever. Nontechnical and technical officials need to continually press to implement existing technologies, and develop new ones, that accelerate the ability to see incidents and mitigate vulnerabilities. The innovation advantage possessed by malicious actors ("black hats") guarantees that any vendor-provided solution to suppress a threat will arrive too late to block the first, most dangerous wave of that threat. Although there are some "zero day" exploits (vulnerabilities that are exploited either before the vulnerability is known or at least before a patch is made available), typically, malicious actors exploit vulnerabilities that have already been publicized and for which patches are available but either were not installed effectively or quickly or were not installed at all).

Many IT infrastructures are rife with common vulnerabilities that make them ripe for attack or exploit; they are accidents waiting to happen. Because of the limitations of conventional tools, exploitation of vulnerabilities can occur without setting off any triggers, thus avoiding detection for a long period of time (if ever). Managers need real-time information on system and device status to protect against exploitation of known vulnerabilities and to see anomalous behaviors as they occur, rather than as part of the "after-action" evaluation and reporting process. Such technology exists. C-level executives and senior managers must be sure that their technical experts are keeping abreast of changing and new technology and are cognizant of the best in breed.

Meaningful risk-management capabilities, whether for financial or cyber security/information risk or assurance, require regular, independent assessment of risk and risk mitigation. Too few organizations subject their in-house teams, much less their outsourced providers, to regular independent audits of their risk posture (threats, vulnerabilities, and consequences if vulnerabilities are exploited) and adequacy of deployed security technologies and processes to provide situational awareness, assess vulnerabilities and noncompliance, remediate noncompliance, and mitigate risk. Many organizations do not even do penetration testing or independent assessments, sometimes because they already know they are vulnerable and do not want to spend precious resources.

As in other areas of the organization, it is important to periodically bring in outside, objective expertise to determine whether security programs are adequately assessing and mitigating risk and effectively and efficiently meeting organizational needs.

The reasons for independent audits and the use of outside experts are just as strong in this area as in others. Organizations can become too set in their ways to be objective. Incumbent vendors and those within the organization who manage them want to maintain the status quo. Personal relations with outside vendors invariably lead to a tendency to fail to view them objectively. This "account control" does not serve the best interests of the organization, only the interests of the vendor-provider and those within the organization who would have to go to significant lengths to find a replacement.

SUMMARY AND CONCLUSION

When one looks at the standard-setting and compliance program strictures of the last few years, it appears that at least some of this activity has been structured primarily to deal with specific problems that received widespread publicity and that would require relatively minimal effort by government and private companies, rather than helping to drive progress toward effective risk-management programs to maintain acceptable levels of information security risk.

One thing has become apparent to increasing numbers of officials in government and the private sector: information risk is more than just an annoyance of the information age; our economy, institutions, and society depend on information systems. We can no longer say that an attack on a bank is just a problem for the bank, or a slip-up at a state Department of Motor Vehicles means merely a busy day for its public affairs department. An attack on any one of them is potentially an attack on all of us. Information security, then, is a matter of national public interest and needs to be treated as such.

We are all in this together. Public and private institutions need to join together to build and implement information risk programs and processes that reduce vulnerabilities to information security disasters. This needs to be done in a suspicion-free atmosphere of shared purpose; it should not be seen as a shrewdly played negotiation between adversaries. As with other historic challenges in our nation's history, we must work together with a sense of shared responsibility and commitment toward addressing information risk.

Individual organizations must make information risk a part of their overall risk-management challenge. Although it is critical for any organization to comply with statutory and regulatory compliance imperatives, the most forward-looking organizations will ensure that their risk-management programs dynamically address information risk, with a focus on the primary mission and critical business drivers and functions of the organization. Risk itself should be the focus, not compliance.

Information risk-management programs need to utilize the people and processes and, yes, the technologies that can help them create and deploy appropriate policies and controls, track compliance with them, and rapidly remediate instances of noncompliance. Such programs need regular (at least annual) independent assessments and robust, after-action, lessons-learned processes following incidents.

Risk management by individual private and public organizations will be a key component involved in meeting the challenge that President Obama said the United States must face to secure the digital information infrastructure.

CHAPTER 6

Information Protection

by James W. Conrad, Jr.

This chapter explains what sorts of legal protections may exist to prevent the public release of private security documents in the possession of a federal agency. The chapter begins by discussing the Freedom of Information Act (FOIA). The next part addresses a variety of labels that may appear to justify the government withholding information but really do not. Finally, the chapter explains at varying lengths a number of statutes that give the government the ability to protect certain types of security infor- mation from public release, focusing on sensitive security infor- mation (SSI), chemical-terrorism vulnerability information (CVI), and protected critical infrastructure information (PCII).

INTRODUCTION

Based on an unscientific polling of fellow lawyers with "homeland secu- rity" practices, the most common questions that clients ask involve the confusing welter of laws, rules, guidance, and folk wisdom involved in protecting security-sensitive information. This area of the law has al- ways been complex, but it has become especially so since September 11, 2001, for several reasons:

- Congress keeps enacting similar but not identical authorizations to protect particular types of information;
- Agencies keep issuing rules and policies that heighten rather than minimize the differences between these authorities and resist ef- forts to rationalize them;

- The field continues, despite reforms, to be cluttered with a distracting profusion of labels that have some practical (albeit inconsistent) meaning within government agencies but provide no legal basis for withholding information from disclosure; and
- All concerned continue to struggle to find the appropriate balance between three competing needs: (i) to avoid giving actionable information to would-be malefactors; (ii) to give governmental and private actors in the security world the information they need to do their jobs; and (iii) to respect our nation's long tradition of public access to governmental and risk-related information.

As the last reason implies, information protection in the security context requires a cultural shift from the traditional binary notion that information in a government agency's possession should be releasable either to anyone outside it or to no one. Security planning, particularly in the area of response, cannot be conducted effectively unless federal, state, local, and private actors are aware of one another's capabilities and have cooperated in defining scenarios, roles, and actions. Accordingly, the public and private sectors need simultaneously both to secure information and to share it. In addition to explaining what legal protections may exist to prevent the public release of private security documents once they are in the possession of an executive branch agency of the federal government, this chapter also notes when these protections (i) may impose obligations on the business that generated the information, and (ii) envision the government sharing information with other entities while not releasing it to the public at large.

THE FREEDOM OF INFORMATION ACT

FOIA provides the overarching framework for deciding whether a federal agency may or must release information in its possession.[1] FOIA generally embodies a congressional policy decision that all government records should be made publicly available unless one of nine exemptions applies. Five of these are potentially relevant to businesses' security information. How useful any of them may prove to be in a given case is uncertain, however, for several important reasons:

- First, the exemptions are from FOIA's mandate to disclose, meaning that the government retains the discretion under FOIA to

---

1. 5 U.S.C § 552.

disclose exempt information unless some other legal authority limits the agency's power to release it.

- Second, most FOIA exemptions have been construed narrowly by agencies and courts in their efforts to effectuate Congress's openness policy. Whether a given agency will protect a given document, and whether a court will agree, are uncertain.
- Finally, each exemption has its own peculiarities deriving from statutory language and years of evolving (and divergent) agency practice and judicial interpretations.

"Other Laws" Exemption

The most reliable FOIA exemption potentially relevant to private security information is the (b)(3) exemption, which exempts from FOIA's disclosure mandate any information the release of which is controlled by another federal law.[2] A multitude of statutes come in through this door, most notably those enacting the SSI, CVI, and PCII programs, discussed in Part IV below in the concluding sections of this chapter.

National Security Exemption

FOIA exempts from disclosure documents that have been properly classified for reasons of national defense or foreign policy.[3] Thus, government records that are "top secret," "secret," or "confidential" need not be disclosed under FOIA—and in fact other authorities establish a range of sanctions if they are disclosed.[4] While at first glance this "(b)(1)" exemption might seem like an ideal way for the government to protect privately generated "homeland security" documents, classification actually has a number of serious limitations:

- *Only some federal agencies can classify a document.* The only way a document can become classified is if a federal agency that has "original classification authority" affirmatively acts to classify it.[5] A private entity cannot classify its own document. Nor is there any established process for private entities to request an agency to classify a document.

---

2. *Id.* § 552(b)(3).
3. *Id.* § 552(b)(1).
4. *See, e.g.,* 18 U.S.C. § 798.
5. Exec. Order 12,958, § 1.1(a)(1), *as amended by* Exec. Order 13,292, 68 Fed. Reg. 15,315 (Mar. 28, 2003).

- *Access to classified documents is very tightly controlled.* Once a document has been classified, the only people who can see it are those who have an active security clearance at the requisite level (e.g., "secret" level for documents that have been classified at the secret or confidential level), have a "need to know," and have signed a nondisclosure agreement.[6]
- *No one else can see the document—even the person who prepared it.* For example, if a private person without a security clearance prepared a vulnerability assessment of his facility and submitted it to a government agency, and the agency classified the document, the submitter could not get it back. Obviously, this is not conducive to effective security or information sharing.
- *Agency rules and procedures regarding access to classified documents are quite burdensome and cumbersome.* Someone who meets the three access requirements listed above has to construct an appropriately secure facility where the documents must remain at all times, with access controls and recordkeeping requirements.[7] People cannot even discuss classified information over the telephone unless they have secure telecommunications capabilities, which are expensive and time-consuming to install.[8]

Law Enforcement Exemption

Another FOIA exemption of partial use in protecting private security documents covers information compiled for civil or criminal law enforcement purposes (conventionally referred to as "law enforcement sensitive" information). This exemption applies to a half-dozen categories of documents, but one is of particular relevance to the facility security predicament: records the release of which "could reasonably be expected to endanger the life or physical safety of any individual."[9] While this "(b)(7)" exemption was originally crafted to protect law enforcement personnel, it has been broadly interpreted to justify agencies' refusal to disclose law enforcement records whenever their release could reason-

---

6. Exec. Order 12,958, § 4.1(a), *as amended by* Exec. Order 13,292, 68 Fed. Reg. 15,324.
7. 32 C.F.R. §§ 2001.41(a), 2001.43.
8. *Id.* §§ 2001.41(c), 2001.49.
9. 5 U.S.C § 552(b)(7)(F).

ably be expected to result in harm to *any* person.[10] In the homeland security context, a federal court has held that Bureau of Reclamation "inundation maps" detailing areas that might be flooded if the Hoover or Glen Canyon dams failed catastrophically were covered by this exemption, because disclosure of the maps "could reasonably place at risk the life or physical safety of . . . individuals," communities, or infrastructure downstream of the dams.[11] A business's security vulnerability assessment could well fall into this category also, and federal agencies have made known their intention to assert this defense where relevant.[12]

The main problem with this exemption is that it can only be asserted when the private information in question could plausibly be argued to have been generated or compiled in connection with some law enforcement purpose. This is likely to be only sporadically true in the security context. Many facilities whose security could be important are not subject to any laws on the topic, and many federal agencies do not have law enforcement authority associated with facility security.

Confidential Business Information Exemption

The Exemption

One FOIA exemption does offer potential protection to any private business: the "(b)(4)" exemption for "trade secrets and commercial or financial information [that is] privileged or confidential," also known as "confidential business information" or CBI.[13] The landmark *Critical Mass* case interpreting this exemption holds that where the information in question is voluntarily supplied to the agency, the only question an agency need ask is whether the information is of a kind that "would customarily

---

10. *See* U.S. DEP'T OF JUSTICE, FREEDOM OF INFORMATION ACT GUIDE 840 n.28 (March 2007) (citing the Attorney General's 1986 Amendments Memorandum).

11. Living Rivers, Inc. v. U.S. Bureau of Reclamation, 272 F. Supp. 2d 1313, 1321–22 (D. Utah 2003).

12. For example, when the FBI housed the National Infrastructure Protection Center (NIPC), it stated that it would assert this defense, among others, if anyone sought information supplied by private facilities regarding threats or similar incidents. *See* CHEMICAL SECTOR INFORMATION SHARING & ANALYSIS CENTER AND NATIONAL INFRASTRUCTURE PROTECTION CENTER, INFORMATION SHARING PROGRAM STANDARD OPERATING PROCEDURE (Apr. 24, 2002).

13. 5 U.S.C. § 552(b)(4).

not be released to the public by the person from whom it was obtained."[14] Since no business in its right mind would customarily release actionable security information to the public, this means that voluntarily submitted private security information should categorically be covered by this exemption. Pursuant to executive order, all federal agency FOIA regulations provide that the agency will notify a submitter if someone has requested information provided by the submitter for which the submitter has claimed CBI protection, giving the submitter a reasonable period of time to object.[15] If the agency decides to release the information notwithstanding an objection, it must notify the submitter in advance of a specified release date so the submitter can file a "reverse FOIA" lawsuit to block release.[16]

Concerns about the Exemption

While the (b)(4) exemption, as construed in *Critical Mass*, would seem to provide clear protection for voluntarily submitted business security information, many representatives of private interests have expressed skepticism about whether this is really the case. As discussed below, some of these concerns are probably unfounded or overwrought, but others have at least some merit.

Is it really discretionary?

Some representatives of potential CBI submitters note with concern the seemingly discretionary nature of the CBI exemption—meaning that an agency may, but is not required to, refuse to disclose information covered by that (or any other) FOIA exemption. While this is technically true, looking only within the four corners of FOIA, it is also true that courts have construed the federal Trade Secrets Act[17] to be coextensive with the CBI exemption.[18] This means that if information falls within the scope of the CBI exemption, it is a federal crime—a felony, in fact—for a federal employee to release it under FOIA. So the "discretionary" nature of the (b)(4) exemption should not be a basis for concern among

---

14. Critical Mass Energy Project v. Nuclear Regulatory Comm'n, 975 F.2d 871, 878 (D.C. Cir. 1992) (en banc).

15. *See* Exec. Order (June 23, 1987), 52 Fed. Reg. 23,781 (June 25, 1987).

16. *Id.*

17. 18 U.S.C. § 1905.

18. *See., e.g.*, CNA Fin. Corp. v. Donovan, 830 F.2d 1132, 1151 (D.C. Cir. 1987).

would-be submitters; but it is, in the author's experience, by some who do not appreciate the Trade Secrets Act angle.

Will courts follow Critical Mass?

A second basis for concern is that the *Critical Mass* decision, while of great persuasive value, is binding precedent only within the D.C. Circuit, and there does not appear to be any trend among other federal courts to follow it.[19] Thus it is entirely possible that a court somewhere in the United States would decline to follow *Critical Mass* and instead direct the agency to follow prior law, which required agencies to assay whether disclosure would likely "impair the Government's ability to obtain necessary information in the future" or "cause substantial harm to the competitive position of the person from whom the information was obtained."[20] Needless to say, many are uncomfortable risking the disclosure of vital information on the outcome of such subjective tests.

Is security information really "commercial or financial"?

A third concern may be that potential submitters do not think of security-related information as commercial or financial information, since for the most part it does not involve cost or price data, product formulas, or other sorts of information that would typically be regarded as valuable to competitors. Most courts have concluded that commercial information covers anything "pertaining or relating to or dealing with commerce."[21] However, one federal district court has concluded that "factual information [supplied to the FAA by airlines] regarding the nature and frequency of in-flight medical emergencies" was not commercial information.[22] How such cases might apply to threat information, and potentially some vulnerability information, is thus uncertain.

---

19. *See* FOIA GUIDE, *supra* note 10, at 372–96. A lawsuit seeking to compel disclosure of a business's security plan could be filed by a plaintiff anywhere he or she resides. *See* 5 U.S.C. § 552(a)(4)(B).

20. *See* Nat'l Parks & Conserv. Ass'n v. Morton, 498 F.2d 765, 770 (D.C. Cir. 1974).

21. *See* Am. Airlines, Inc. v. Nat'l Mediation Bd., 588 F.2d 863, 870 (2d Cir. 1978).

22. *See* Chicago Tribune v. FAA, 1998 WL 242611 (N.D. Ill. May 7, 1998).

The culture of disclosure

Finally, some potential submitters are no doubt put off by associations that they have with the (b)(4) exemption deriving from their experience with it in other contexts. Many agencies, especially the Environmental Protection Agency (EPA), have zealously followed judicial admonitions to interpret exemptions from FOIA narrowly. Persons who are familiar with these agencies' policies and practices likely will impute them to the Department of Homeland Security (DHS) or other agencies and be reluctant to trust them with such sensitive information. For all these reasons, the (b)(4) exemption is potentially applicable to a broad range of business security information, but of uncertain reliability in the eyes of many.

"Risk of Circumvention" Exemption

A somewhat unlikely FOIA exemption that may have limited utility in protecting private security documents is the "(b)(2)" exemption (also known as Exemption 2) protecting records "relat[ing] solely to the internal personnel rules and practices of an agency."[23] Over the years, many courts have interpreted this exemption to cover not only agency papers that literally address "internal personnel rules and practices" (called "low 2" materials), but also what are called "high 2" materials: that is, those "predominantly internal" records that are effective only if they remain confidential.[24] Immediately after 9/11, the Justice Department advised other federal agencies that this exemption is well suited for application to the sensitive information contained in vulnerability assessments, and that agencies should "avail themselves of the full measure of Exemption 2's protection for their critical infrastructure information as they continue to gather more of it, and assess its heightened sensitivity, in the wake of the September 11 terrorist attacks."[25] On the other hand, not all circuit courts have adopted the "high 2" concept, and a district court has refused to apply it to the inundation maps discussed above.[26] Moreover, it is not at all clear whether this exemption could apply to a report developed by a private business.

---

23. *See* 5 U.S.C. § 552(b)(2).

24. *See* FOIA GUIDE, *supra* note 10, at 273–305; U.S. Dep't of Justice, *OIP Guidance: Protecting Vulnerability Assessments Through Application of Exemption 2*, FOIA UPDATE, Vol. X, No. 3, at 3–4.

25. U.S. Dep't of Justice, *FOIA Post* (Oct. 15, 2001), *available at* www.usdoj.gov/oip/foiapost/2001foiapost19.htm. *See also* FOIA GUIDE, *supra* note 10, at 299–305.

26. *See Living Rivers, supra* note 11, 292 F. Supp. 2d at 1317.

"PROTECTIONS" THAT AREN'T

Understanding the rules for when government agencies can withhold information is complicated by the existence of several labels that, while frequently referenced by government agencies seeking to protect information, do not actually authorize those agencies to withhold records from release under FOIA. Many government documents are prominently captioned "For Official Use Only," or FOUO, and contain ominous legends.[27] While it may sound gravely important, FOUO does not represent a category of information that is exempt from release under FOIA. If no FOIA exemption applies, an FOUO document would have to be produced in response to a FOIA request that adequately describes it. A similarly intimidating but legally ineffectual label that is commonly used in and out of government is "Sensitive But Unclassified," or SBU. As described in the section above on national security exemption, there are three types of classified information, and a document properly classified at one of these levels is exempt from disclosure under FOIA thanks to the (b)(1) exemption. But there is no "Sensitive But Unclassified" exemption to FOIA.

FOUO, SBU, and similar labels are basically intra- or intergovernmental tools for "safeguarding" documents—that is, ensuring that they are closely held and not disseminated more broadly than intended.[28] There are over 100 of these labels, and their decentralized proliferation inspired the president to issue a memorandum requiring federal agencies to consolidate all of their labels for sensitive unclassified information into a

---

27. For example:

   Warning: This document is FOR OFFICIAL USE ONLY (U// FOUO). It contains information that may be exempt from public release under the Freedom of Information Act (5 U.S.C. § 552). It is to be controlled, stored, handled, transmitted, distributed, and disposed of in accordance with [agency] policy related to FOUO information and is not to be released to the public or other personnel who do not have a valid "need-to-know" without prior approval of an authorized [agency] official. No portion of this document should be furnished to the media, either in written or verbal form.

28. Other common labels that do not necessarily correlate with any FOIA exemption are "Official Use Only" (OUO), "Sensitive Homeland Security Information" (SHSI), and "Limited Official Use" (LOU).

dramatically simpler framework. After overcoming much bureaucratic resistance, the administration in May 2008 finally unveiled its framework for "controlled unclassified information (CUI)."[29] Under this framework, all prior labels such as FOUO are abolished, and unclassified information requiring any particular restrictions on handling or dissemination is to be categorized and labeled in one of three ways: "controlled/ standard dissemination," "controlled specified dissemination," or "controlled enhanced/specified dissemination." This framework encompasses information that is exempt from disclosure under FOIA and information that is not exempt; in the former case, the conditions of the applicable exemption provide the "specified dissemination" limitations. The framework is unfortunately not comprehensive; DHS and the Department of Energy (DOE) succeeded in getting four categories of information exempted from the CUI framework, including the "Safeguards Information" (SGI), SSI, CVI, and PCII programs discussed below.[30]

OTHER LAWS THAT MAY PROTECT A BUSINESS'S SECURITY INFORMATION

As noted earlier, the (b)(3) exemption from FOIA protects documents from being released when some other statute governs their disclosure. A number of these statutes are specifically designed to protect security-sensitive information. The most comprehensive were enacted (or dramatically expanded) after 9/11, and the responsible agencies in some cases are still struggling to define their scope and operation—as are organizations that generate or may possess covered information. The first section below summarizes information protections applicable to particular types of facilities or operations. The following sections describe three much more broadly applicable regulatory programs for protecting three kinds of information: "Sensitive Security Information," "Chemical-terrorism Vulnerability Information," and "Protected Critical Infrastructure Information."

---

29. Presidential Memorandum *re* Designation & Sharing of Controlled Unclassified Information (May 9, 2008), *available at* http://www.whitehouse.gov/news/releases/2008/05/20080509-6.html. The memorandum effectuated several congressional directives to promote information sharing. *See* 6 U.S.C. §§ 482, 485(d)(3)(A).

30. Memorandum, *id.* ¶ 27.

Laws Applicable to Particular Classes of Business Activities

The "law enforcement" exemption from FOIA may apply where particular agencies have the ability to regulate security at particular types of facilities or transportation modalities. The laws granting such authority often contain their own information protections applicable to information generated pursuant to their authorities. This part of the chapter discusses five such programs, as well as innovative programs for managing security sensitive information related to energy infrastructure.

Large Public Drinking Water Systems

The Safe Drinking Water Act requires large public drinking water systems to certify to EPA that they have conducted vulnerability assessments, and to provide it with those assessments.[31] The identity of a facility submitting an assessment and the date of the certification must be made public.[32] Otherwise, however, these assessments, and information derived from them, must be kept in a secure location, and EPA is prohibited from making this information "available to anyone other than an individual designated by the [EPA] Administrator."[33] These designated individuals need not be government employees. Criminal penalties are provided if such an individual knowingly or recklessly releases the information in an unauthorized fashion.[34] The statute further provides that covered drinking water systems do not have to provide these assessments to a state or local entity "solely by reason of the requirement" that they submit them to EPA[35]—but it does not prevent state or local entities from passing enactments that specifically require submission of these assessments. The law also authorizes designated individuals who are govern-

---

31. *See* 42 U.S.C. § 300i-2(a)(2).

32. *Id.* § 300i-2(a)(3).

33. *Id.* § 300i-2(a)(5).

34. *Id.* § 300i-2(a)(6)(A). Such an individual can disclose the information (i) to another designated individual, (ii) for purposes of conducting inspections or taking actions in response to imminent hazards, or (iii) in administrative or judicial enforcement actions under the act. *Id.*

35. *Id.* § 300i-2(a)(4). This provision was designed to preempt state or local laws that say, in effect, "you must submit to us anything you have to submit to EPA."

ment employees to "discuss the contents of a vulnerability assessment" with state or local officials.[36]

Ports, Facilities, and Vessels Regulated by the Maritime Transportation Security Act

The Maritime Transportation Security Act (MTSA), enacted in 2002, charges the Coast Guard with comprehensively regulating security at ports, maritime facilities, and vessels.[37] The act declares that, "[n]otwithstanding any other provision of law, information developed under [it] is not required to be disclosed to the public, including . . . facility security plans, vessel security plans, . . . port vulnerability assessments; and . . . other information related to security plans, procedures or programs for vessels or facilities authorized under [it]."[38] Scattered provisions of the Coast Guard's MTSA rules flesh out this declaration (which does not require regulations to be effective) by stating that various types of information generated under the MTSA are "sensitive security information" (SSI) under regulations jointly published by the Department of Transportation (DOT) and the Transportation Security Administration (TSA).[39] The SSI rules—which impose obligations on the generators of this information, not just agencies—are discussed below.

Shippers and Carriers of Hazardous Materials Required to Prepare Security Plans

Shippers and carriers of certain hazardous materials are required by DOT's HM-232 rules to prepare transportation security plans (including "an assessment of possible transportation security risks") and to provide awareness and in-depth security training to relevant employees.[40] None of these documents is required to be submitted to DOT.[41] DOT has stated that it "[g]enerally . . . will not collect or retain security plans," and "in the rare instance" where it does, it will "analyze all applicable laws and Freedom of Information Act exemptions to determine whether the information or portions of information in the security plan can be withheld from re-

---

36. *Id.* § 300i-2(a)(6)(B).
37. *See* Chapter 11.
38. 46 U.S.C. § 70103(d).
39. *See, e.g.,* 33 C.F.R. § 105.400(c).
40. *See* Chapter 10.
41. *See* 49 C.F.R. §§ 172.704, 172.802.

lease."[42] There is no question that, to the extent such plans involve aviation or maritime transportation, they are covered by the SSI rules. These rules, however, define many types of information (including vulnerability assessments) as SSI without regard to mode of transportation, and so at least the assessment portions of any HM-232 plans should be protected by the SSI rules.

Facilities Regulated under the Chemical Weapons Convention Implementation Act

The Chemical Weapons Convention (CWC) Implementation Act provides that any confidential business information supplied to or otherwise acquired by the U.S. government under the act or the convention "shall not be disclosed" under FOIA.[43] "Confidential business information" is defined under the act to include CBI as defined under FOIA and specifically also includes "any plant design process, technology, or operating method," which could well include plant security practices or procedures.[44] Exceptions to this prohibition allow the government to supply CBI:

- to the CWC Technical Secretariat or other states that are parties to the Convention (which has its own Annex on the Protection of Confidential Information);[45]
- to congressional committees and subcommittees, upon written request of the chair or ranking member (though committees and staff are prohibited from disclosing this information except as required or authorized by law);[46]
- to other federal agencies for enforcement of any law, or when relevant to any proceeding under any law (but in either case must be managed "in such a manner as to preserve confidentiality to the extent practicable without impairing the proceeding");[47] or
- when the government determines it is in the national interest to do so.[48]

---

42. 68 Fed. Reg. 14,517 (Mar. 25, 2003).
43. 22 U.S.C. § 6744(a).
44. *Id.* § 6713(g). *See also* 15 C.F.R. § 718.
45. *See* 22 U.S.C. § 6744(b)(1).
46. *Id.* § 6744(b)(2).
47. *Id.* § 6744(b)(3).
48. *Id.* § 6744(c)(1).

Nuclear Power and Atomic Weapons Activities

The Atomic Energy Act (AEA) gives rise to two related categories of information protection:

- *Safeguards Information* (SGI).[49] The AEA authorizes the Nuclear Regulatory Commission (NRC) to issue rules or orders exempting from disclosure under FOIA information generated by NRC licensees (commercial nuclear facility owners and operators, principally) "if the unauthorized disclosure of such information could reasonably be expected to have a significant adverse effect on the health and safety of the public or the common defense and security by significantly increasing the likelihood of theft, diversion, or sabotage of [nuclear] material or . . . facilit[ies]." Such safeguards information includes:
  - "security measures (including security plans, procedures, and equipment) for the physical protection of [nuclear] material or plant equipment vital to the safety of production or utilization facilities involving nuclear materials"; and
  - the location of such equipment.

SGI cannot include "information pertaining to the routes and quantities of shipments" of nuclear material. Civil penalties can be imposed on anyone violating the NRC's SGI rules.[50]

- *Unclassified Controlled Nuclear Information.*[51] The AEA also authorizes the secretary of energy to issues rules or orders exempting from disclosure under FOIA unclassified information regarding atomic weapons programs "only if and to the extent that the Secretary determines that the unauthorized dissemination of such information could reasonably be expected to have a significant adverse effect on the health and safety of the public or the common defense and security by significantly increasing the likelihood of (A) illegal production of nuclear weapons, or (B) theft, diversion, or sabotage of nuclear materials, equipment, or facilities." This includes information on "security measures (including security plans, procedures, and equipment) for

---

49. 42 U.S.C. § 2167(a).
50. These rules are contained at 10 C.F.R. § 73.21.
51. 42 U.S.C. § 2168(a).

the physical protection of (i) production or utilization facilities, (ii) nuclear material contained in such facilities, or (iii) nuclear material in transit." Civil and criminal penalties can be imposed on any person who violates one of these rules or orders.[52]

Facilities Regulated by the Federal Energy Regulatory Commission

Shortly after September 11, the Federal Energy Regulatory Commission (FERC) initiated two innovative though controversial approaches for managing information related to the security of energy infrastructure.[53] While these approaches do not provide a separate basis for withholding information from disclosure, they remain worth discussing in the interest of comprehensiveness and because they show the maturation of an agency's efforts to balance information protection and access.

First, FERC has established special FOIA rules for critical energy infrastructure information (CEII), defined as information about critical infrastructure that: "relates details about the production, generation, transportation, transmission or distribution of energy; . . . could be useful to a person in planning an attack on critical infrastructure; . . . is exempt from mandatory disclosure under [FOIA]; . . . and does not simply give the general location of the critical infrastructure."[54] The CEII program does not expand the scope of information exempt from FOIA, since it only applies to information that already falls into a FOIA exemption (usually, the (b)(4) exemption for CBI). The purpose of the CEII rules is actually to facilitate the limited, but not general, disclosure of information that FERC could simply refuse to release to anyone. Under the rules, a person submitting information to FERC—whether voluntarily or not—who believes the information qualifies as CEII must file, along with the information, a statement justifying special treatment of the information.[55] Persons who can substantiate why they need particular CEII (typically, to participate in a ratemaking or similar FERC proceeding involving the infrastructure in question) can receive access to it, provided they provide FERC with personally identifying information and, in most cases, sign a

---

52. These rules are contained at 10 C.F.R. § 1017.

53. 18 C.F.R. §§ 388.112–388.113.

54. *Id.* § 388.113(c)(1). FERC's definition of "critical infrastructure" closely tracks the definition in DHS's PCII rules. *Compare* 18 C.F.R. § 388.113(c)(2) *with* 6 C.F.R. § 29.2.

55. 18 C.F.R. § 388.112(b).

nondisclosure agreement.[56] As with any FOIA request for CBI, FERC will provide the submitter of information with five days' notice of the request (in case the submitter wants to object) and five days' notice of a decision to release (in case the submitter wants to sue).[57]

FERC's second experiment was a category of "non-Internet public" (NIP) information for "maps or diagrams that reveal the location of critical energy infrastructure . . . but do not rise to the level of CEII."[58] A submitter was required to request NIP treatment as it would have CEII treatment.[59] FERC treated NIP like any other public information, except that it did not include it in its online Federal Energy Regulatory Records Information System.[60] In 2007, however, FERC abolished the category on the bases that much of the information was available online from other sources and all of it was available in FERC's Public Reference Room.[61]

Sensitive Security Information

Background

In 1974, the Federal Aviation Administration was given the power to prohibit the disclosure of information that, if released, could jeopardize the safety of passengers in air transportation. This authority has been revised and expanded several times since that date. At present, both DOT and TSA have statutory authority to issue regulations restricting the dissemination of information[62] and have jointly issued Sensitive Security Information rules implementing this authority.[63] The current rules largely address aviation security (regulated by TSA) and maritime security (regulated by the Coast Guard under the MTSA).[64] Land modes of transporta-

---

56. *Id.* § 388.113(d)(4).
57. *Id.* § 388.112(d), (e).
58. *Id.* § 388.112(a)(3).
59. *Id.* § 388.112(b)(1).
60. *See* 68 Fed. Reg. 46,457 (Aug. 6, 2003).
61. *See* 72 Fed. Reg. 63,980 (Nov. 14, 2007).
62. *See* 49 U.S.C. §§ 114(s)(1), 40119(b)(1). While the DOT language refers to transportation "safety" rather than "security," the difference is probably not legally significant.
63. 49 C.F.R. Parts 15 (DOT) and 1520 (TSA). These rules have been successfully applied to block disclosure of government-generated security information. *See* Judicial Watch v. DOT, 2005 WL 1606915 (July 7, 2005).
64. *See supra* page 106.

tion (e.g., rail and truck) are not expressly referenced in the rules, but a few are written so generally that they apply in any transportation setting.

Scope

The SSI rules have both general and particular applicability. In general, they track the statutes by defining sensitive security information as "information obtained or developed in the conduct of security activities, including research and development, the disclosure of which TSA [or the secretary of DOT] has determined would . . . [r]eveal trade secrets or privileged or confidential information obtained from any person; or . . . be detrimental to the security [or safety] of transportation."[65]

The rules also identify several categorical inclusions: if information falls into one of these categories, it is automatically SSI. Two of these categories are not limited to aviation or maritime transportation:

- *"Vulnerability assessments* . . . directed, created, held, funded, or approved by the DOT [or] DHS, or that will be provided to DOT or DHS in support of a Federal security program."[66]
- *"Threat information.* Any information held by the Federal government concerning threats against transportation or transportation systems and sources and methods used to gather or develop threat information, including threats against cyber infrastructure."[67]

The other categorical inclusions are restricted to aviation and maritime security. The rules list over a dozen, including:

- *"Security programs and contingency plans* . . . issued, established, required, received, or approved by DOT or DHS." Security programs, at least, are largely limited to aviation and maritime operations.[68] These specifically include vessel and maritime facility security plans.[69]
- *"Security inspection or investigative information* . . . Details of any security inspection or investigation of an alleged violation

---

65. 49 C.F.R. §§ 15.5(a)(2), (3); 1520.5(a)(2), (3).
66. *Id.* §§ 15.5(b)(5), 1520.5(b)(5) (emphasis in original).
67. *Id.* §§ 15.5(b)(7), 1520.5(b)(7) (emphasis in original).
68. *Id.* §§ 15.5(b)(1), 1520.5(b)(1) (emphasis in original).
69. *Id.* §§ 15.5(b)(1)(ii), 1520.5(b)(1)(ii).

of aviation or maritime transportation security requirements of Federal law that could reveal a security vulnerability . . . ."[70]

- *"Security measures.* Specific details of aviation or maritime transportation security measures, both operational and technical, whether applied directly by the Federal government or another person . . . ."[71]

- *"Security training materials.* Records created or obtained for the purpose of training persons employed by, contracted with, or acting for the Federal government or another person to carry out any aviation or maritime transportation security measures required or recommended by DHS or DOT."[72]

- *"Critical aviation or maritime infrastructure asset information.* Any list identifying systems or assets, whether physical or virtual, so vital to the aviation or maritime transportation system that the incapacity or destruction of such assets would have a debilitating impact on transportation security, if the list is—
  - Prepared by DHS or DOT; or
  - Prepared by a State or local government agency and submitted by the agency to DHS or DOT."[73]

- *"Trade secret information* . . . and *[c]ommercial or financial information* . . . obtained by DHS or DOT in carrying out aviation or maritime transportation security responsibilities, but only if the source of the information does not customarily disclose it to the public."[74]

Information that clearly falls into one of the foregoing categories is SSI by definition, and qualifies for automatic protection. Information not falling into one can be SSI if DOT or TSA determines that it meets the statutory criteria for SSI; that is, that improper disclosure of the information would be detrimental to transportation security.[75] Conversely, the rules authorize DOT or DHS to determine that information does not

---

70. *Id.* §§ 15.5(b)(6), 1520.5(b)(6) (emphasis in original).
71. *Id.* §§ 15.5(b)(8), 1520.5(b)(8) (emphasis in original).
72. *Id.* §§ 15.5(b)(10), 1520.5(b)(10) (emphasis in original).
73. *Id.* §§ 15.5(b)(12), 1520.5(b)(12) (emphasis in original).
74. *Id.* §§ 15.5(b)(14)(ii), (iii); 1520.5(b)(14) (emphasis in original).
75. Note: The DHS rules speak of TSA making these determinations on behalf of DHS, but in practice the Coast Guard can and does make SSI determinations as well. *See supra* p. 106.

meet the definition of SSI, even though it appears to fall into one of the categorical inclusions listed above.[76]

Persons Able to Obtain SSI

The federal government has purposefully designed the SSI rules to facilitate the protection of privately held or operated activities such as commercial aviation and maritime commerce. As a result, the rules allow DOT and DHS to make SSI available to the relevant players in these areas. In the maritime security context, these "covered persons" include:

- owners, operators, and charterers of vessels required to have a security plan;
- owners and operators of facilities required to have a security plan;
- persons participating on national, area, or port security committees;
- industry trade associations representing the foregoing (if they have entered into a nondisclosure agreement with DOT or DHS);
- DHS and DOT themselves; and
- persons employed by, contracted to, or acting for any of the above.[77]

Without regard to transportation mode, the rules also provide that any person for whom DOT or DHS has "directed, created, held, funded, or approved" a vulnerability assessment, or who provides an assessment to either department, can obtain SSI.[78]

In any case, access to specific SSI is limited to persons with a "need to know" that SSI. Under the SSI rules, these include the following private-sector actors:

- persons carrying out, in training to carry out, or supervising any transportation security activities approved, accepted, funded, recommended, or directed by DHS or DOT;
- persons providing technical or legal advice to a covered person regarding any federal transportation security requirements; and

---

76. 49 C.F.R. §§ 15.5(b), 1520.5(b).
77. *Id.* §§ 15.7(c), (d), (f), (g), (h), (k) (2004), 1520.7(c), (d), (f), (g), (h), (k).
78. *Id.* §§ 15.7(l), 1520.7(l).

- persons representing covered persons in connection with any judicial or administrative proceeding regarding those requirements.[79]

Federal employees can have access to SSI whenever it is necessary for performance of their official duties. Federal contractors and grantees can have access if it is necessary for performance of the contract or grant.[80]

The SSI Rules Bind Private Persons

Like the procedures for classified information, the SSI rules impose obligations on private-sector persons who possess SSI, including the persons who generate the information in the first place. These include:

- Taking reasonable steps to safeguard it from unauthorized disclosure (this includes storage in a secure container, such as a locked desk or file cabinet or in a locked room);
- Disclosing it only to covered persons who have a need to know, unless otherwise authorized in writing by the TSA, the Coast Guard, or the secretary of DOT;
- Complying with marking requirements; and
- Reporting unauthorized disclosures to the applicable DOT or DHS component.[81]

Violations of the SSI rules by private actors are "grounds for a civil penalty and other enforcement or corrective action" by the relevant agency.[82] Notably, each agency with authority regarding SSI is responsible for policing compliance with the rules by entities under its jurisdiction. So, for example, the Coast Guard interprets and enforces compliance with the SSI rules at MTSA-regulated facilities.

Litigation

The SSI rules provide that, in enforcement actions, DOT/DHS reserve to themselves "sole discretion" to provide SSI to a defendant in order for

---

79. *Id.* §§ 15.11(a), 1520.11(a).
80. 49 C.F.R. §§ 15.11(b), 1520.11(b).
81. *Id.* §§ 15.9(a)(1), (2), (4), 15.9(c); 1520.9(a)(1), (2), (4), 1520.9(c).
82. *Id.* §§ 15.17, 1520.1.

the person to respond.[83] The rules do not address other litigation, but DOT/DHS have intervened in private lawsuits to prevent the disclosure of SSI.[84] In response to concerns that courts have been too quick to deny litigants access to SSI in such cases, Congress in 2007 provided a means for civil litigants or their counsel to obtain SSI under a protective order under the same circumstances that justify obtaining fact work product, unless TSA can demonstrate that such access would present a risk of harm to the nation.[85]

The SSI rules also do not address preemption, but DOT/DHS have taken the position that the SSI rules preempt state open records laws.[86]

Chemical-Terrorism Vulnerability Information

In the DHS spending bill for fiscal year 2007, Congress created a new federal program regulating security at "chemical facilities that . . . present high levels of security risk."[87] This short enactment added that "information developed under this section, including vulnerability assessments, site security plans, and other security related information, records, and documents shall be given protections from public disclosure consistent with" the SSI rules just discussed, with the additional proviso that, in enforcement cases, this information is to be treated as if it were classified.[88]

DHS called its rules implementing this new statute the Chemical Facility Anti-Terrorism Standards (CFATS). Rather than narrowly amending the SSI rules to expand their scope to cover CFATS facilities, however, DHS in Subpart D of CFATS established yet another category of information protection: chemical-terrorism vulnerability information (CVI). Subpart D states that "the following information, whether transmitted verbally, electronically, or in written form, shall constitute CVI," referring to specific sections of the CFATS rules:

- Security Vulnerability Assessments under § 27.215;
- Site Security Plans under § 27.225;

---

83. *Id.* §§ 15.15(d)(1), 1520(d)(1).
84. Pub. L. No. 109-295, § 525(d).
85. *E.g., In re* Sept. 11 Litig., 431 F. Supp. 2d 405 (S.D.N.Y. 2006).
86. *See* 68 Fed. Reg. 60,469 (Oct. 22, 2003).
87. Pub. L. No. 109-295, § 550(a) (Oct. 4, 2006). *See* Chapter 12.
88. *Id.* § 550(c).

- Documents relating to the Department's review and approval of Security Vulnerability Assessments and Site Security Plans, including Letters of Authorization, Letters of Approval and responses thereto; written notices; and other documents developed pursuant to Sec. 27.240 or 27.245;
- Alternate Security Programs under Sec. 27.235;
- Documents relating to inspection or audits under Sec. 27.250;
- Any records required to be created or retained under Sec. 27.255;
- Sensitive portions of orders, notices or letters under Sec. 27.300;
- Information developed pursuant to Sec. Sec. 27.200 and 27.205; and
- Other information developed for chemical facility security purposes that the Secretary, in his discretion, determines is similar to the [foregoing] information . . . and thus warrants protection as CVI.[89]

The first eight of these elements are self-implementing, so that any person who properly comes into possession of CVI, and anyone else who "gains access to what they know or reasonably should know constitutes CVI"—collectively called "covered persons"—must comply with the CVI requirements.[90]

As with the SSI rules, access to CVI is limited to persons with a "need to know," such as:

- persons carrying out, in training to carry out, or supervising any chemical facility security activities approved, accepted, funded, recommended or directed by DHS;
- persons providing technical or legal advice to a covered person regarding any federal chemical facility requirements; and
- with DHS approval, persons representing covered persons in connection with a judicial or administrative proceeding regarding those requirements.[91]

A federal employee can have access to CVI whenever it is necessary for performance of the employee's official duties.[92] Federal contractors and grantees can have access if it is necessary to performance of the

---

89. 6 C.F.R. § 27.400(b).

90. *Id.* § 27.400(c). The CVI rules dispense with the SSI rule's approach of listing "covered persons."

91. *Id.* § 27.400(e)(1).

92. *Id.* § 27.400(e)(2)(i).

contract or grant.[93] DHS can find that only specific persons or classes of persons have a need to know particular CVI, or that persons not meeting the foregoing list have a need to know.[94] DHS can condition access to CVI on satisfactory completion of a background check and can further condition non-federal persons' access to CVI to execution of a nondisclosure agreement.[95]

Also as with the SSI rules, the obligations of the CVI rules include:

- Taking reasonable steps to safeguard it from unauthorized disclosure (this includes storage in a secure container, such as a safe);
- Disclosing it only to covered persons who have a need to know;
- Complying with marking requirements; and
- Reporting unauthorized disclosures to the Assistant Secretary for Infrastructure Protection.[96]

As noted earlier, the only significant statutory difference between SSI and CVI is the requirement that CVI be treated in enforcement actions as if it were classified. To implement that requirement, the CFATS rules adopt an approach modeled on the current statutory provision governing access to classified information in civil litigation involving charges of supplying material support to terrorist organizations.[97] These provisions give great power to DHS; for example:

- DHS has reserved to its sole discretion whether to provide CVI to counsel or other persons necessary for the conduct of administrative or judicial enforcement;[98]
- The rules purport to tell courts what actions they shall take in response to particular DHS motions;[99]
- Defendants are assigned the obligation to establish the relevance and materiality of any CVI they seek to introduce;[100] and

93. *Id.* § 27.400(e)(2)(ii).

94. *Id.* § 27.400(e)(4)–(5).

95. *Id.* §§ 27.400(e)(2)(iii), (3).

96. *Id.* § 27.400(d).

97. 71 Fed. Reg. 78,289 (Dec. 28, 2006) (citing 18 U.S.C. § 2339B); 72 Fed. Reg. 17,717 (April 9, 2007).

98. 6 C.F.R. §§ 27.400(h), (i).

99. *Id.* §§ 27.400(i)(3), 27.400(i)(7)(ii).

100. *Id.* § 27.400(i)(7)(iii).

- DHS reserves the right, in addition to the procedures set out in the rule, to seek protective orders or assert privileges like the state secrets privilege.[101]

Through its implementation of the CVI program, DHS has imposed further, extra-regulatory requirements. Most notably, DHS has declared that a covered person with a need to know CVI must also become an "Authorized User," which requires completion of Web-based DHS training.[102] (There is no similar concept under the SSI rules.) This training originally required the trainee to execute a nondisclosure agreement (NDA), more demanding than the NDA that one must sign to obtain classified information, in order to obtain an Authorized User number. After much criticism, DHS rescinded the NDA requirement when it issued its current CVI procedural manual.[103] That manual recommends additional restrictions and practices, gives guidance regarding what constitutes CVI,[104] and explains DHS's policy regarding how and when state and local government entities should obtain access to facilities' CVI. Finally, it states that "[t]he DHS Office of General Counsel will consider recommending U.S. Government intervention in litigation relating to the disclosure of CVI on a case-by-case basis."[105]

The Critical Infrastructure Information Act

Background

The foregoing notwithstanding, no federal agency regulates the security of the great bulk of the nation's privately held critical infrastructure, e.g., banking and finance, telecommunications, electric power, oil and gas, agriculture and food, etc. As discussed in Chapter 12, the fundamental orientation of the Homeland Security Act regarding protection of this infrastructure is a voluntary one of cooperation among all levels of gov-

---

101. *Id.* § 27.400(i)(8).

102. The training is available at https://csat.dhs.gov/dana/home/index.cgi.

103. *Safeguarding Information Designated as Chemical-Terrorism Vulnerability Information (CVI)* (Sept. 2008), *available at* http://www.dhs.gov/xlibrary/assets/chemsec_cvi_proceduresmanual.pdf. The manual reserves the right in the future to require an NDA, *id.* at 3, which the CVI rules authorize, *see* note 94 *supra.*

104. In particular, information developed for other regulatory purposes cannot become CVI. *Id.* at 8.

105. *Id.* at 23.

ernment and private owners and operators of infrastructure. For this approach to work, those private entities have to be willing to share information regarding their vulnerabilities and security measures with government. That willingness in turn depends on the trust such entities have that this extraordinarily sensitive information will not be publicly disclosed or used against them for other, extraneous regulatory purposes. The Critical Infrastructure Information Act of 2002 (CIIA)[106] attempts to encourage this sharing by providing such voluntarily shared security information with an unprecedented type of protection. DHS has implemented the CIIA through regulations that establish its Protected Critical Infrastructure Information (PCII) Program.

Scope

The PCII Program applies to *critical infrastructure information* that is *voluntarily* submitted, directly or indirectly, to the PCII Program Office at DHS.

- *Critical infrastructure information* basically means information not customarily in the public domain regarding threats, vulnerabilities, and related problems or solutions affecting critical infrastructure or the physical or cyber resources that support it.[107]
- *Voluntarily* means not in response to DHS's exercise of its power "to compel access to or submission of the information."[108] The Homeland Security Act does not give DHS any general power to do this, though various elements of DHS (e.g., the Coast Guard) have that power.

Notably, the PCII program does not apply to information that regulated entities must report to the federal government, and federal, state, and local agencies continue to have all their existing powers under other laws to obtain records and other information that regulated entities are required to make available to them.[109]

---

106. *See* 6 U.S.C. §§ 131–134.
107. 6 C.F.R. § 29.2(a).
108. *Id.* § 29.2(o).
109. 6 U.S.C. § 133(c), (d).

Information Protections

The law creates a variety of protections applicable to critical infrastructure information that the business submits to DHS, including the identity of the submitter:[110]

- *FOIA exemption.* The information is exempt from disclosure under FOIA. Criminal penalties are established for federal employees who knowingly release the information.[111]
- *Preemption of state and local open records laws.* The information is also exempt from disclosure under any state or local FOIA or "sunshine" laws.[112]
- *Ex parte exclusion.* The operation of any rules about ex parte communications with agency officials does not subject the information to disclosure.
- *Civil liability protection.* If submitted in good faith, the information cannot be used by any party in any proceeding except a criminal prosecution.[113]
- *No waiver of privilege.* The submitter, by the act of submitting information, does not waive any applicable privileges or protections, e.g., attorney-client privilege, work-product doctrine, and trade secret protection.
- *Restrictions on sharing and use.* DHS can share the information within the federal government and with state and local governments—and contractors working for them—but all of these entities can only use it for purposes of infrastructure protection or investigating or prosecuting crimes.

The CIIA rules also lay out detailed physical and procedural protections regarding safeguarding of the information.[114]

---

110. All of these bullets are drawn from 6 U.S.C. § 133(a)(1) unless otherwise noted.

111. 6 U.S.C. § 133(f).

112. A California intermediate appellate court has erroneously held that PCII is subject to the state's FOIA statute when a state agency is the submitter. County of Santa Clara v. Super. Ct., 170 Cal. App. 4th 1301, 90 Cal. Rptr. 3d 374 (2009).

113. 6 C.F.R. § 29.2(p).

114. *Id.* §§ 29.7, 29.8.

Implementation

Unlike the SSI and CVI programs, the PCII program is not self-implementing, and no information is PCII by operation of law. Rather, to be eligible for protection, information must be submitted directly or indirectly to the PCII Program Office, accompanied by an "express statement" referencing the CIIA.[115] Once a business submits information, DHS reviews it and validates it as PCII. (It protects the information presumptively as PCII pending that determination.) If DHS determines that the information does not qualify as PCII, it will, at the submitter's direction, return it or destroy it in accordance with the Federal Records Act.[116] Also unlike the SSI and CVI rules, the PCII rules do not impose any obligations on persons generating PCII, who remain free to disclose or otherwise do what they choose with it.[117]

---

115. *Id.* § 29.5.
116. *Id.* § 29.6.
117. DHS will stop protecting PCII that has been disclosed "generally or broadly to the public." *Id.* § 29.2(b), (d).

CHAPTER 7

2008: The Year of Increased Worksite Enforcement

By Dawn M. Lurie, Mahsa Aliaskari, and Joe Whitley

The year 2008 saw a dramatic increase in the "culture of compliance" called for by former Homeland Security Secretary Michael Chertoff. Increased and forceful worksite enforcement actions put issues of immigration enforcement front and center on the national political stage, while also making the best of the absence of immigration legal reforms from Congress. The Department of Homeland Security also attempted to implement the Social Security No-Match regulation and expand application of the E-Verify program. With this heightened environment of enforcement comes a real need for employers to ensure that they have the benefit of specialized and able counsel to track the rapidly changing enforcement landscape and ensure compliance.

If 2007 was "The Year of Failed Comprehensive Immigration Reform (CIR)," we can accurately characterize 2008 as "The Year of Increased Worksite Enforcement." With the failure of CIR, Immigration and Customs Enforcement (ICE), the enforcement agency within the Department of Homeland Security[1] (DHS), forged ahead with the Bush

---

1. DHS, the successor to legacy Immigration and Naturalization Service (INS), houses the three distinct agencies now charged with providing security along with immigration-related services and benefits and enforcement of federal immigration laws, customs laws, and air security law. ICE is the enforcement arm of the agency whose mission is to protect national security and uphold public safety by targeting criminal networks and terrorist organizations that seek to exploit vulnerabilities in our immigration system, in our financial networks, along our border, at federal facilities, and elsewhere in order to do harm to the United States. *See* http://www.ice.gov/about/index.htm.

administration's new mission, which included changes to the ICE worksite enforcement program. The approach was no longer piecemeal with case-specific efforts; instead, ICE viewed its mission as part of a comprehensive, layered approach that focused on how illegal aliens entered the United States, the ways in which they obtained identity documents allowing them to become employed, and the employers who knowingly hired and continue to employ them.

In this vein, under section 274A of the Immigration and Nationality Act, 8 U.S.C. Sec. 1324 (a)(3)(A), ICE worksite investigations began to produce felony charges and not just the traditional misdemeanor worksite violations.[2] In 2008, the public witnessed a dramatic refinement of the department's approach to include nationally coordinated worksite raids, the vigorous defense of the Social Security No-Match regulation, and expansion of the E-Verify program. This multifaceted, multiagency effort is unlikely to change with the Obama administration. Without an effective, comprehensive approach, the U.S. immigration system will remain broken, where employers are left with more confusion and new questions rather than straightforward answers.[3] History has taught us that enforcement policies alone do not work; they can only succeed as part of a comprehensive, long-term approach to immigration reform.

ENFORCEMENT-ONLY STRATEGY

During 2008, ICE made worksite enforcement a priority, as the agency targeted the businesses and industries deliberately employing illegal aliens.

---

2. *See* Statement of Julie L. Myers, Assistant Secretary U.S. Immigration & Customs Enforcement, U.S. Dep't of Homeland Security, Regarding a Hearing on *Immigration Enforcement at the Workplace: Learning from the Mistakes of 1986,* before the U.S. Senate Comm. on the Judiciary Subcomm. on Immigration, Border Security and Citizenship, June 19, 2006.

3. This article focuses on employer-related issues and does not address the hardships and issues faced by an estimated 11.9 million unauthorized workers in the United States (figure derived from *Undocumented Immigration Now Trails Legal Inflow, Reversing Decade-Long Trend,* by Jeffrey S. Passel, senior demographer, Pew Hispanic Center, and D'Vera Cohn, senior writer, Pew Research Center, Oct. 2, 2008). Our historical experience also teaches us that there must be practical solutions to the very real problems employers in certain parts of the United States and in certain industries face when attempting to attract a legal, viable, and long-term workforce where fair and reasonable rates of pay are already offered. The scope of this article does not cover this issue at any great length, but it should be considered a point of contention on both sides of the debate.

For the first time since 1988, there were significant increases in worksite raids, criminal arrests, fines, and felony indictments. Hundreds of aliens, many of whom had committed no crime other than working unlawfully in the United States, were taken into custody and placed into the U.S. correctional system.

With no success in obtaining the much-needed legislative reform, the Bush administration moved forward and implemented policies within the only regulatory framework that was available. With the administration's support, DHS dusted off dormant regulations and implemented newer and stricter regulations. Professor Peter Markowitz, director of the Immigration Justice Clinic at the Benjamin N. Cardozo School of Law at Yeshiva University in New York, expressed this sentiment as well, stating, "[s]omething really shifted in the Bush Administration once it realized comprehensive immigration reform was not going to pass on its watch . . . . When they saw the public policy battle was lost, they moved instead to public relations."[4] With enforcement surging, the culture of compliance was born.

The culture of compliance and enforcement and the tone of the agency were solidified early on when President Bush nominated Julie Myers as Assistant Secretary of Homeland Security in June 2005.[5] ICE was already pouring resources into interior worksite operations and beefing up border security after September 11, 2001. However, it was not until a stakeholders' meeting on August 10, 2007, when Secretary of Homeland Security Michael Chertoff officially announced the agency's policy shift vis-à-vis the failure of comprehensive immigration reform in the legislature, that employers really began to understand what was at stake. Chertoff clarified the government's purpose and game plan, stating:

> Let me be very clear about what we're doing here. I have said with absolute consistency from before we started the immigration reform effort earlier this year that I was determined to enforce the laws of this country to the utmost of my vigor. And we've done that . . . ever since I've been Secretary. We had hoped that immigration reform on a comprehensive basis would

---

4. Moira Herbst, *Immigration: Enforcement or Politics?* BUSINESSWEEK (Aug. 20, 2008), *available at* http://www.businessweek.com/print/bwdaily/dnflash/content/aug2008/db20080819_105143.htm.

5. Myers served as the face of ICE's serious and highly publicized enforcement culture until Nov. 15, 2008. http://www.dhs.gov/xnews/releases/pr_1225920873224.shtm.

give us a much wider set of tools. We don't have that. We still think Congress can act on it. But until the laws change, we are enforcing the laws as they are to the utmost of our ability using every tool that we have in the tool box, and we're going to sharpen some of those tools.[6]

It was also in August 2007 that Chertoff announced the agency's plans for 26 "administrative reforms" to improve border security and immigration within the existing structure and tapestry of laws and regulations.[7] This provided the framework for what was to come in 2008: a policy that included both border security and interior enforcement, with worksite enforcement as the linchpin.

During fiscal year 2008, ICE made 5,173 administrative immigration arrests at worksites nationally and carried out 1,101 criminal arrests.[8] Under the leadership of Assistant Secretary Myers, ICE focused on securing America's borders by implementing a new comprehensive interior enforcement strategy. This initiative included concentrating on the basic infrastructure that supported the business of illegal immigration in the United States: the employers of the undocumented and those who furthered the crimes of identity theft and document fraud. To that end, one of ICE's greatest accomplishments has been its aggressive efforts in targeting the "job magnets" that attract illegal aliens seeking employment in U.S. workplaces—efforts that have been widely publicized and, at times, criticized.

The failed attempt at comprehensive immigration reform also focused attention on the U.S. border with Mexico, as well as on the challenges of cracking down on illegal border crossings and cross-border crime. To support this focus, the Bush administration increased border

6. News Conference with Sec'y of Homeland Security Michael Chertoff and Sec'y of Commerce Carlos Gutierrez on Border Security and Immigration Administrative Reforms (Aug. 10, 2007), http://www.fnsg.com/transcripta.htm?id=20070810t7008&query.

7. Michael Chertoff, Sec'y of Homeland Security, Testimony before the House Committee on the Judiciary (Mar. 5, 2008), http://www.dhs.gov/xnews/testimony/testimony_1204746985090.shtm.

8. Press Release, U.S. Immigration & Customs Enforcement, Kentucky restaurant owner sentenced to 8 months for employing illegal aliens (Jan. 7, 2009), http://www.ice.gov/pi/nr/0901/090107louisville.htm (135 business owners, managers, supervisors, or human resource employees were charged with crimes arising out of these raids).

patrol funding, deployed new technologies, and built additional physical barriers at the border.

WORKSITE ENFORCEMENT

In remarkably forceful ways, Secretary Chertoff's initiatives were intended to create "a culture of compliance."[9] Secretary Myers analogized the new policy to IRS tax audits, saying that "[t]he IRS doesn't audit every tax return in the country, but the *threat* of an IRS audit is enough to compel most people to do the right thing."[10]

The administration's policies, coupled with the agency's actions, instantly affected public perception and knowledge of worksite compliance and enforcement. The previously "benign" punishments outlined in the Immigration Reform and Control Act (IRCA) morphed into a heavy-handed compliance medium. In fact, one of the most effective transformations of the agency's tactics was the elevation and use of fines and forfeitures. The change was a drastic one from the relatively insignificant civil penalties of the past. Now substantial criminal fines, prison terms, and multimillion-dollar settlements became commonplace. Bad faith and egregious actors could no longer consider immigration compliance penalties, enforcement investigations, and fines as an acceptable cost of doing business.

Increases in penalties and fines were not the only changes. Over the course of the last several years, ICE's enforcement and investigation methods were refined to include the use of undercover informants and agents placed at worksites for months at a time. Investigation tactics became more sophisticated, and administrative reviews were also improved through the use of forensic documents experts assigned to local ICE offices. ICE also initiated and intensified cooperation with other agencies and publicly acknowledged that "[t]he presence of illegal aliens at a business does not necessarily mean the employer is responsible. Developing sufficient evidence against employers requires complex, white-collar crime investigations that can take years to bear fruit."[11]

---

9. Moira Herbst, *Immigration: Enforcement or Politics?* BUSINESSWEEK (Aug. 20, 2008), http://www.businessweek.com/print/bwdaily/dnflash/content/aug2008/db20080819_105143.htm.

10. *Id.* [emphasis added].

11. Press Release, U.S. Immigration & Customs Enforcement, Worksite Enforcement, Nov. 25, 2008, *at* http://www.ice.gov/pi/news/factsheets/worksite.htm (Feb. 4, 2009).

Keeping its word, ICE surpassed all expectations with the number and magnitude of investigations, audits, raids, and criminal charges that were filed in 2008. The agency began to develop internal standards to standardize I-9 reviews in an effort to ensure that the same parameters were used in audits conducted nationwide. The leadership at ICE also attempted to ensure that the same standard of review was used in determining fines for I-9 violations. Discretion of the local special agent in-charge offices began to disappear as headquarters solidified its control. Training increased, bringing together agents and auditors in an attempt to ensure continuity and correctness in the field.

With big worksite raids, ICE continued to make a splash, and the mainstream media continued to respond and publicize the department's actions. This coverage also started to include and uncover alleged abuses of aliens during the raids. In response to this attention and the new lawsuits, ICE reviewed its detention policies following worksite raids and made provisions for sole caregivers to ensure the safety of family members caught in the middle of these massive raids.

With the support of U.S. attorneys, imprisonment of managers and executives, as well as aggravated felony charges against aliens using fraudulent identification, flourished. In 2008, ICE made more than 1,100 criminal arrests tied to worksite enforcement investigations, targeting critical infrastructure and suspect industries. Out of those charged criminally, 135 were business owners, managers, supervisors, or human resource employees.[12] The agency's tactics evidenced a remarkable strategy shift.

In an effort to level the playing field, ICE made sure to investigate not only the larger companies, but also the smaller businesses that had normally flown under the enforcement radar. From large multistate companies to small mom-and-pop shops, no egregious employer was exempt, as those unauthorized aliens working for them were arrested and hauled off to confinement.[13]

---

12. Press Release, U.S. Immigration & Customs Enforcement, ICE multifaceted strategy leads to record enforcement results, *Removals, criminal arrests, and worksite investigations soared in fiscal year 2008* (Oct. 23, 2008). *See* http://www.ice.gov/pi/nr/0810/081023washington. htm.

13. Often these aliens received long sentences after unknowingly pleading guilty to aggravated felonies (including the use of false Social Security numbers). After they serve their federal prison time they will be returned to ICE's custody and then deported back to their home countries.

The widely publicized raids of IFCO Systems North America (IFCO) in 2006 presaged the seriousness of ICE compliance and the resources the agency was willing to invest in 2008. The IFCO investigation focused on the largest pallet-management services company in the United States. ICE executed search warrants or consent searches simultaneously at more than 40 IFCO locations nationwide in 26 states, serving as a harsh example to would-be violators. The raids resulted in the arrest of nearly 1,200 undocumented workers.[14] In December 2008, IFCO reached a historic settlement agreement with the government in which the company agreed to pay $20.7 million in civil forfeitures, back pay, and penalties.[15] Sixteen of IFCO's management officials, including two vice presidents, continue to face criminal charges for their alleged role in the conspiracy. John Torres, acting assistant secretary for ICE, confirmed that nine of those individuals have already entered guilty pleas.[16] In January 2009, a federal grand jury returned superseding indictments on the remaining seven employees.

Through this multistate investigation, ICE found that IFCO's systematic, willful violations of the law went back as far as 1990.[17] However, the U.S. attorney agreed not to pursue *corporate* criminal charges against IFCO for hiring illegal alien workers at IFCO pallet plants prior to April 19, 2006.[18]

---

14. Press Release, U.S. Immigration & Customs Enforcement, ICE multi-faceted strategy leads to record enforcement results, *Removals, criminal arrests, and worksite investigations soared in fiscal year 2008* (Oct. 23, 2008). *See* http://www.ice.gov/pi/nr/0810/081023washington. htm.

15. Press Release, U.S. Immigration & Customs Enforcement, IFCO Systems enters into record $20.7 million settlement of claims for employment of illegal aliens (Dec. 19, 2008), www.ice.gov/pi/nr/0812/081219albany.htm. The settlement is scheduled to be paid over the course of a four-year period.

16. Press Release, U.S. Immigration & Customs Enforcement, Superseding indictments charge 7 IFCO managers with violating federal immigration law (Jan. 23, 2009).

17. Press Release, U.S. Immigration & Customs Enforcement, Guilty plea in government's probe of immigration violations at IFCO Systems (Nov. 17, 2008), http://www.ice.gov/pi/news/newsreleases/articles/070716albany.htm.

18. Press Release, U.S. Immigration & Customs Enforcement, IFCO Systems enters into record $20.7 million settlement of claims for employment of illegal aliens (Dec. 19, 2008), http://www.ice.gov/pi/nr/0812/081219 albany.htm.

THE NEXT WAVE OF ENFORCEMENT: AGRIPROCESSORS

The next display of enforcement muscle took place in Iowa on May 12, 2008, when ICE raided the Postville plant of the meat processor Agriprocessors, Inc. The impact of the raids was truly devastating to the company, and partially as a result of the large-scale enforcement action, Agriprocessors filed for bankruptcy in November 2008.[19]

ICE referred to this Agriprocessor raid as "the largest criminal worksite enforcement operation in history."[20] A total of 389 illegal workers were arrested, 305 of whom were arrested on criminal charges of identity theft and use of false documents and Social Security numbers. In November 2008, the company's former CEO, a human resources employee, and three company managers, two of whom were deemed fugitives, were indicted on multiple criminal charges, including harboring illegal aliens, identity theft, bank fraud, and document fraud.[21]

Agriprocessors was a memorable raid for its magnitude and consequent press coverage. However, raids of various sizes continued consistently, as evidenced by a snapshot of just a few more enforcement activities by ICE that took place in 2008:

- *El Pollo Rico*—Owner Juan Francisco Solano and sister Consuelo Solano forfeited $7.2 million in assets, including 13 bank accounts, eight properties, and $2.1 million in cash. Juan Solano was sentenced to 15 months in prison.[22]
- *Action Rags USA*—Owner and two managers indicted and facing 10 years for alien harboring among other charges, as well as a $250,000 fine.[23]

---

19. Julia Preston, *Large Iowa Meatpacker in Illegal Immigrant Raid Files for Bankruptcy*, N.Y. TIMES, Nov. 6, 2008, at A21.

20. Press Release, U.S. Immigration & Customs Enforcement, 297 convicted and sentenced following ICE worksite operation in Iowa (May 15, 2008), http://www.ice.gov/pi/news/newsreleases/articles/080515waterloo.htm.

21. Press Release, U.S. Immigration & Customs Enforcement, Agriprocessors and management criminally indicted (Nov. 21, 2008), http://www.ice.gov/pi/nr/0811/081121cedarrapids.htm.

22. Press Release, U.S. Immigration & Customs Enforcement, El Pollo Rico restaurant owners sentenced for money laundering and harboring illegal aliens (Sept. 29, 2008), http://www.ice.gov/pi/nr/0809/080929greenbelt.htm.

23. Press Release, U.S. Immigration & Customs Enforcement, Indictment returned against Action Rags USA owner and 2 managers (July 31, 2008), http://www.ice.gov/pi/nr/0807/080731houston.htm.

- *RCI*—Three former top executives sentenced to prison for alien harboring and defrauding the United States. The former president of the company was sentenced to 10 years in prison and ordered to pay close to $17 million in fines.[24]
- *Proffer Wholesale*—This investigation not only focused on the employment of illegal aliens, but also targeted a company taking advantage of the temporary employment visa program. The discovery of H-2B visa fraud on the part of Proffer Wholesale, a Missouri product distribution company, led to a $350,000 fine, along with a felony guilty plea by Proffer to one count of conspiracy to commit visa fraud.[25]

OTHER COMPLIANCE TOOLS

IMAGE

On the gentler and more conciliatory side of its compliance efforts, DHS also expanded the IMAGE program, originally put forth in 2007. The ICE Mutual Agreement Between Government and Employers (IMAGE) program presents employers with the opportunity to partner with ICE against the employment of illegal workers by adopting a set of best practices. These practices include volunteering for an I-9 audit, enrolling in E-Verify, establishing a tip line, and using the Social Security Number Verification Service (SSNVS).

While local ICE offices provide outreach and information on IMAGE, the program is truly limited in capacity due to a current lack of resources. At present, there are only 46 participating U.S. employers.[26] Given that the Department of Labor estimates the number of U.S. employers at 10 million,[27] the IMAGE program may never become as wide-

---

24. Press Release, U.S. Immigration & Customs Enforcement, Leaders of multimillion-dollar immigration and tax scam sentenced to hard time (Mar. 4, 2008), http://www.ice.gov/pi/news/newsreleases/articles/080304 grandrapids.htm.

25. Press Release, U.S. Immigration & Customs Enforcement, Eastern Missouri company pleads guilty to visa fraud charges (Dec. 18, 2008), http://www.ice.gov/pi/nr/0812/081217stlouis.htm.

26. U.S. Immigration & Customs Enforcement, Members, http://www.ice.gov/partners/opaimage/members.htm.

27. U.S. DEP'T OF LABOR, OFFICE OF THE SECRETARY, SUMMARY OF THE MAJOR LAWS OF THE DEPARTMENT OF LABOR (Jan. 23, 2009), http://www.dol.gov/opa/aboutdol/lawsprog.htm.

spread as ICE projects. In fairness to ICE, all interested employers may make an application to the program; however, ICE simply does not have the manpower to fully vet and conduct even sample I-9 audits for a large number of potential employer-partners.

Social Security No-Match Rule[28]

DHS's actions on the Social Security No-Match Rule remained a hot-button issue in 2008. The No-Match saga started on June 14, 2006, when DHS published a proposed rule purporting to create a "safe harbor" for employers who received no-match letters and followed a specific policy to respond to such letters.[29] The No-Match Rule has in part been DHS's attempt to provide guidance to employers on what it believes is a "correct" response to a no-match letter from the Social Security Administration (SSA) or the equivalent notification letter from DHS. But that is not where the "guidance" stops, and therein lies the controversy.

The No-Match Rule seeks to broaden the definition of "constructive knowledge"[30] as it is used in reference to the employment of individuals who are not authorized to work in the United States to include receipt of a no-match letter. Under the rule, an employer who receives a no-match letter would be deemed to have "constructive knowledge" that the individual in question may not be authorized to work. This broadening of the definition of constructive knowledge and the use of the no-match letter subjects employers to penalties if they do not take certain steps once they are in receipt of a no-match letter.

On August 15, 2007, after much controversy and politically charged discussion with the administration, DHS published a final rule (2007 Rule) providing guidance to employers on how to respond to Social Security no-match letters while also broadening the legal definition of constructive knowledge.[31] The rule was scheduled to take effect on Sep-

---

28. This section derived from Dawn Lurie, Greenberg Traurig LLP, The DHS No-Match Rule (2008), http://www.gtlaw.com/portalresource/lookup/wosid/contentpilot-core-401-10826/pdfCopy.pdf?view=attachment.

29. A no-match letter refers to a letter issued by the SSA noting that the Social Security number reported to the IRS by the employer does not match with SSA records and therefore does not allow for the processing of with-held taxes.

30. "Constructive knowledge is knowledge that may fairly be inferred through notice of certain facts and circumstances that would lead a person, through the exercise of reasonable care, to know about a certain condition." 8 C.F.R. § 274a.1(l)(1).

31. 72 Fed. Reg. 45,611 (Aug. 15, 2007).

tember 14, 2007. However, a number of groups, including the U.S. Chamber of Commerce, National Roofing Contractors Association, and the American Nursery and Landscape Association, challenged the final rule. The suit successfully challenged some of the procedural aspects of how the 2007 Rule was issued, leading to a preliminary injunction issued on October 10, 2007. On November 23, 2007, DHS requested that the court delay the proceedings until March 1, 2008, in order to allow it to reissue the 2007 Rule in a new rulemaking effort—asking the court, in effect, to freeze the litigation to allow it to correct the record that served as the basis for the court's injunction.

On March 21, 2008, DHS's response to (though some may say disregard of) the court's decision and injunction was apparent when the agency continued its rulemaking journey and released a Supplemental Proposed Rule. The Supplemental Proposed Rule was published in the *Federal Register* on March 26, 2008. In October 2008, DHS published its Supplemental Final Rule, stating in no uncertain terms that it "finalized the additional legal analysis set out in the supplemental notice of proposed rulemaking, and determined that the rule should issue without change."[32] While the rule called for implementation upon publication in the *Federal Register*, DHS acknowledged that it will not be enforced until the court lifts the existing injunction. The department expressed confidence that the additional steps it took in this newly "revised" form of the regulation would address the concerns the court raised in granting the injunction.

From DHS's perspective, this supplement resolved all of the issues and concerns that the court presented. At the time of this writing, the injunction remains in place, the regulations are not being enforced, and SSA continues to refrain from sending no-match letters to employers.

E-Verify

Formerly known as the Basic Pilot/Employment Eligibility Verification Program, E-Verify is the United States Citizenship and Immigration Services' (USCIS)[33] free Web-based system that, through partnering with

---

32. Dep't of Homeland Security, Safe Harbor Procedures for Employers Who Receive a No-Match Letter: Clarification; Final Regulatory Flexibility Analysis, at 7 [DHS Docket No. ICEB-2377-06; ICE 2377-06] (2008); *see also* 71 Fed. Reg. 209 (Oct. 28, 2008) (Supp. Final Rule).

33. U.S. Citizenship & Immigration Services is the agency within DHS that provides immigration benefits to people who are entitled to stay in the United States on a temporary or permanent basis. These benefits include the

the SSA and the Department of State, comprises a software product that allows employers to verify the employment eligibility of their workers. USCIS markets the program as "the best means available for determining employment eligibility of new hires and the validity of their Social Security Numbers."[34]

For the most part, E-Verify is a voluntary program.[35] However, the implementation of revised regulations and executive orders mandating its use for government contractors drew controversy leading to yet more litigation. On June 6, 2008, President Bush issued an executive order requiring all federal contractors to use E-Verify.[36] On June 9, 2008, Secretary Chertoff announced that the Office of Management and Budget (OMB) had completed review of a rulemaking to amend the Federal Acquisitions Regulations (FAR) to impose the same requirement on all federal contractors.[37] The new rules were originally scheduled to go into effect on January 15, 2009.[38] In December 2008, the U.S. Chamber of Commerce, together with other members of the business community, including the Associated Builders and Contractors, the Society for Human Resource Management, the American Council on International Personnel, and the HR Policy Association, filed a lawsuit challenging the legality of the new rules issued through the executive order, arguing that they were the product of the Bush administration's circumvention of the federal immigration and procurement laws.[39] The chamber requested that the government agree to suspend the rule until a resolution was reached

granting of U.S. citizenship to those who are eligible to naturalize, authorizing individuals to reside in the U.S. on a permanent basis, and providing aliens with the eligibility to work in the United States.

34. U.S. Citizenship & Immigration Services, E-Verify (search http://www.uscis.gov/portal/site/uscis; then follow "E-Verify" hyperlink).

35. *Id.*

36. EFREN HERNANDEZ III & DAWN LURIE, E-VERIFY WILL SOON BE REQUIRED FOR FEDERAL CONTRACTORS (2008) (http://www2.gtlaw.com/practices/immigration/index.asp, then follow "News Flashes" hyperlink; then follow "2008" hyperlink).

37. *Id.*

38. Press Release, U.S. Chamber of Commerce, Mandatory E-Verify Use for Government Contractors Postponed Until Feb. 20 (Jan. 9, 2009), http://www.uschamber.com/press/releases/2009/january/090109_everify.htm.

39. Press Release, U.S. Chamber of Commerce, U.S. Chamber Lawsuit Challenges Massive Extension of E-Verify Program to Federal Contractors (Dec. 23, 2008), http://www.uschamber.com/press/releases/2008/december/081223_lawsuit.htm.

in the U.S. district court. On January 9, 2009, the chamber reported that the government had in fact agreed to suspend the rule from going into effect until February 20, 2009.[40] The Obama administration pulled back the regulation temporarily by another 60 days, thereby ensuring that federal contract awards and solicitations would not include the clause committing government contractors to use E-Verify until April 21, 2009. This brief suspension of the E-Verify requirement is providing federal contractors with some time to review their obligations under the rule and develop a better understanding of how the requirements will impact their businesses as the effective date of the regulations quickly approaches.

Due to changes in requirements for utilizing E-Verify for both current and new employees, in essence, the FAR created a second E-Verify program changing all the rules of the original E-Verify program. USCIS spent an enormous amount of time and money educating employers and urging them to sign on to the original E-Verify program and to use it correctly and within the parameters of IRCA. By asserting different guidelines for federal contractors, the government has left employers dazed and confused during a time when resources and budgets are being slashed.

The most confusing differences between Federal Contractor E-Verify (FCEV) and Basic E-Verify (BEV) is evident in the FCEV requirement to run *existing* employees through the E-Verify system. BEV participants are prohibited from doing so and could face a daunting investigation by the Department of Justice's Office of Special Counsel if current employees are run in the system. FCEV also mandates a review and update of *existing* Form I-9s for U.S. citizens and legal permanent residents, normally taboo for employers. The list of differences is expansive, but the critical issue to understand is that these actions do not in any way assist in ensuring or increasing compliance.

Notwithstanding the controversy surrounding the federal contractor provisions, the core E-Verify program rapidly expanded in 2008. Many states mandated E-Verify for either all employers or for those employers having contracts with public entities or state agencies. A relatively small number of employers signed up voluntarily. At the time of this writing, USCIS reported the number of participating employers at over 100,000.[41]

---

40. U.S. Chamber of Commerce, Mandatory E-Verify Use for Government Contractors Postponed Until Feb. 20 (Jan. 9, 2009), http://www.uschamber.com/press/releases/2009/january/090109_everify.htm.

41. Press Release, U.S. Citizenship & Immigration Services, 100,000 Employers Use E-Verify Program (Jan. 8, 2009) (http://www.uscis.gov/portal/site/uscis, then follow hyperlink under "100,000 Employers Use E-Verify Program.").

The year 2008 also spotlighted internal reviews on E-Verify. The USCIS Ombudsman issued a report, "Immigration Services Ombudsman, Observations on the E-Verify Experience in Arizona and Recommended Customer Service Enhancements (Dec. 22, 2008)," which noted that, by the end of 2008, 12 states had made E-Verify mandatory either statewide or in connection with state and local government contractors.[42] The growth of the program will be fueled further as funding increases and anticipated improvements take effect, including state partnerships and user-based improvements geared at smaller and medium-sized businesses.

E-Verify's most serious and fundamental flaw is that it does not adequately safeguard against fraud or identity theft. Identity theft is a growing concern that has proliferated into many arenas, causing the government to crack down by using strict laws with harsh penalties, including those found in the Identity Theft Penalty Enhancement Act of 2004 (18 U.S.C. 1028A(a)(1)).[43] In the wake of workplace raids, many foreign nationals had no intention of stealing an identity but rather used false documents, names, and numbers to obtain work authorization—a lesser offense. However, in recent years the government moved forward with the more serious identity theft charges, even when there was no indication that the undocumented worker actually knew that the counterfeit Social Security and other fake identification numbers they were using belonged to an actual person.

The critical distinction between the two types of charges was argued in February 2009 before the Supreme Court. The government has used the identify theft charge, which carries a mandatory two-year minimum prison term, to persuade aliens to plead guilty to the lesser immigration charges and accept prompt deportation. "There's a basic problem here," said Chief Justice John G. Roberts, Jr. "You get an extra two years if it just so happens that the number you picked out of the air belonged to somebody else."[44]

---

42. As of the time of this writing, these states include Arizona, Colorado, Georgia, Idaho, Minnesota, Mississippi, Missouri, North Carolina, Oklahoma, Rhode Island, South Carolina, and Utah. *Id.* at 3

43. In general, the law provides that whoever, during and in relation to any felony violation enumerated in subsection (c), knowingly transfers, possesses, or uses, without lawful authority, a means of identification of another person shall, in addition to the punishment provided for such felony, be sentenced to a term of imprisonment of two years.

44. Adam Liptak & Julia Preston, *Supreme Court Hears Challenge to Identity-Theft Law in Immigration Cases,* N.Y. TIMES, Feb. 25, 2009.

THE YEAR OF INCREASED WORKSITE ENFORCEMENT: WHAT WE HAVE LEARNED

In 2008, ICE stepped up criminal enforcement actions as well as administrative reviews and I-9 audits. Legacy INS, the agency that accepted pennies on the dollar for I-9 fines, is long gone, and ICE is no longer interested in negotiating fines. ICE's budget for worksite enforcement continues to grow, and agents are aggressively pursuing compliance issues, particularly in identified critical infrastructure sites and targeted industries. While raids, including massive incarceration of unlawful workers, are likely not to be as prominent in the coming Obama years, investigations and government audits will undoubtedly continue with a focus on employers, executives, and managers. ICE has devoted $34 million of its fiscal year 2009 budget to worksite enforcement alone.[45]

Worksite enforcement measures translate into the need for employers to ensure companywide compliance. A company can no longer make the business decision to wait until the government knocks on its door. Internal I-9 audits and compliance plans should become an integral part of any responsible company's best practices—being proactive is no longer an option, it is a necessity. The Obama administration is not likely to move away from this enforced compliance culture. While the new administration may tweak its tactics, investigations of employers are certain to continue and most likely increase. Eliminating the magnet of illegal employment and interagency cooperation will continue to be a focus, along with information sharing.

LOOKING FORWARD: WORKSITE ENFORCEMENT

Regardless of the outcome of the litigation over E-Verify and the No-Match Rule, enforcement activity will continue to increase. The focus is likely to be on the employers that employ the undocumented and the vendors who sell fraudulent identification cards rather than on the workers who purchase them. After-the-fact damage control and remedial action is not as effective for employers as is proactively addressing the issues in a preventive fashion.

Worksite compliance and enforcement tactics will certainly be revisited by the new administration and the tone may change, but the goal is

---

45. Fact Sheet, U.S. Immigration & Customs Enforcement, Fiscal Year 2009 (Oct. 23, 2008), www.ice.gov/doclib/pi/news/factsheets/2009 budgetfactsheet.doc.

likely to remain the same: protecting U.S. borders, security, and U.S. workers. The American public may expect an Obama administration to focus on exploitative employers, critical infrastructure, and continuation of the fight against criminal aliens.

President Obama's choice for secretary of labor, California Representative Hilda Solis, is another clear indication of the likely direction of enforcement. Secretary Solis's recent DOL investigation of an H-2B employer opened in cooperation with DHS is a sure signal of what is to come. Increased cooperation and joint task forces between the two agencies will likely begin a sophisticated attack on employers that are taking advantage of employees or the system. Compliance efforts will spill into the labor arena as U.S. workers will continue to be protected more zealously than ever before. H-1B, H-2A, H-2B, and other visa-driven investigations are sure to become more prevalent to ensure that unscrupulous employers are caught.

The goals and methods to be used by this administration will likely be geared toward noncompliant employers. ICE may take a backseat to many DOL investigations but will certainly provide critical support. DOL and DHS are sure to work together and increase efforts to protect the labor rights of all American workers and to penalize employers using and abusing undocumented workers for profit, especially at a time when the U.S. economy is in such a fragile state. Maintaining workplace wage and hour standards, as well as health and safety standards, is sure to be another tool used by the new administration to reduce an employer's incentive to hire undocumented workers.

CONCLUSION

The move to enforcement in 2008 without the much-needed legislative reform did not solve our nation's immigration problems. Instead, the initiatives of the last year left U.S. companies bewildered, with no practical guidance or viable solutions to legalize unlawful workers. Admittedly, while good-faith employers were faced with difficult situations, including how to ensure that their current workforce was legally eligible to work, bad-faith employers were put on notice—they would be targeted and severely punished. Following the failure of CIR, DHS undeniably sharpened its existing tools and added some new ones.

As we look forward to the changes promised by the new administration, comprehensive immigration reform and interior border enforcement must be among its first priorities in order to protect the prosperity and safety of the American people. With global financial times uncertain and unprecedented loss of jobs, downsizing, and predictions that things will get much worse before they get better, both pro- and anti-immigration advocates note the importance and interplay between legal and illegal immigration and the economy.

CHAPTER 8

Succession Planning and Business Continuity

by James P. Gerkis and Adam Klepack

Part I introduces the concepts of succession planning and business continuity planning and discusses the developments in these areas since the events of September 11, 2001. Part II discusses the federal and state legislative developments in succession planning and business continuity planning. Part III discusses the reactions from the private sector to business continuity planning. Finally, Part IV discusses potential corporate liability for failing to implement a business continuity plan or failing to monitor the effectiveness of an existing plan.

ADMINISTRATIVE AND REGULATORY DEVELOPMENTS IN BUSINESS CONTINUITY PLANNING

Introduction

The United States Constitution contains automatic succession provisions to ensure orderly lines of command and control in the event of a catastrophic disaster.[1] The Presidential Succession Act of 1947 establishes the line of succession to the office of President of the United States if neither the president nor vice president is able to discharge the powers and duties of the office.[2] The lack of a clear line of succession would have a devastating effect on the operations of the United States in times

---

1. U.S. CONST. art. II, § 1, cl. 6.
2. U.S. CONST. art. II, § 1, cl. 6; U.S. CONST. amend. XXV; 3 U.S.C.A. § 19.

of emergency if high-level officers were incapable of discharging the powers and duties of office.

Similarly, the operations of a business would be adversely affected if its board of directors or executive officers were incapable of discharging their managerial duties. All businesses should have a clear line of succession before an emergency and an appropriate business continuity plan in case disaster strikes and the unimaginable becomes reality.

The goal of succession planning and business continuity planning is to ensure that business operations face minimal disruption and continue to run efficiently following an event on the scale of a significant terrorist attack or natural disaster. Succession planning and business continuity planning do not aim to prevent disasters, but rather help ensure that corporations are in a position to mitigate the effects on their operations. The Federal Emergency Management Agency (FEMA) lists 17 types of disasters, including earthquakes, floods, hurricanes, terrorism, and release of or exposure to hazardous materials.[3] This list does not include other types of events that could significantly disrupt business operations, including data security breaches, identity theft, and loss of key personnel. Without proper planning, the occurrence of any one of these events could cause significant operational disruptions that may undermine a business's relationships with customers, suppliers, stockholders, or other third parties.

The events of September 11, 2001, awakened the country to the vulnerabilities of our financial institutions and the need for planning that would enable such institutions to continue to provide service to their customers, notwithstanding the occurrence of a major national disaster. Although most major business firms had business continuity plans prior to September 11, the scope of those attacks exposed the weaknesses of such plans. For example, some firms transmitted records off-site only at occasional intervals or stored their off-site records at a nearby facility that was destroyed, along with their primary facility, by the September 11 attacks.[4] Subsequent to September 11, large corporations that are heavily reliant on the transmission of data, such as banks and telecommunications companies, have increasingly devoted substantial resources to de-

---

3. JAMES W. SATTERFIELD & HARRY W. RHULEN, DISASTER READY PEOPLE FOR A DISASTER READY AMERICA 31 (Firestorm Solutions LLC, 2006).

4. U.S. SECURITIES & EXCHANGE COMMISSION, SUMMARY OF 'LESSONS LEARNED' FROM EVENTS OF SEPTEMBER 11 AND IMPLICATIONS FOR BUSINESS CONTINUITY, *available at* http://www.sec.gov/divisions/marketreg/lessonslearned.htm (Feb. 13, 2002).

velop computer disaster recovery measures to guard against and mini-mize the effects of such an occurrence affecting their electronic data.[5]

The devastation of the Gulf Coast region's economic infrastructure following Hurricane Katrina reinforced the need for comprehensive plans that will allow businesses and financial institutions to continue to func-tion in the aftermath of widespread geographic destruction. In today's world, business continuity plans that contemplate disruptions of varying severity are part of sound corporate governance practices.

Sarbanes-Oxley's Effect on Business Continuity Planning

The Sarbanes-Oxley Act of 2002 (SOX), the goal of which is to "protect investors by improving the accuracy and reliability of corporate disclo-sures," does not specifically require companies to implement business continuity plans.[6] Its effect on business continuity planning is indirect at best. In the event of a significant business disruption, a corporation sub-ject to SOX without a continuity plan may be unable to comply with SOX's filing requirements. Because SOX requires corporate CEOs and CFOs to certify their filings on a quarterly basis, the inability to make proper filings could create problems for those corporate officers.[7] Rec-ognizing the potential complications posed by this issue, external audi-tors have pushed executives to implement business continuity plans for purposes of their financial reporting functions.

Additionally, federal securities laws require that corporations iden-tify risks, as well as internal controls to deal with those risks, in their periodic filings with the Securities and Exchange Commission (SEC).[8] Risks include natural events, such as hurricanes or earthquakes.[9] Depend-ing on the location of a corporation's operations, the risk of a highly destructive natural disaster could be a relevant consideration. Under SOX, the corporation must accurately identify such a risk and the controls implemented to ameliorate the risk, and the officer signing the report

---

5. Monique C.M. Leahy, *American Jurisprudence Proof of Facts 3d Database*, 29 Am. Jur. 3d 53.

6. Sarbanes-Oxley Act (2002).

7. *Id.* § 302 (2002).

8. *See* Tim J. Leech, Sarbanes-Oxley Sections 302 & 404: A White Pa-per Proposing Practical, Cost-Effective Compliance Strategies, April 2003, *available at* http://www.sec.gov/rules/proposed/s74002/card941503.pdf.

9. *Id.*

must take responsibility for the internal controls.[10] A control to ameliorate the risk of detrimental effects to a corporation following a natural disaster would, of course, include a sound business continuity plan.

New York Stock Exchange and Financial Industry Regulatory Authority, Inc.: Business Continuity Rules

In April 2004, the SEC approved rules requiring members of the New York Stock Exchange (NYSE) and the members of the Financial Industry Regulatory Authority, Inc. (FINRA) to implement business continuity plans and designate emergency points of contact.[11] NASD Rule 3520 became effective for all members as of June 14, 2004, and Rule 3510 became effective for clearing firms on August 11, 2004, and for introducing firms on September 10, 2004. NYSE Rule 446 became effective as of August 5, 2004.[12] Under these rules, business continuity plans must address 10 areas of operations: data backup and recovery (both electronic and hard copy); mission-critical systems;[13] financial and risk assessments; alternate communications between customers and the member; alternate communications between the member and its employees; alternate physical location of employees; critical constituent, bank, and counter-party impact; regulatory reporting; communications with regulators; and how the member will ensure customers' prompt access to their funds and securities if the member is unable to continue its business.[14] If one or more of the 10 categories is inapplicable to a member's business, it need not include the category in its plan but must explain the reason for its omission.[15] Both the NYSE and FINRA require members to provide contact information concerning a person (FINRA requires two such persons) whom the NYSE or FINRA may contact in case of an emergency.[16]

---

10. Sarbanes-Oxley Act § 302(a)(4)(A) (2004).

11. NYSE Rule 446 (2004); NASD Rules 3510, 3520 (2004).

12. *See* Richard Ketchum, Rule 446—Business Continuity and Contingency Plans, Letter to Members and Member Organizations, *available at* http://www.disasterrecovery.com/NYSE_Rule446.pdf (last visited Oct. 26, 2005).

13. For purposes of the rules, "mission-critical system" means a system that is necessary to process transactions, deliver funds and securities, and maintain and permit access to customer accounts. NYSE Rule 446(e) (2004); NASD Rule 3510(f)(1) (2004).

14. NYSE Rule 446 (2004).

15. NYSE Rule 446(c)(10) (2004); NASD Rule 3510(c)(10) (2004).

16. NASD Rule 3520(a)–(b).

The emergency contact(s) must be a senior officer, in the case of NYSE members, or a senior manager, in the case of FINRA members.[17]

NYSE and FINRA rules also strive to protect customers and ensure that the plans are kept up to date. FINRA requires each member to designate a member of senior management to conduct an annual review of its business continuity plan.[18] The NYSE requires members to designate a senior officer to conduct a yearly review.[19] Both the NYSE and FINRA rules state that members must update their plans in the event of a material change to the entity.[20] Each member also, at a minimum, must furnish its plan to its customers in writing when they open their accounts, post its plan on the company Web site, and mail the plan to customers upon request.[21] Members must state whether they plan to continue to do business in the event of a disruption (whether isolated, as in the case of a fire in the building, or widespread).[22] If they plan to continue operations, they must state their planned recovery time. The NYSE has stated that its purpose in requiring disclosure is twofold: first, disclosure allows investors to take business continuity plans into consideration when deciding whether to invest their funds with a particular institution; and second, it deters companies from enacting inadequate plans.[23]

The SEC interprets its Rule 206(4)-7 to require investment advisers to prepare business continuity plans. In a release dated February 5, 2004, the SEC stated that investment advisers have a fiduciary obligation to protect their clients' interests where they are unable to provide services following a natural disaster (or other significant disruption).[24] Following Hurricane Katrina, the SEC established a Web site directory listing the alternate contact information for registered investment advisers located in cities throughout the affected areas.[25]

---

17. NYSE Rule 446(g); NASD Rule 3520(b).

18. NASD Rule 3510(b).

19. NYSE Rule 446(g).

20. NYSE Rule 446(b); NASD Rule 3510(b).

21. NYSE Rule 446(d); NASD Rule 3510(e).

22. NYSE Rule 446(d) (2004); NASD Rule 3510(e) (2004).

23. U.S. Securities & Exchange Comm'n Release No. 34-48502, NYSE Rulemaking re: Business Continuity and Contingency Planning, Sept. 17, 2003, *available at* http://www.sec.gov/rules/sro/34-48502.htm.

24. U.S. Securities & Exchange Comm'n, Release No. IA-2204, Final Rule: Compliance Programs of Investment Companies and Investment Advisers, Feb. 5, 2004, *available at* http://www.sec.gov/rules/final/ia-2204.htm.

25. U.S. Securities & Exchange Comm'n, SEC Provides Alternate Contact Information for Registered Investment Advisers Displaced by Hurricane Katrina, Sept. 9, 2005, *available at* http://www.sec.gov/news/press/2005-128.htm.

As a policy matter, the SEC expects that trading markets and electronic communications networks (ECNs) will establish their own business continuity plans.[26] ECNs are computer systems that automatically match buy and sell orders at specified prices.[27] In a 2003 statement, the SEC wrote that each market or ECN should have a plan in place no later than the end of 2004 that contemplates resumption of trading on the day following a significant disruption.[28]

National Futures Association: Business Continuity Rules

On April 28, 2003, the National Futures Association (NFA) issued Compliance Rule 2-38: Business Continuity and Disaster Recovery Plan, and an Interpretive Notice to NFA Compliance Rule 2-38 that requires all NFA members to establish a written business continuity and disaster recovery plan that outlines the procedures to be followed during an emergency or significant business disruption.[29] In addition, each NFA member must provide the NFA with the contact information for an individual whom the NFA can contact in the event of an emergency, and the NFA member must update that information upon request.[30] Each NFA member may adopt a business continuity plan tailored to its individual needs based on the size and complexity of the member's operations.[31] However, to comply with NFA Compliance Rule 2-38, the plan must, at a minimum, be designed to allow the NFA member to continue or transfer its operations in the event of an emergency and to minimize disruption to other NFA members and the futures market generally.[32]

The Interpretive Notice to NFA Compliance Rule 2-38 states that an NFA member's plan should address the following, as applicable:

- establishing backup facilities, systems, and personnel that are located in one or more reasonably separate geographic areas from the NFA member's primary facilities, systems, and personnel (e.g., primary and backup facilities should be located in differ-

---

26. U.S. Securities & Exchange Comm'n, Release No. 34-48545, Policy Statement: Business Continuity Planning for Trading Markets, Oct. 1, 2003, *available at* http://www.sec.gov/rules/policy/34-48545.htm.

27. *See* http://www.sec.gov/answers/ecn.htm.

28. *Id.*

29. NFA Compliance Rule 2-38(a).

30. NFA Compliance Rule 2-38(b).

31. Interpretive Notice to Rule 2-38.

32. NFA Compliance Rule 2-38(a).

ent power grids and different telecommunication vendors should be used), which may include arrangements for the temporary use of facilities, systems, and personnel provided by third parties;

- backing up or copying essential documents and data (e.g., general ledger) on a periodic basis and storing the information off-site in either hard-copy or electronic format;
- considering the impact of business interruptions encountered by third parties and identifying ways to minimize that impact; and
- developing a communication plan to contact essential parties, such as employees, customers, carrying brokers, vendors, and disaster recovery specialists.[33]

An NFA member must periodically review and update its business continuity plan.[34] Although NFA Compliance Rule 2-38 and the Interpretive Notice to Rule 2-38 do not expressly require an annual review, NFA members should be encouraged to review the effectiveness of their business continuity plans on an annual basis. Each NFA member should distribute its business continuity plan to key employees and effectively communicate the proper procedures in the event of a disaster or significant business disruption. Copies of the business continuity plan should be kept at one or more off-site locations and should be accessible to key employees.[35]

LEGISLATIVE DEVELOPMENTS IN SUCCESSION PLANNING AND BUSINESS CONTINUITY PLANNING

Disaster Planning and Corporation Law: Emergency Bylaws

The General Corporation Law of the State of Delaware (DGCL) expressly provides emergency bylaws that permit corporations to have proper succession planning. Section 110 of the DGCL provides that boards of directors may adopt emergency bylaws, which shall be operative if a quorum of the board cannot be convened during an "emergency," which includes:

---

33. Interpretive Notice to Rule 2-38.
34. *Id.*
35. *Id.*

- any emergency resulting from an attack on the United States or on a locality in which the corporation conducts its business or customarily holds meetings of its board of directors or its stock-holders;
- during any nuclear or atomic disaster; or
- during the existence of any catastrophe or other similar emergency condition.[36]

Emergency bylaws may become operative regardless of anything to the contrary in the corporation's bylaws or certificate of incorporation.[37]

Section 110 of the DGCL also expressly addresses the issue of director succession. Section 110 provides that "officers or other persons designated on a list approved by the board of directors before the emergency, all in such order of priority and subject to such conditions . . . as may be provided in the emergency bylaws . . . shall, to the extent required to provide a quorum at any meeting of the board of directors, be deemed directors for such meeting."[38] If a corporation does not have such a list prepared, Section 110 provides for default succession. Unless otherwise stated in the emergency bylaws, Section 110 states that "the officers of the corporation who are present shall . . . be deemed, in order of rank and within rank in order of seniority, directors."[39] The board of directors may, either before or during an emergency, provide lines of succession in times of emergency that render directors or officers incapable of discharging their duties to the corporation.[40]

Additionally, Section 110 provides for the possibility of emergency bylaws addressing methods for calling board meetings, reduced quorums, and relaxed notice requirements.[41] If officers, directors, or employees act in accordance with the corporation's emergency bylaws, they can only be held liable for willful misconduct.[42] In addition to Delaware, other states have adopted laws that provide for the operation

---

36. 8 DEL. CODE REGS. § 110(a).

37. *Id.*

38. 8 DEL. CODE REGS. § 110(a)(3).

39. 8 DEL. CODE REGS. § 110(g).

40. J. ROBERT BROWN JR. & HERBERT B. MAX, RAISING CAPITAL: PRIVATE PLACEMENT FORMS AND TECHNIQUES, Form 1-38 (Aspen Publishers Online, 2002).

41. 8 Del. CODE REGS. § 110(a)(1); 8 Del. CODE REGS. § 110(f).

42. 8 Del. CODE REGS. § 110(d).

of emergency bylaws and provide for lines of succession in the event of an emergency.[43]

Because of the importance of succession and disaster planning, several large corporations have provisions for emergency bylaws within their incorporation documents. For example, Bank of America Corporation has an entire section in its bylaws dedicated to emergency bylaws that provide for, among other things, special meeting and quorum rules in the event of an emergency.[44] In addition, the emergency bylaws give the board of directors the authority to modify, amend, or add to the emergency bylaws to make any provision that may be practical or necessary under the circumstances of the emergency. Halliburton Company's bylaws contain a similar section.[45] Another example of succession and disaster planning is contained in the amended and restated bylaws of Kraft Foods, Inc., which provide, among other things, that if an officer is unavailable to perform his or her duties for any reason, the board of directors is authorized to elect any director or officer of the company to fill such position on a temporary basis.[46]

The Emergency Securities Response Act of 2004

In December 2004, Congress passed the Emergency Securities Response Act (ESRA) as part of the Intelligence Reform and Terrorism Prevention Act.[47] ESRA extends the SEC's authority to act in case of an emergency under the Securities Exchange Act of 1934, as amended.[48] If an emergency arises (defined to include "a major disturbance that substantially disrupts or threatens to disrupt" the functioning of the securities markets), the SEC may suspend or impose requirements under securities laws (its own or those of a self-regulatory organization, such as the NYSE or FINRA) for up to 10 days.[49] The SEC may extend the order if

---

43. FLA. STAT. tit. VI, ch. 607, §§ 0207, 0303; KAN. STAT. ch. 17, art. 60, pt. 10; VA. CODE tit. 13.1, ch. 9, pts. 824 & 827; Model Bus. Corp. Act §§ 2.07 & 3.03; N.Y. BUS. CORP. LAW ch. 4, art. 2, § 202(11).

44. http://sec.gov/Archives/edgar/data/70858/000119312507011657/dex31.htm.

45. http://sec.gov/Archives/edgar/data/45012/000004501206000343/amendedbylaws.htm.

46. http://sec.gov/Archives/edgar/data/1103982/000119312508196014/dex31.htm.

47. Pub. L. No. 108-458, § 7803.

48. Pub. L. No. 108-458, § 7803(b)(1).

49. Pub. L. No. 108-458, § 7803(b)–(c).

the emergency lasts beyond 10 days, but it may not extend the order for more than a total of 30 days.[50] ESRA also requires the SEC, the Board of Governors of the Federal Reserve, and the Comptroller General of the Currency to report on the efforts of the private sector to implement business continuity practices suggested in their Interagency Paper on Sound Practices to Strengthen the Resilience of the U.S. Financial System (the Interagency Paper).[51] The Interagency Paper sets forth business continuity practices with which securities market participants should comply. Recognizing the interdependent nature of the U.S. financial system, the goal of the Interagency Paper was to encourage institutions to develop plans that would help the system stabilize if some significant securities dealers were unable to function.[52] The practices identified included intraday resumption or recovery goals to be set by each participant, maintenance of resources to meet those goals, and routine testing of business continuity plans.[53] The agencies suggested that market participants should have backup facilities at least 200 to 300 miles away from their primary facilities.[54] Their suggestion contemplates an event causing widespread destruction (like the events of September 11) rather than a destructive incident confined to a single facility.

In response to ESRA, in April 2006, the SEC, the Board of Governors of the Federal Reserve, and the Comptroller General of the Currency rendered a joint report. The report concluded that the financial industry's core clearing and settlement organizations had substantially implemented the sound practices from the Interagency Paper. According to the report, significant firms had achieved or should have completed substantial implementation by the end of 2006. The agencies believed that there was no need to expand the Interagency Paper to cover additional private-sector financial services firms or to adopt other legislative

---

50. Pub. L. No. 108-458, § 7803(b)(2)(C).

51. Pub. L. No. 108-458, § 7830(e)(1).

52. *See* Mary Ann Gadziala, Speech by SEC Staff: Disaster Recovery and Business Continuity Planning, given to the Financial Markets Association 2003 Compliance Seminar, May 1, 2003, *available at* http://www.sec.gov/news/speech/spch050103mag.htm.

53. *Id.*

54. *See* Anue Systems, Solutions, *available at* http://www.anuesystems.com/regulatory_requirements.htm.

or regulatory requirements for supervised financial institutions. Overall, significant progress had been made within the financial sector.[55]

PRIVATE-SECTOR DEVELOPMENTS IN BUSINESS CONTINUITY PLANNING

How the Private Sector Has Reacted

Although there have been great strides within the private sector on this issue, many companies have not taken the necessary steps in disaster preparedness and business continuity planning. In June 2008, AT&T reported in its annual AT&T Business Continuity Survey that on average, nearly 30 percent of U.S. businesses do not consider business continuity planning a priority. Companies recently have become more likely to make business continuity planning a priority—43 percent compared to 34 percent in 2005. Accordingly, more companies have been adopting business continuity plans, with 80 percent indicating that they have a business continuity plan compared to 67 percent in 2005. Among the companies that do have a plan, 60 percent have made some type of business change in the past year that would warrant updating their business continuity plans, but only 28 percent updated their plans due to such changes. The AT&T Business Continuity Survey also found that companies are more likely to update their plans than to test their effectivenes: 59 percent have had their plans updated in the last year, but only 46 percent have had their plans tested during the same period.

In response to a January 23, 2004, letter from the 9/11 Commission, the American National Standards Institute (ANSI) convened safety, security, and business continuity experts from a wide range of industries and associations, as well as from federal, state, and local government stakeholders, to consider the need for standards for private-sector emergency preparedness and business continuity. ANSI recommended that the Department of Homeland Security (DHS) recognize as the national standard the National Fire Protection Association Standard 1600 (NFPA 1600). This is a voluntary code that sets forth a process for creating and implementing a crisis management plan.

---

55. *See* Joint Report on Efforts of the Private Sector to Implement the Interagency Paper on Sound Practices to Strengthen the Resilience of the U.S. Financial System—April 2006, *available at* http://www.sec.gov/news/press/studies/2006/soundpractices.pdf.

For a number of reasons, some believe that NFPA 1600 in time may become mandatory and lead possibly to legal exposure for employers. In the Intelligence Reform and Terrorism Prevention Act, Congress urged the DHS to promote the adoption of voluntary national preparedness standards for the private sector. The 9/11 Commission report also encouraged the credit-rating and insurance industry to rate companies based on NFPA 1600 compliance. The 9/11 Commission strongly suggested that companies failing to comply with NFPA 1600 are operating their businesses in a negligent manner. Even if Congress does not implement NFPA 1600 as the statutory duty of care for companies, some courts could adopt this standard in negligence suits as the measure of reasonable expectation.[56]

An example of the positive strides that have been made within the private sector was the Financial Services Industry Business Continuity Test. The Securities Industry Association, the Bond Market Association, the Futures Industry Association, and the Financial Information Forum successfully completed an industry-wide business continuity planning test on October 14, 2006. More than 250 securities firms, exchanges, markets, service bureaus, and industry utilities participated. These parties collectively handled more than 80 percent of normal market trading volume. During the test, firms and service bureaus were able to connect by utilizing backup data centers and communications links, alternative trading sites, and alternative operations facilities to place test orders, receive simulated executions, and conduct payment and settlement interactions. The test achieved a 95 percent overall success rate and did not encounter any significant problems.[57]

Business Continuity Planning for Pandemics

Even after multiple wakeup calls from the events of September 11 and Hurricane Katrina, many American companies have not even attempted to address business continuity and disaster preparedness planning. But even within the ones that have, there remains a gap between what has been done and what needs to be done regarding appropriate business

---

56. *See* Kevin Lindsey, *Crisis alert! Plan for emergencies to avoid losses of life, property and profits—and liability under a heightened duty of care; Legal Trends*, HRMAGAZINE, Aug, 1, 2006, at 121(4).

57. *See* Melissa Buden, *Financial Services Industry Conducts Successful Business Continuity Test*, Oct. 20, 2006, *available at* http://www.bondmarkets.com/story.asp?id=2660.

continuity planning. Unfortunately, many of these businesses do not give enough thought to what many experts believe could be the next U.S. disaster, the worldwide outbreak of a pandemic such as avian (bird) flu. Every state and many localities have devised plans to respond to an outbreak.[58] However, a Deloitte & Touche survey of more than 100 executives in January 2006 found that two-thirds have done virtually nothing to prepare for a pandemic. Traditional business continuity plans tend to address technology breakdowns or the collapse of physical structures. But a pandemic is a personnel crisis with no geographic boundaries, and waves of the infections could come in year-long periods of time.[59]

The Financial Services Sector Coordinating Council for Critical Infrastructure Protection and Homeland Security has stated that many financial institutions are concerned that their current planning for business continuity may not address the unusual circumstances that could arise during an outbreak of flu or other highly infectious disease. The council cautioned that financial service organizations ought to reexamine their current business continuity plans with a view to surviving a long-running outbreak of a highly infectious disease. The following were some of the recommendations suggested by the council:

- Identify which operations could be suspended and which are critical;
- Segregate critical staff into separate office locations;
- Plan for possible governmental actions that would cause large numbers of employees to remain home;
- Expand telecommuting and videoconferencing capabilities to avoid travel and face-to-face contact;
- Increase security due to police and security services' potential compromise by the illness; and
- Implement emergency plans that can be phased to deal with different degrees of an outbreak.[60]

---

58. *See* Allan H. Weitzman & Kimmone M. Ottley, *Asian Flu Pandemic: A Legal Framework for the Wary Employer*, HR ADVISOR LEGAL & PRACTICE GUIDE, Vol. 13, No. 5, September/October 2007.

59. *See* Janet H. Cho, *When bird flu hits*, PLAIN DEALER (Cleveland), June 26, 2006, at B1.

60. *See FSSCC Says, 'Avian Flu' Outbreak Poses Unique Threat; Council Issues Paper Outlining Guidelines to Prepare Financial Industry*, BUS. WIRE, Jan. 24, 2006.

Additionally, in a May 5, 2006 Information Memo, the NYSE addressed the issue of "Guidance pertaining to Business Continuity and Contingency Plans relating to a Potential Pandemic" with its members.[61] The memo encouraged all members to assess whether their business continuity plans would be suitable for a prolonged, widespread public health emergency. The memo stated five specific risks regarding a pandemic and the disruption it could cause: (1) pandemics can have multiple strains that arrive in multiple waves; (2) the government has indicated that it may resort to quarantines; (3) pandemics can have a multinational or global scale; (4) pandemics can impact large percentages of the company's workforce; and (5) a pandemic could result in the loss of multiple personnel within the same business unit (succession planning). The NYSE's goal was to initiate change within those companies that have not considered this rather new and alarming possibility when attempting to abide by NYSE Rule 446.[62]

CORPORATE LIABILITY

Introduction

Since the events of September 11, business continuity planning has become imperative for some corporations to protect themselves from unknown and unforeseeable risks. Given that business continuity planning has become prevalent among certain types of corporations based on size, complexity, and geographic location, it raises the issue of whether the failure to implement a business continuity plan could expose directors and officers to liability. Traditional notions of tort liability suggest that corporations and their directors and officers may have a defense to tort claims based on foreseeability requirements,[63] although personal liability for directors and officers is not beyond the realm of possibil-

---

61. *See* NYSE Info. Memo, No. 06-30, Guidance Pertaining to Business Continuity and Contingency Plans Relating to a Potential Pandemic (May 5, 2006); and Financial Services Sector Coordinating Council for Critical Infrastructure Protection and Homeland Security, Statement of Preparations for "Avian Flu" and related paper, Issues for Consideration Regarding Preparations for "Avian Flu" (Jan. 23, 2006).

62. NYSE Reg. Info. Memo, No. 06-30, May 5, 2006.

63. PROSSER & KEETON ON TORTS § 43 (5th ed. 1984).

ity.[64] Even though corporations and their directors and officers may not be liable to third parties on tort theories, state corporation law imposes fiduciary duties of loyalty and care[65] on directors that could form the basis of liability.

Under Delaware corporation law, the business judgment rule protects directors from liability for bad business decisions made in good faith, upon reasonable information, and with a rational basis.[66] The policy of the business judgment rule prevents courts from review of the merits of a business decision made in good faith and with due care.[67] However, the business judgment rule applies only to *decisions* made by the board of directors; inaction or failure to make any decision generally is outside the scope of the protection afforded to directors.[68] It follows that the business judgment rule conceivably would not be available to protect directors from allegations that the board failed to implement a business continuity or disaster recovery plan to protect the corporation from preventable harm.[69]

Oversight Liability: Board of Directors and Officers

In *In re Caremark*,[70] the Delaware Supreme Court applied the traditional notions of fiduciary duties and crafted a general rule for oversight liability. In *Caremark*, the court held that the fiduciary duty of care owed by directors includes an obligation to implement adequate information and reporting systems to ensure compliance with the key regulatory regimes

---

64. Monique C.M. Leahy, *American Jurisprudence Proof of Facts 3d Database*, 29 AM. JUR. 3D 53, § 35 (explaining that personal liability for corporate officers for failure to provide computer disaster recovery measures is unlikely but possible under traditional theories of negligence).

65. *In re* Walt Disney Derivative Litig., 906 A.2d 27 (Del. 2006).

66. Smith v. Van Gorkom, 488 A.2d 858, 872 (Del. 1986).

67. EDWARD P. WELCH, ANDREW J. TUREZYN & ROBERT S. SAUNDERS, FOLK ON THE DELAWARE GENERAL CORPORATION LAW, FIFTH ED., § 141.2.2.2 (2006, supplemented 6/08).

68. Rales v. Blasband, 634 A.2d 927 (Del. 1993); EDWARD P. WELCH, ANDREW J. TUREZYN & ROBERT S. SAUNDERS, FOLK ON THE DELAWARE GENERAL CORPORATION LAW, FIFTH ED., § 141.2.2.10. Note that a conscious decision to refrain from acting may be a valid exercise of business judgment and would be protected under the business judgment rule.

69. Kevin P. Cronin, *As Courts Increasingly Hold Firms Liable for Losses Caused by Computer Failures, Recovery Capabilities Are Fast Becoming a Legal Necessity*, DISASTER RECOVERY JOURNAL, Vol. 6 #2 (1997).

70. *In re* Caremark Int'l Deriv. Litig., 698 A.2d 959 (Del. 1996).

under which it operates.[71] Specifically, the board "has a responsibility to assure that appropriate information and reporting systems are established by management" to ensure compliance with applicable law.[72] Under *Caremark*, directors have an affirmative duty to the corporation to set up a monitoring system to ensure that the corporation does not violate law; passivity is not permitted.

Ten years after *Caremark,* the Delaware Supreme Court in *Stone v. Ritter* reaffirmed and recast the *Caremark* standard for liability in corporate oversight matters.[73] *Stone* involved a derivative action against the corporation's present and former directors relating to $50 million in fines and penalties paid by the corporation for violations of the Federal Bank Secrecy Act. Despite the existence of an information and reporting system that was designed to monitor legal compliance (although inadequate in this instance), the plaintiffs alleged that the directors failed to implement adequate controls that would have enabled them to learn of violations of the law.

In dismissing the plaintiffs' claims, the court concluded that the board established reasonable reporting systems to supervise compliance with relevant law, even though those systems failed to prevent the violations at issue.[74] Plaintiffs must show more than a substantial financial loss to establish oversight liability. The court concluded that oversight liability may be imposed only if "(a) the directors utterly failed to implement any reporting or information system or controls; or (b) having implemented such a system or controls, consciously failed to monitor or oversee its operations, thus disabling themselves from being informed of risks or problems requiring their attention."[75] That a monitoring system fails to detect serious misconduct does not necessarily demonstrate a conscious disregard of oversight duties to impose liability.

Although the Delaware Supreme Court reaffirmed the principles of oversight liability in *Caremark*, the court also recast the theory of liability in a way to prevent indemnification in certain cases.[76] While the court in *Caremark* framed the oversight liability analysis in terms of a duty of

---

71. 698 A.2d 959, 970.
72. 698 A.2d 959, 969–70.
73. 911 A.2d 362 (Del. 2006).
74. 911 A.2d 362, 370–71.
75. 911 A.2d 362, 370.
76. *See* http://www.businessassociationsblog.com/lawandbusiness/comments/stone_v_ritter_directors_caremark_oversight_duties/ (last visited Sept. 23, 2008).

care, the court in *Stone* framed the issue in terms of good faith and loyalty rather than the duty of care.[77] This may have the practical effect of moving oversight liability claims outside the purview of Section 102(b)(7) of the DGCL, which allows corporations to adopt charter provisions that eliminate or limit the personal liability of directors for monetary damages for breach of the duty of care.[78]

It was assumed that the duties imposed by *Caremark* and its progeny applied to corporate officers as well as directors. Recently, a bankruptcy court in Delaware confirmed this assumption.[79] At issue in *Miller v. McDonald* was whether the corporation's general counsel and vice president could be held liable for failing to implement a system to detect and report wrongdoing by the president of the corporation. The court held that officers also have the duty to exercise reasonable care in oversight of corporate operations in their area of responsibility. Officers, like directors, owe an affirmative duty to implement a monitoring system by which management misconduct can be detected and reported. Accordingly, officers and directors should work together to devise a plan for ameliorating any potential risk of loss to the corporation.

Oversight Liability and Business Continuity Planning

Generally speaking, a director may be held liable to the corporation for a loss arising from an unconsidered failure by the board to act in circumstances in which due attention might have prevented the loss.[80] The Delaware courts have not had the opportunity to decide whether a director or officer would be liable to the corporation for the failure to implement a business continuity plan or the failure to monitor the effectiveness of such a plan. Directors and officers are obligated to ensure that the corporation has adequate policies, procedures, and systems for managing the affairs of the corporation.[81] Applying the reasoning of *Caremark* and its progeny, directors and officers could be held to an affirmative duty to

---

77. 911 A.2d 362, 370.

78. 8 DEL. CODE § 102(b)(7).

79. Miller v. McDonald, 385 B.R. 576 (Bankr., Del. Apr. 9, 2008). Although Florida law governed the breach of fiduciary duty claim, the court cited *Caremark* and *Stone* in its analysis and stated that Delaware law was relevant because the Florida courts have relied upon Delaware corporate law to establish their own body of corporation law.

80. *Caremark*, 698 A.2d 959, 968.

81. Judah Best & Bruce E. Yannett, Practicing Law Inst. Corp. Legal Dep'ts, *Crisis Management, in* PLIEF-CORPLEG 13 Exh. 13A, § I.B.

plan for disasters.[82] Depending on the size, complexity of operations, and geographic area of the corporation, directors and officers (at a minimum) should have a business continuity plan and establish procedures to test its effectiveness on a regular basis.

Best Practices

To guard against potential liability, directors and executive officers of a company that does not already have a business continuity plan or succession plan should adopt such plans and give careful consideration to the type of plans that would be appropriate for their company. As part of sound corporate governance, all business entities, regardless of size and geographic location, should assess their risk of, and their vulnerability to, certain disasters that could adversely affect their business operations. Almost every type of organization is under some pressure (e.g., from the government or customers) to demonstrate that they have a viable plan to mitigate the risks of disastrous events.[83] Companies that have a business continuity plan and succession plan should periodically review and test those plans. For companies without a business continuity plan, high-ranking officers should, at a minimum, coordinate with the IT department, familiarize themselves with the risks to the business, and design a plan to mitigate those risks. In addition, companies should review their insurance policies and determine whether they are covered for loss of earnings, off-premise power failures, electronic data failures, or valuable papers insurance for the cost of reconstructing destroyed documents.[84]

---

82. *Id.* § IV.

83. HOWARD MUSON, PREPARING FOR THE WORST: A GUIDE TO BUSINESS CONTINUITY PLANNING FOR MID-MARKETS, The Conference Board, Executive Action Series, No. 179, February 2006.

84. JEAN BARR, PUTTING TOGETHER A DISASTER RECOVERY PLAN, January/February 1993.

Critical Infrastructure

CHAPTER 9

The SAFETY Act—
A Practioner's Guide to the
Homeland Security
Technology Catalyst

by Mark J. Robertson and Jeffrey Kaliel

The following chapter aims to familiarize counsel with the liability protections available under the Support Anti-Terrorism by Fostering Effective Technologies Act of 2002 (SAFETY Act, passed by Congress as a part of the Homeland Security Act of 2002. The chapter addresses the background of the SAFETY Act, provides a detailed discussion of the system of risk and litigation management provided under the act, and summarizes the responsibilities of companies offering SAFETY Act–approved technologies. The chapter also aims to put the SAFETY Act in context with other liability protection devices and addresses practicalities involved in obtaining SAFETY Act approvals.

The Support Anti-Terrorism by Fostering Effective Technologies Act of 2002 (the SAFETY Act) was passed by Congress as part of the Homeland Security Act of 2002 (Subtitle G of Title VIII), which created the U.S. Department of Homeland Security (DHS).[1] Congress designed the SAFETY Act to encourage the rapid development and fielding of anti-terror technologies. The SAFETY Act removes a recognized hindrance

---

1. 6 U.S.C. §§ 441–444

to companies that wish to invest in and deploy technologies helpful in homeland security: the potentially catastrophic liability that could result if their technology were to become the subject of litigation following a terror attack. The SAFETY Act largely eliminates this concern. A firm with DHS approval under the SAFETY Act would have protections against liability if, in the event of a terror attack, its product or service failed to perform as intended. The SAFETY Act provides important liability protections not only for a selling company and its shareholders, but also for those who purchase and deploy protected technologies, and sharply limits the possibility of costly liability for both.

The SAFETY Act is a tool that should be considered by every provider of an anti-terrorism "technology" as that term is expansively defined by the SAFETY Act and its implementing regulations.[2] Those who procure and utilize homeland security technologies are increasingly insisting that technology providers obtain SAFETY Act coverage. Although delays in promulgating regulatory guidance and a somewhat convoluted initial application process adversely affected early implementation efforts, DHS has since taken action that has engendered greater confidence in, and paved the way for, more robust implementation of the SAFETY Act. DHS has to date granted SAFETY Act coverage to approximately 250 different anti-terrorism technologies. Whatever the history of the SAFETY Act and its implementation, companies today should recognize that the act essentially offers them a relatively inexpensive insurance policy against catastrophic risk. Moreover, the SAFETY Act's limit of potential liability in itself can allow firms to offer technologies at a more competitive price, and it can free companies to design products that provide at least some meaningful level of protection while shielding them from the specter of overzealous plaintiffs and juries.

There is also a growing sense that SAFETY Act approval is seen in industry as a de facto seal of approval affording advantages in marketing a product or service, as it indicates a substantial level of government

---

2. *See* Regulations Implementing the Support Anti-terrorism by Fostering Effective Technologies Act of 2002 (the SAFETY Act), 71 Fed. Reg. 33,147–68 (June 8, 2006); "The term 'Technology' means any product, equipment, service (including support services), device, or technology (including information technology) or any combination of the foregoing. Design services, consulting services, engineering services, software development services, software integration services, threat assessments, vulnerability studies, and other analyses relevant to homeland security may be deemed a Technology under this part." 6 C.F.R. § 25.2.

review and assessment of a technology and its safety and effectiveness. Further, recent changes to the Federal Acquisition Regulations (FAR) integrate the SAFETY Act into the federal acquisition process, effectively extending advantages to SAFETY Act–approved technologies. Some also argue that corporate officers have a duty to their shareholders to seek SAFETY Act liability protection when fielding homeland security technologies. In sum, there are a host of reasons for companies to obtain SAFETY Act protections.

This article aims to familiarize in-house and outside counsel with the protections available under the SAFETY Act, so that they might in turn advise clients in the broader homeland security community. We will discuss the background of the SAFETY Act, then discuss in detail the protections offered and responsibilities of companies that offer SAFETY Act–approved technologies. We will also put the SAFETY Act in context with other liability protection devices, such as the Public Readiness and Emergency Preparedness Act (PREP Act) and the Government Contractor Defense. Finally, we will address practicalities involved in advancing a SAFETY Act application.

THE SAFETY ACT'S PROTECTIONS

The SAFETY Act, it should be emphasized, offers its liability protections well beyond the actual vendors who sell their technologies to the federal government. The benefits of the SAFETY Act's liability protection flow up and down the supply chain, in both government and private markets. Both users and suppliers of anti-terror technologies are covered by SAFETY Act protections if the technology they are fielding has been "Designated" or "Certified" by DHS. Excluding government indemnification for unusually hazardous risks pursuant to P.L. 85-804, before the SAFETY Act was enacted, the great majority of technologies could access liability protections only when they were sold to the U.S. military and when their designers complied with strict government requirements (the Government Contractor Defense is discussed below). These protections, limited as they were, led to incentives for the defense industry to aggressively and creatively work to meet some of the Department of Defense's technological requirements. One could argue that a large part of the American defense industry's success in developing new defense technologies can be traced back to its liability protections, which allowed for greater risk-taking.

After September 11, 2001, Congress recognized that similar incentives did not exist for technologies that could protect civilian populations in the homeland, and the industrial base for those technologies remained small. Even technologies designed for the Department of Defense (DoD) with potential crossover applications could not be brought to the civilian market without losing critical liability protections.

As such, one potential major effect of the SAFETY Act is to allow the movement of existing defense and homeland security technologies from mere federal agency use to the broader civilian homeland security marketplace—to all those transportation hubs, stadiums, office towers, shopping malls, and manufacturing and chemical facilities that have real and immediate security needs. Toward this end, SAFETY Act protections are available to both newly developed and existing technologies, whether they have been specifically developed for anti-terror purposes or not.[3] This is no small accomplishment, as the homeland security community has increasingly recognized that the government alone cannot fully defend the nation from a terror attack. The involvement of the private sector is crucial, especially in light of the fact that as much as 85 percent of the nation's critical infrastructure is privately held. Still, after verdicts like the one that held the Port Authority of New York and New Jersey more than two-thirds responsible for the 1993 World Trade Center bombing, many in the security and technologies industries faced a high barrier to entering the civilian homeland security market.[4]

Under the SAFETY Act, the "seller"[5] of an anti-terror technology may apply to DHS for protection from civil liability following a terrorist attack. To date, SAFETY Act approval has been awarded to technologies ranging from video surveillance systems to explosive detection technol-

---

3. 6 U.S.C. § 444 allows for SAFETY Act designation of technology that is "designed, developed, modified, or procured for the specific purpose of preventing, detecting, identifying, or deterring acts of terrorism or limiting the harm" caused by acts of terrorism.

4. *See* Nash v. Port Auth. of N.Y. & N.J., #129074/93, 2008 N.Y. App. Div. LEXIS 374, 2008 N.Y. slip op. 03991 (1st Dept.). Victims of the 1993 World Trade Center bombings sued the Port Authority of New York and New Jersey for damages. A New York appellate panel affirmed the jury verdict that the Port Authority was more than two-thirds responsible for the 1993 terrorist bombing of the World Trade Center.

5. *See* 6 C.F.R. § 25.2. For purposes of the SAFETY Act, the term "seller" means any person, firm, or other entity that sells or otherwise provides Qualified Anti-Terrorism Technology to any customer(s) and to whom or to which (as appropriate) a designation and/or certification has been issued.

ogy, from software and IT applications to radiological detection equipment.[6] Protection, in short, is available for virtually any product or service that can effectively deter, mitigate, or help respond to a terrorist attack. The definition of technology for purposes of the SAFETY Act and its implementing regulations is expansive and includes "any product, equipment, service (including support services), device, or technology (including information technology) or any combination of the foregoing."[7] Further, the regulatory definition specifies that "[d]esign services, consulting services, engineering services, software development services, software integration services, threat assessments, vulnerability studies, and other analyses relevant to homeland security may be deemed a Technology . . ." under the SAFETY Act.[8]

DESIGNATION AS A QUALIFIED ANTI-TERRORISM TECHNOLOGY

The SAFETY Act provides two potential classes of protection for approved anti-terrorism technologies. First, products or services may be *designated* as a Qualified Anti-Terrorism Technology (QATT). In evaluating whether a technology should be designated as a QATT, DHS must consider the following factors:

1. Prior U.S. government use or demonstrated substantial utility and effectiveness.
2. Availability of the technology for immediate deployment in public and private settings.
3. Existence of extraordinarily large or extraordinarily unquantifiable potential third-party liability risk exposure to the seller or other provider of such anti-terrorism technology.

---

6. Recently designated technologies include: cargo and vehicle inspection systems, criminal information sharing services, Smarttech Chem system, protective services, rail transportation security services, Sulf-N® 26 fertilizer process and product, multi-threat risk analysis and physical perimeter protection system for the federal secure border initiative network program, and explosive trace detection inspection services. A full list of certified technologies is available on the Web site of the Office of SAFETY Act Implementation at www.safetyact.gov.

7. *See* note 2 above.

8. *Id.*

4. Substantial likelihood that such anti-terrorism technology will not be deployed unless protections under the system of risk management provided under [the SAFETY Act] are extended.

5. Magnitude of risk exposure to the public if such anti-terrorism technology is not deployed.

6. Evaluation of all scientific studies that can be feasibly conducted in order to assess the capability of the technology to substantially reduce risks of harm.

7. Anti-terrorism technology that would be effective in facilitating the defense against acts of terrorism, including technologies that prevent, defeat or respond to such acts.

8. A determination made by federal, state, or local officials that the technology is appropriate for the purpose of preventing, detecting, identifying, or deterring acts of terrorism or limiting the harm such acts might otherwise cause.

9. Any other factor that the Under Secretary [of DHS's Science and Technology Directorate] may consider to be relevant to the determination or to the homeland security of the United States.[9]

The SAFETY Act's implementing regulations provide for broad discretion in determining whether to designate a particular technology as a QATT. Further, in conducting his analysis, the DHS Under Secretary for Science and Technology has discretion to give greater weight to certain factors over others, and he may determine that failure to meet one or more of the criteria does not necessary disqualify a technology from being designated as a QATT.[10]

Upon designation by DHS, the seller and all users of the approved QATT enjoy the benefits of the system of risk management and litigation management established by the SAFETY Act. Together, the risk and litigation management provisions provide the following protections:

1. A limitation on the liability of sellers of Qualified Anti-Terrorism Technologies to an amount of liability insurance coverage specified for each Qualified Anti-Terrorism Technology, pro-

---

9. *See* 6 C.F.R. § 25.4(b)(1).

10. *See* 6 C.F.R. § 25.3; all of the responsibilities, powers, and functions of the Secretary of Homeland Security under the SAFETY Act, except the authority to declare that an act is an act of terrorism for purposes of the SAFETY Act have been delegated to the DHS Under Secretary for Science & Technology.

vided that sellers cannot be required to obtain any more liability insurance coverage than is reasonably available "at prices and terms that will not unreasonably distort the sales price" of the technology;[11]

2. A prohibition on joint and several liability such that sellers can only be liable for the percentage of noneconomic damages that is proportionate to their responsibility;[12]
3. A complete bar on punitive damages and prejudgment interest;[13]
4. The reduction of a plaintiff's recovery by the amount of collateral source compensation, such as insurance benefits or government benefits, such plaintiff receives or is eligible to receive;[14]
5. Exclusive jurisdiction in federal court for suits against the sellers of Qualified Anti-Terrorism Technologies;[15] and
6. A rebuttable presumption that sellers are entitled to the Government Contractor Defense.[16]

The designation of a technology as a QATT confers each of the aforementioned liability protections except for the rebuttable presumption in favor of the Government Contractor Defense, or GCD. That specific liability protection is conferred only upon an additional certification by the secretary, as discussed below.

Those who deploy QATTs are protected from liability for punitive damages if the technology allegedly fails to perform as intended in a terror attack. Liability is restricted to noneconomic damages in direct proportion to the seller's percentage of responsibility.[17] Noneconomic damages under the SAFETY Act are defined as "damages for losses for physical and emotional pain, suffering, inconvenience, physical impairment, mental anguish, disfigurement, loss of enjoyment of life, loss of society and companionship, loss of consortium, hedonic damages, injury to reputation, and any other nonpecuniary losses."[18]

Further, compensatory damages may not exceed a predetermined amount of liability insurance coverage that the seller is obligated to main-

---

11. *See* 6 U.S.C. § 443 (c); 6 U.S.C. § 443(a)(2).
12. *See* 6 U.S.C. § 442 (b)(2).
13. *See* 6 U.S.C. § 442(b)(1).
14. *See* 6 U.S.C. § 442(c).
15. *See* 6 U.S.C. § 442(a)(2).
16. 6 U.S.C. § 442(d).
17. 6 U.S.C. § 442(b)(2)(A).
18. 6 U.S.C. § 442(b)(2)(B).

tain. The SAFETY Act provides that in connection with designation of a QATT, the seller is obligated to obtain liability insurance of such types and amounts that DHS has determined is appropriate "to satisfy otherwise compensable third-party claims arising out of, relating to, or resulting from an act of terrorism when qualified anti-terrorism technologies have been deployed in defense against or response or recovery from such act."[19] The SAFETY Act provides that "[n]otwithstanding any other provision of law, liability for all claims against a Seller arising out of, relating to, or resulting from an act of terrorism when [QATTs] have been deployed in defense against or response or recovery from such act and such claims result or may result in loss to the Seller . . ." shall not be in an amount greater than the limits of liability insurance that the seller is obligated to maintain.[20] Further, any recovery by a plaintiff in this context shall be offset by the amount of plaintiff's collateral source compensation.[21] The SAFETY Act's insurance requirement and how the appropriate amount of insurance is calculated is discussed below.

In addition, exclusive jurisdiction in federal court is granted for all suits against the sellers of Qualified Anti-Terrorism Technologies.[22] This is an especially important provision, as DHS interprets it to mean that in any suit arising out of a terrorism incident, not only can the seller be sued exclusively in federal court (itself an important protection against inflated damages awarded by some state jurisdictions), but further that it is *only* against the *seller* of a QATT that any suit can be upheld. As DHS states in the preamble to the SAFETY Act final rule, "[I]t is clear that the Seller is the only appropriate defendant in this exclusive Federal cause of action."[23] That is, no lawsuit shall proceed against any user, vendor, or subcontractor employing a QATT, according to DHS interpretation. As DHS explains in the preamble to the final rule implementing the SAFETY Act, "[I]f the Seller of the Qualified Anti-Terrorism Technology at issue were not the only defendant, would-be plaintiffs could, in an effort to circumvent the statute, bring claims (arising out of or relating to the performance or non-performance of the Seller's Qualified Anti-Terrorism Technology) against arguably less culpable persons or entities, including but not limited to contractors, subcontractors, suppliers, vendors, and customers of the Seller of the technology. Because the claims in the

---

19. 6 U.S.C. § 443(a).
20. 6 U.S.C. § 443(c).
21. 6 U.S.C. §§ 442(c).
22. 6 U.S.C. § 442(a).
23. 6 C.F.R. § 25 at 33150.

cause of action would be predicated on the performance or nonperformance of the Seller's Qualified Anti-Terrorism Technology, those persons or entities, in turn, would file a third-party action against the Seller."[24] It is for this reason that DHS interprets the SAFETY Act to bar claims against entities other than the seller.

CERTIFICATION OF A QATT

Following designation, the second class of protection is SAFETY Act *certification*.[25] Certification provides all the benefits of the systems of risk and liability management of designation, plus an additional layer of liability protection. DHS has interpreted this bi-level scheme to mean that a designation must be granted in order for a certification to be granted, but both may be granted simultaneously, if warranted. A seller of a Certified QATT is entitled to assert the Government Contractor Defense (GCD) in product liability or other litigation involving its SAFETY Act–certified technology resulting from an act of terrorism.[26] SAFETY Act certification of a QATT creates the rebuttable presumption that the GCD applies, which can only be overcome if a plaintiff proves that the seller acted "fraudulently" or "with willful misconduct" in applying for SAFETY Act protections.[27]

The GCD, which exists in no statute but has been created in case law by the federal judiciary, essentially immunizes contractors that supply goods to the government provided they have met certain conditions. It has been used primarily by military contractors in cases involving allegations of defective military equipment. We will discuss the GCD in more detail below, but for now it is important to bear in mind that certification under the SAFETY Act entitles the seller to assert the affirmative GCD and thus serves as important protection against potential liability.

DESIGNATION VS. CERTIFICATION UNDER THE SAFETY ACT

As discussed above, the SAFETY Act creates two classes of protections. The broader classification is the designation of QATTs. The stricter classi-

---

24. *Id.*
25. 6 U.S.C. § 442(d).
26. *Id.*
27. 6 U.S.C. § 442(d)(1).

fication is certification, which serves to establish "[a] rebuttable presumption that the Seller is entitled to the 'government contractor defense.'" The SAFETY Act mandates that the review culminating in a technology's Certification must be "comprehensive," and it must allow the DHS Secretary to determine "whether it will perform as intended, conforms to the Seller's specifications, and is safe for use as intended."[28] The Seller is also required to conduct "safety and hazard analyses on such technology, and . . . supply the Secretary with all such information."[29]

Just as the requirements for QATT certification are more rigorous than those for designation, the benefits attendant SAFETY Act certification are comparatively sweeping. In short, the SAFETY Act has, for the first time, codified the GCD—something that until now had been entirely a judicial construct.

Government Contractor Defense

Much has been written about the GCD, and while we will not attempt to provide exhaustive analysis, it is important, for purposes of understanding the SAFETY Act, to know the reach and limitations of the GCD. The leading case for the GCD is *Boyle v. United Technologies Corp.*, 487 U.S. 500 (1988). In that case, a U.S. Marine was killed in a crash of a helicopter manufactured by United Technologies. The Supreme Court held that the government contractor may invoke the GCD "when (1) the United States approved reasonably precise specifications; (2) the equipment conformed to those specifications; and (3) the supplier warned the United States about the dangers in the use of the equipment that were known to the supplier but not to the United States."[30]

The first prong is satisfied when the contractor shows that the government provided the technical requirements for the equipment or service, and that the government had exclusive control over the design, use, and application of the product. The second prong is a question of fact. The third prong ensures that the government knew about the dangers of a product before use. Many courts, like the U.S. Court of Appeals for the Ninth Circuit, have interpreted *Boyle* to apply only in the context of military procurement.[31] Other courts have broadened the scope slightly.

---

28. 6 U.S.C. § 442(d)(2).

29. *Id.*

30. 487 U.S. 500, 512 (1988).

31. Nielsen v. George Diamond Vogel Paint Co., 892 F.2d 1450, 1454–55 (9th Cir. 1990).

Whether the defense can be invoked against, for example, manufacturing defects is also controversial. On this and other issues, there has been an uneven and sometime unpredictable application of the GCD in our courts. What is clear is that where the GCD applies, state tort law is displaced: the Supreme Court in *Boyle* held that "state law which holds Government contractors liable for design defects" can present a conflict with federal policy and therefore "must be displaced."[32]

The decision clearly stated some important protections for defense contractors, but the doctrine was painstakingly limited by the Court. As one commentator has noted, "[w]hile the *Boyle* decision recognized the need to provide some litigation protections to private entities that help reduce public risk, the decision was quite limited in its application: it related only to contracts entered into directly with the federal government to provide goods that furthered the military's conducting of the national defense. Yet, in light of recent developments in the war on terrorism and the threat posed by a potential avian flu pandemic, it becomes clear that the general policy justification for the government contractor defense in *Boyle* is compelling in contexts well beyond those presented in *Boyle*."[33]

Public Readiness and Emergency Preparedness Act

The SAFETY Act is not the only legislation that provides broad liability protections. Congress adopted a similar approach of shielding companies from liability when it passed the Public Readiness and Emergency Preparedness Act (PREP Act) enacted as Division C of the Defense Appropriations Act for fiscal year 2006, Pub. L. No. 109-148.[34] The PREP Act grants makers of drugs, vaccines, and devices immunity from civil liability for anything related to the development and production of drugs, vaccines, or devices. Just as Congress was concerned that not enough anti-terror technologies would make it to market without liability protections, so too was it concerned that vital protections against bioterrorism like vaccines and drugs would not become available absent protections against potential liability.

---

32. 487 U.S. 500, 512 (1988)

33. Paul Taylor, *We're All in This Together: Extending Sovereign Immunity to Encourage Private Parties to Reduce Public Risk*, 75 U. CIN. L. REV. 1595.

34. The PREP Act may be found in sections 319F-3 and 319F-4 of the Public Health Service Act and is codified at 42 U.S.C. §§ 247d-6d, 247d-6e.

Companies covered under the PREP Act are granted even broader protection from liability than the coverage available under the SAFETY Act. Under the PREP Act, so-called "covered entities" are "immune from suit and liability under Federal and State law with respect to all claims for loss caused by, arising out of, relating to, or resulting from the administration to or the use by an individual of a covered countermeasure."[35] The process by which a countermeasure becomes "covered" is quite different from that under the SAFETY Act, however. Under the PREP Act, a countermeasure is covered if the secretary of HHS "makes a determination that a disease or other health condition or other threat to health constitutes a public health emergency, or that there is a credible risk that the disease, condition, or threat may in the future constitute such an emergency" and makes a declaration, through publication in the *Federal Register*, recommending, under such conditions as the secretary may specify, the manufacture, testing, development, distribution, administration, or use of one or more covered countermeasures.[36]

Such government interventions in the private marketplace are rare and not without controversy. To a certain extent, such actions build upon the much less controversial, and long-established, common law principle of sovereign immunity, which provides that a government is immune from lawsuits unless it consents. The theory is that the government must be able to perform its essential functions, using the judgment of its elected officials and their subordinates, free from the prospect of litigation that would necessarily second-guess governmental decisions. Though the *Boyle* Court made clear that the government contractor defense is not based on sovereign immunity and expressly declined to decide whether such contractors enjoy such immunity, it reasoned that "it makes little sense to insulate the Government against financial liability for the judgment that a particular feature of military equipment is necessary when the Government produces the equipment itself, but not when it contracts for the production."[37] The Court explained that "[t]he financial burden of judgments against the contractors would ultimately be passed through, substantially if not totally, to the United States itself, since defense contractors will predictably raise their prices to cover, or to insure against, contingent liability for the Government-ordered designs."[38] Generally, the idea

---

35. 42 U.S.C. § 247d-6d.
36. *Id.*
37. *See Boyle*, 487 U.S. 512 (1988).
38. *See id.* at 511–12.

is that the government should be able to accomplish its most pressing national defense goals with the help of private companies, if it so chooses, without sacrificing its sovereign immunity. Until the SAFETY Act and the PREP Act, however, this line of reasoning had only rarely been extended to non-military functions.

The final rule implementing the SAFETY Act attempts to clarify the relationship between the SAFETY Act and the GCD: "The Department believes with the SAFETY Act that Congress incorporated government contractor defense protections outlined in the Supreme Court's *Boyle* line of cases as it existed on the date of enactment of the SAFETY Act, rather than incorporating future developments of the government contractor defense in the courts."[39] This interpretation begs several questions, especially since the GCD is not evenly applied across courts. Further, DHS has taken a firm stance as to the application of the GCD in the SAFETY Act context: "The Act does not permit judicial review of the Secretary's exercise of discretion in this context. When the Secretary determines that a Certification is appropriate, that decision creates a rebuttable presumption that the government contractor defense applies. This presumption may only be rebutted "by clear and convincing evidence showing that the Seller acted fraudulently or with willful misconduct in submitting information to the Department during the course of the consideration of such Technology."[40]

In the same way the GCD has been the subject of varying judicial interpretation, there will likely be no uniform national application of SAFETY Act protections in the event they are tested following a terrorist attack. Any SAFETY Act protections will be raised as an affirmative defense before a court, and it will ultimately be the courts that determine whether DHS's interpretation of its authority is valid. For example, DHS's interpretation in the final rule is that lawsuits may only be brought for claims for injuries that are proximately caused by sellers that provide qualified antiterrorism technology:

> The best reading of § 863(a), and the reading the Department
> has adopted, is that (1) Only one cause of action exists for loss
> of property, personal injury, or death for performance or non-
> performance of the Seller's Qualified Anti-Terrorism Technol-
> ogy in relation to an Act of Terrorism, (2) Such cause of action
> may be brought only against the Seller of the Qualified Anti-

---

39. 6 C.F.R. § 25.
40. 6 C.F.R. § 25.8(b).

Terrorism Technology and may not be brought against the buyers, the buyers' contractors, downstream users of the Qualified Anti-Terrorism Technology, the Seller's suppliers or contractors, or any other person or entity, and (3) Such cause of action must be brought in Federal court. The exclusive Federal nature of this cause of action is evidenced in large part by the exclusive jurisdiction provision in § 863(a)(2).[41]

That said, what is beyond doubt is that the SAFETY Act is the first time the GCD has been expanded to non-military situations. In fact, the act applies even where the government is not a party at all to any transaction involving the technology. The protections are available not only to federal government contractors, but also to those who sell to state, local, and tribal governments—or to the private sector. With the SAFETY Act, the "government contractor defense" becomes the "seller of qualified anti-terror technology defense."

Another way the SAFETY Act diverges significantly from the GCD is in the area of product design. Sellers of QATTs need not have designed their technologies to government specifications in order to obtain SAFETY Act protections. In fact, it works in the opposite manner, where a fully designed and potentially market-ready product is submitted to DHS for review.

One way the SAFETY Act's protections are more restrictive than the GCD is that the SAFETY Act's liability protections are effective only in the event of an act of terrorism. Under the GCD, contractors can use the shield whether or not there has been an act of terrorism or war or any other national security crisis. Accordingly, for the purposes of the SAFETY Act, the definition of an "Act of Terrorism" is crucial.[42]

---

41. 6 C.F.R. § 25.

42. Relying upon the statute, DHS defined "Act of Terrorism" in the SAFETY Act Final Rule as follows: "any act determined to have met the following requirements or such other requirements as defined and specified by the Secretary: (1) Is unlawful; (2) Causes harm, including financial harm, to a person, property, or entity, in the United States, or in the case of a domestic United States air carrier or a United States-flag vessel (or a vessel based principally in the United States on which United States income tax is paid and whose insurance coverage is subject to regulation in the United States), in or outside the United States; and (3) Uses or attempts to use instrumentalities, weapons or other methods designed or intended to cause mass destruction, injury or other loss to citizens or institutions of the United States." See 6 C.F.R. § 25.2.

SAFETY ACT RESPONSIBILITIES

In addition to the benefits that SAFETY Act protection affords, there are also responsibilities for the sellers of the anti-terrorism technologies who receive SAFETY Act protection. Chief among these are the requirements to inform DHS of material modifications to QATTs and to maintain specified insurance. Section 443 of the SAFETY Act requires persons who "sell or otherwise provide a qualified anti-terrorism technology to Federal and non-Federal Government customers . . . [to] obtain liability insurance . . . in such amounts as shall be required."[43] DHS has clarified that such insurance need not protect the seller's contractors, subcontractors, suppliers, vendors, and customers.[44] The seller of the anti-terrorism technology may not be required to obtain insurance that is not "available on the world market [or] that would unreasonably distort the sales price of the Seller's anti-terrorism Technology."[45]

The SAFETY Act final rule sets forth the following factors that should be considered in determining the requisite amount of liability insurance sellers are obligated to maintain in connection with their QATT:

1. The particular technology at issue;
2. The amount of liability insurance the seller maintained prior to application;
3. The amount of liability insurance maintained by the seller for other technologies or for the seller's business as a whole;
4. The amount of liability insurance typically maintained by sellers of comparable technologies;
5. Information regarding the amount of liability insurance offered on the world market;
6. Data and history regarding mass casualty losses;
7. The intended use of the technology; and

---

43. 6 U.S.C. § 443(a)(1).

44. "The Department recognizes that an action for recovery of damages proximately caused by a QATT that arises out of an Act of Terrorism may only be properly brought against a Seller. Accordingly, the Department has specified, and will continue to specify in particular Designations, that the liability insurance required to be obtained by the Seller shall not be required to provide coverage for the Seller's contractors, subcontractors, suppliers, vendors or customers." 6 C.F.R. § 25 at 33154.

45. 6 C.F.R. § 25.5.

8. The possible effects of the cost of insurance on the price of the product, and the possible consequences thereof for development, production, or deployment of the technology.

If the seller fails to maintain coverage at the requisite level, a designation may be terminated.[46]

Clearly, there are challenges inherent in a process to determine an appropriate level of insurance to be maintained by a seller of a particular QATT. The insurance component of the SAFETY Act has proven among the most difficult in the program's implementation. DHS has made recent progress through its utilization of a risk-based methodology and maintaining a high degree of flexibility in working with applicants to address the insurance component.

CHANGES TO DHS REGULATIONS IN 2007— STREAMLINING AND EXPANSION

DHS had been operating under an interim SAFETY Act regulation until 2007. In the SAFETY Act final rule, DHS applied industry and public comments and lessons learned from the first years of the SAFETY Act program. In the preamble to the final rule, DHS explained that the Final Rule:

1. further clarifies the liability protections available under the SAFETY Act;
2. states with greater specificity those products and services that are eligible for Designation as a Qualified Anti-Terrorism Technology;
3. clarifies the Department's efforts to protect the confidential information, intellectual property, and trade secrets of SAFETY Act applicants;
4. articulates the Department's intention to extend SAFETY Act liability protections to well-defined categories of anti-terrorism technologies by issuing "Block Designations" and "Block Certifications;"
5. discusses appropriate coordination of SAFETY Act consideration of anti-terrorism technologies with government procurement processes; and

---

46. 6 C.F.R. § 25.5(h).

6. takes other actions necessary to streamline processes, add flexibility for applicants, and clarify protections afforded by the SAFETY Act.[47]

To increase flexibility, DHS provided for Developmental Testing and Evaluation Designations, as well as Block Designations and Block Certifications, which provide more flexible options for both companies with unproven technologies and those with proven technologies, respectively.

The incorporation of Developmental Testing and Evaluation (DT&E) Designations makes it possible to grant SAFETY Act protections to anti-terrorism technologies that are still in the development process. For example, promising technologies—including those developed by DHS's own Science and Technology Directorate researchers in cooperation with the private sector—that have yet to be field-tested could qualify for a DT&E Designation.[48] The litigation and risk management protections of the SAFETY Act could be made available, though with some limitations. DT&E Designations would have limitations on the use and deployment of the subject technology, remain terminable at-will by the department should any concerns regarding the safety of technology come to light, and have a limited term not to exceed a reasonable period for testing or evaluating the technology. Such a provision could also allow for rapid fielding of technologies in exigent circumstances, where there simply was not enough time to fully test certain technologies. As DHS has said, "The Department may issue a DT&E Designation for anti-terrorism technologies that show promise but that may not yet meet the requirements for Designation as a QATT."[49]

Where DT&E Designations can help provide protection for unproven technologies, the use of Block Designations or Block Certifications can provide easy access to protections for sellers of technologies that have an

---

47. 6 C.F.R. § 25 at 33148.

48. About half of S&T's research and development budget goes toward identifying and developing technologies that have been specifically requested by field agents. To accomplish this, the S&T Directorate created "customer-led" Capstone Integrated Product Teams (IPTs) charged with identifying technological capability requirements across the department. This model is intended to ensure that investments meet up with actual homeland security requirements.

49. SAFETY Act Application Kit, July 2006, p.8.

established record of success. Such designations and certifications recognize technologies that meet technical criteria and established performance standards. When DHS issues such Block Designations or Certifications, it signals to sellers of covered technologies that the particular QATT already satisfies all relevant technical criteria—and no further technical analysis will be necessary before approval.[50] As DHS has stated, "[A]pplications from sellers of a QATT that is the subject of a Block Designation or Block Certification will receive expedited review and will not require submission of information concerning the technical merits of the underlying technology."[51] In short, entire classes of technology makers can receive the valuable protections of the SAFETY Act with minimum effort in this streamlined process. It should be noted that such Block Designations or Certifications can be issued either in response to an application to DHS or on DHS's own initiative. Trade associations and industry groups would be well-advised to consider a relevant request to DHS. Similarly, an aggressive use of this provision by DHS could give a boost to the SAFETY Act program.

NEW DEVELOPMENTS—FAR AMENDMENT AND COORDINATION OF PROCUREMENTS

With an important addition to the Federal Acquisition Regulation (FAR), the Civilian Agency Acquisition Council and the Defense Acquisition Regulations Council (the councils) have enhanced the significance of the SAFETY Act across the range of government procurements. In so doing, the councils built upon and expanded tools provided by the SAFETY Act final rule. In that rule, DHS had promised that it "recognize[d] the need to align consideration of SAFETY Act applications and the government procurement process more closely. Accordingly, the final rule incorporates provisions that establish a flexible approach for such coordination."[52]

In November 2007, the councils issued an Interim Rule that incorporated the SAFETY Act into the FAR.[53] To start, the rule ensures that SAFETY Act considerations are made an integral part of each agency's acquisition planning procedures, and that contracting officers give ad-

---

50. 6 C.F.R. § 25.6(h); 6 C.F.R. § 25.9(j).
51. *Id.*
52. 6 C.F.R. § 25, preamble, at 33156.
53. 72 Fed. Reg. 63,027.

equate lead time in their acquisition plans to account for DHS's review process of SAFETY Act applications.[54] The Interim Rule emphasizes two other points: 1) it streamlines SAFETY Act approval in some cases, and 2) it gives government contracting officers the authority to allow companies to submit proposals that they can make *contingent* on SAFETY Act approval. Therefore, it is possible for a contractor to limit its financial exposure of proposing an otherwise risky technology to be fielded for the government.[55]

The rule creates a new section in the FAR that requires agencies across the federal government—not only in the homeland security arena—to determine whether the technology or service they are procuring may be eligible for SAFETY Act coverage.[56] In most cases, this will require that the contracting officer consult with DHS's Office of SAFETY Act Implementation. If DHS decides that SAFETY Act protection is not appropriate, a clause must be included in the Request for Proposal (RFP) or Solicitation stating that SAFETY Act coverage is not applicable. The procurement then proceeds as every other procurement does.[57]

But if DHS determines that the technology or service is appropriate for SAFETY Act coverage, and it does not already fall under a Block Designation or a Block Certification approval for similar technologies, all potential offerors would have to stand up and take note. The procuring agency would get a "pre-qualification decision" from DHS—essentially a preview of what DHS will do with a certain technology once it receives a full SAFETY Act application. The pre-qualification decision, transmitted to the contracting officer, can be in one of two forms, both of which offer important benefits for offerors: first, DHS could say the particular product or service will be awarded SAFETY Act coverage once an application is received; second, DHS could give a presumptive

---

54. FAR 50.205-2.

55. The rule permits offerors to submit offers contingent on DHS issuing a SAFETY Act Designation or Certification. Under this first alternative, contracting officers may permit such contingent offers only if DHS has issued, for offers contingent upon SAFETY Act Designation, a prequalification Designation Notice or a Block Designation, or for offers contingent upon SAFETY Act Certification, a Block Certification.

56. FAR Part 50.204.

57. Contracting officers are required to insert FAR 52.250-2, SAFETY Act Coverage Not Applicable, if, after consultation with DHS, the agency has determined that SAFETY Act protection is not applicable for the acquisition, or DHS denies approval of a prequalification Designation Notice.

determination that the technology or service could qualify for SAFETY Act coverage, but it needs more data to be sure. In both cases, all offerors on that particular RFP would be eligible for streamlined SAFETY Act approval process. DHS has successfully used this process prior to the promulgation of the interim rule.

As discussed above, contracting officers can now issue awards on the presumption that the contractor will receive SAFETY Act coverage after the contract is awarded. Based on a clause required in this instance, an eventual decision by DHS to deny SAFETY Act coverage would be a ground for the contractor to seek an equitable adjustment, and to demand that the procuring agency compensate the vendor for its increased financial risk.[58] As further evidence of the federal focus on the SAFETY Act, the Interim Rule further requires agencies to encourage offerors to apply for SAFETY Act protections, even before a solicitation. In addition, it encourages industry outreach on SAFETY Act issues, such as in Requests for Information (RFIs), draft RFPs, and industry conferences.

Notably, the Interim Rule in the FAR builds upon an important development in the SAFETY Act Final Rule discussed above. Section 50.205-1(a) includes coverage for Block Designations and Block Certifications, requiring that the procuring agency verify with DHS whether one exists. If one does, then the requiring activity must inform the contracting officer, who must then incorporate the Block Designations and Block Certifications in any solicitation or advanced public notice to inform potential offerors of this important preexisting benefit.[59]

The FAR addition expands further the intent of the SAFETY Act to encourage development of anti-terror technologies. If the goal of the SAFETY Act in general is to promote the use of the private sector for public homeland security concerns, and if the FAR regulation in particu-

---

58. If DHS does not issue a SAFETY Act Designation or SAFETY Act Certification to the successful offeror by the time of contract award, the contracting officer is then permitted to award the contract with the clause at 52.250-5, SAFETY Act-Equitable Adjustment, which allows for an equitable adjustment in the event DHS denies the contractor's SAFETY Act application.

59. Contracting officers are required to insert 52.250-3, SAFETY Act Block Designation/Certification, or 52.250-4, SAFETY Act Pre-qualification Designation Notice, in solicitations when DHS has issued a block designation/certification or a prequalification designation notice, respectively, for the solicited technologies. These provisions do not permit submission of offers contingent upon SAFETY Act Designation or Certification of the proposed product(s) or service(s).

lar aims to promote the use of the SAFETY Act in the procurement process, we are seeing progress on both fronts. One good example is TSA's Screening Partnership Program (SPP), which allows an airport operator to have screening services performed by a private screening company. The contractor must perform under federal oversight, and the contracted screeners must perform to equal or higher performance levels than federal screeners. TSA has established a SAFETY Act certification process for SPP contractors to help them limit their liability and offer a competitive price to the airport operators procuring their services.[60]

THE OFFICE OF SAFETY ACT IMPLEMENTATION— HOW THE PROCESS WORKS IN PRACTICE

After the SAFETY Act Final Rule went into effect in July 2006, the DHS Office of SAFETY Act Implementation (OSAI) issued a new SAFETY Act Application Kit. The updated application kit contains the required forms for a submission, which request a good amount of detailed technical and financial information. The application requires the disclosure of a nonproprietary description of the technology, the technology's procurement status, the technological and essential elements of the technology (including proprietary information), and the type of terrorist attack the technology is intended to counter.

---

60. As TSA has publicly stated:

> TSA also seeks to address the liability issue through clarification on the applicability of the Support of Anti-terrorism by Fostering Effective Technologies Act of 2002 . . . The Department of Homeland Security (DHS) Office of Science and Technology (OST) makes determinations concerning the applicability of the SAFETY Act. Application of the SAFETY Act does not provide blanket indemnification but limits third-party tort suits in the event of a terrorist incident. Significantly, liability protection pursuant to the SAFETY Act for services 'designated' as a qualified anti-terrorism technology will result in limited liability risks for the private screening company and its contractors, subcontractors, suppliers, vendors,s and customers as well as the contractors, subcontractors, suppliers, and vendors of the customer. TSA, OST, and the Office of General Counsel have been working closely on SAFETY Act determinations. The Department is still reviewing the applicability of the SAFETY Act.

Frequently Asked Questions, http://www.tsa.gov/what_we_do/optout/spp_faqs.shtm, last visited Oct. 7, 2008.

Once an application is received, the DHS under secretary of the S&T Directorate has 30 days to notify an applicant that receipt of the application is complete, 90 days to review a complete application, and the ability to extend without reason the review period for another 45 days.[61] In short, DHS has up to 165 days to complete its review of a SAFETY Act application.

DHS also suggests that applicants submit a preapplication form. Such a form allows for a pre-application consultation, which is "a voluntary means through which OSAI provides helpful guidance to potential applicants without requiring the completion and submission of a full SAFETY Act Application."[62] Such a consultation allows a potential applicant to gauge its likelihood of ultimate approval and is an important safeguard against wasted time and effort.

Applicants should understand that SAFETY Act applications request a fair amount of detailed data, some of which applicants may view as proprietary either due to its technical nature or because it represents sensitive business information. Such data, while necessary for a proper evaluation of the technology, can be extremely sensitive for both business and security purposes. DHS has stated that such submitted information, whether ultimately a part of a successful application or not, will be safeguarded to the fullest extent of the law. "DHS is committed to taking all appropriate steps to protect the proprietary information of applicants consistent with applicable FOIA exemptions and the Trade Secrets Act (18 U.S.C. 1905). As an example of this commitment, those engaged in evaluating applications are required to enter into appropriate nondisclosure agreements. . . . Underlying this commitment to protect an applicant's information are various Federal civil and criminal laws that potentially apply to unauthorized disclosure of SAFETY Act confidential materials, including the Trade Secrets Act and 18 U.S.C. Chapter 90."[63]

With these concerns in mind, applicants should consider consulting a practitioner with experience in SAFETY Act applications ahead of tendering such sensitive information. Moreover, DHS often will ask applicants for additional installments of information following an initial submission, and sometimes these information requests are overly aggressive. Counsel can play an important role in managing the exchange of

---

61. 6 C.F.R. § 25.6.
62. Safety Act Application Kit, July 2006, p.14.
63. 6 C.F.R. § 25.10.

information with DHS and navigating the overall application process. While the discussion above points to real improvement in the SAFETY Act procedures, applicants regularly confront obstacles on the road to receiving designation or certification. For example, disagreements over the appropriate type and amount of insurance coverage is a perennial issue. Experienced SAFETY Act practitioners can help applicants with the overall application process and limit potentially costly and time-consuming delays.

SUMMARY

The SAFETY Act is a valuable tool for litigation and risk management for companies developing and fielding anti-terrorism technologies. By giving companies the assurance they need to develop and deploy cost-effective homeland security technologies, the act has the potential to expand both the number of technologies available and the homeland uses of existing technologies. As discussed above, the SAFETY Act furthers private interests to the benefit of the greater common good by enhancing our nation's security. In-house and outside industry counsel can support both goals by promoting the use and understanding of the SAFETY Act.

CHAPTER 10

Security-Based Reregulation of Transportation after 9/11: Giving Coherent Client Advice in a Volatile Rules Climate

by Joel A. Webber

Since September 11, 2001, federal agencies have been quietly reregulating with security protocols a transportation sector whose pricing and market-entry limits they loudly deregulated 30 years ago. This new climate is marked by (i) a fast pace of new rules releases, (ii) overlapping jurisdiction between departments, and (iii) resulting new constraints across entire supply chains. Consequently, this rules environment calls for an approach to legal advice that (i) is readily translated into operational terms, (ii) is frequently updated, and (iii) captures in a comprehensive matrix all federal requirements imposed on a shipper's or carrier's freight business processes.

SUMMARY

Federal agencies are quietly reregulating the transportation sector that Congress so loudly deregulated 30 years ago. Now addressing post-9/11 security rather than the decades-earlier focus on economic rules, each morning's *Federal Register* presents the possibility of new public-sector directives for the private sector's basic freight processes. For all the administrative activity, it is still early in this process. And, the 2008 election results are likely to take this regulatory transition in new directions before it settles down and becomes more coherent.

To date, this transition has been marked by more than just a proliferation of government demands. This new rules climate often assigns more than one rule maker to a single subject—and then gives two agencies enforcement authority thereafter. For instance, an agency of the U.S. Department of Homeland Security (DHS)—the Transportation Security Administration (TSA)—proposed and then finalized[1] rail-borne hazardous materials (hazmat) rules to guard against asymmetric attacks on targets like tank cars carrying chlorine and other "Poisonous by Inhalation" chemicals.

However, an agency of the U.S. Department of Transportation (U.S. DOT)—the Pipeline and Hazardous Materials Safety Administration (PHMSA)[2]—has issued rules governing hazmat transport for decades. U.S. DOT's Federal Railroad Administration (FRA) has had what amounts to joint jurisdiction with PHMSA for the shipment of such chemicals by rail. Although TSA announced that it had conferred with PHMSA and FRA in this new rule's creation, it was TSA that wrote this 2008 rail-borne hazmat rule. And it will also be TSA that enforces it.

Despite this new guidance and new enforcement authority to go with it, the decades-old regime that traditionally governed rail-borne hazardous materials (HM-232) remains in full force. PHMSA and FRA will continue to have enforcement authority for HM-232, while TSA takes up its own new hazmat enforcement duties.

A second distinctive trait consists in the shorter time between the proposal of anti-terror logistics rules and their final status. At least this period is shorter than those aimed at time-honored concerns like operator fatigue, railcar braking safety, and the reliable preservation of truck accident data. September 11–type threats are urgent enough to sharply reduce the time in which agencies can identify asymmetric threat vectors, identify responsive security protocols for them, and then test technologies and other measures to those ends.

For instance, while DHS's Customs and Border Protection agency (CBP) has deliberated for roughly 10 years on the trade data management system it calls the Automated Commercial Environment (ACE), it

---

1. This took place in November 2008.
2. This refers as well to its predecessor agency within U.S. DOT, the Research and Special Programs Administration, until PHMSA's founding in 2004.

finalized its Advance Manifest rule for ocean shipping within 14 months of the 9/11 attacks. This rule embodied a radical[3] departure from centuries of cargo practice. But now, armed with this manifest's contents well before arrival in port, CBP had ample time to make a risk analysis of container freight prior to allocating CBP agents' time and VACIS® scanning resources to identified containers from that ship.

Within 14 months of the attacks, CBP had altered the business rules of engagement among shippers, consignees, and ocean carriers in an unprecedented way to defend against asymmetric attack. By 2003, if cargo had been loaded abroad without CBP approval, or if it was tendered at a CBP-administered port without having otherwise complied with this advance manifest requirement, CBP barred its entry into the United States.

Yet a third distinctive trait consists in the overlap between Congress and the administrative agencies in the issuance of new protocols and mandates of related technology. Congress has taken this step for two of its post-9/11 security priorities: (i) containers entering the United States on ocean ships, and (ii) freight carried on scheduled passenger air service. While CBP and TSA considered the feasibility of 100 percent machine scanning of containers at seaports and air cargo at airports,

---

3. First, this CBP rule transformed the function of a commercial document called the "manifest." This centuries-old format had—until this rule was promulgated—recorded an ocean vessel's freight contents. Its purpose was to serve as a record for the parties who sent and received the goods, and to provide evidence of the extent of the carrier's responsibility for the goods so recorded. For the first time, this business document designed to record the ship's contents after they had been loaded was transformed into a forward-looking document—not one executed only upon loading and just prior to departure, but one filed with CBP 24 hours before U.S.-bound containers were loaded onto the vessel in a foreign port. Second, this CBP rule barred, for the first time, use of terms that had long been staples of cargo practice. In particular, CBP forbade the usage of "freight all kinds" (or FAK) and "said to contain" (STC). Historically, these might simply save time and effort where parties did not need a written record of freight categories on the face of the manifest for their commercial purposes. Or, the parties' commercial needs did not include a certification of the signer's audit and confirmation of what cargo had been loaded. Post-9/11, however, the lack of specificity as to freight types, or lack of accountability on the part of the person certifying the ship's cargo contents, would defeat CBP's purpose. From this time forward, CBP required a higher level of advance notice and accountability to assist it in ascertaining on which containers to apply agent or VACIS® machine scanning resources when those containers arrive at CBP-administered ports.

respectively, Congress in its 2007 9/11 Commission Implementation Act bypassed them both—simply mandating these measures and the scientific applications they require.[4]

This third distinctive trait goes beyond Congress eclipsing the agencies' traditional role in regulating business processes. The same CBP and TSA whose judgment Congress circumvented on these two points have both since publicly expressed reluctance to implement what the federal statute now mandates.

Finally, this post-9/11 rules climate extends—at least as to cross-border[5] freight moves—to government guidance that cannot really be considered to be "rules" at all. CBP's Customs-Trade Partnership Against Terrorism (C-TPAT) for those involved in importing goods is not, strictly speaking, mandatory—one's goods may be admitted through CBP whether or not the importer, carrier, or other logistics participant is C-TPAT-certified. CBP encourages firms to apply for audit and certification as C-

---

4. While this product of "divided government" may seem obviated by the 2008 election results, Democrats in Congress have for several years been identified with more aggressive measures in their security protocols and in their readiness to require technology than their Republican executive branch counterpart at DHS and DOT would agree to. It may be that the lesson of such controversy is that Democratic homeland security officials—notably House Homeland Security Committee Chair Bennie G. Thompson and, to a lesser degree, Senator Joseph Lieberman—have specific proposals whose passage has been constrained by the Bush administration, which had disagreed with those proposals. More generally, conventional wisdom tends to hold that constraints on business may meet with more support after this election. It would seem that the agencies are not necessarily going to be a check upon or impediment to the security measures that can obtain a majority of votes in Congress.

5. In this category of "voluntary" programs that arguably function in lieu of what would otherwise be imperatives, TSA's Known Shipper program is worthy of note—but will apparently not have the long-term impact of C-TPAT. Prior to the 9/11 Commission Implementation Act's passage, TSA had opposed 100% machine scanning of freight (weighing in excess of 16 ounces) loaded onto scheduled passenger aircraft as unworkable. TSA launched as a substitute a new post-9/11 requirement that if one wished to ship air freight in such circumstance, that person or company must document with TSA that it had been a substantial and regular shipper, and that it was not therefore an "unknown quantity" in the air freight community. While the Known Shipper program remains in effect, its significance would seem to have been reduced to minimal importance by the advent of 100% machine scanning in the future, as federal statute requires (albeit for future implementation).

TPAT members, though it couches this encouragement in words like "voluntary" and "non-mandatory." CBP styles C-TPAT as its offer of expedited treatment at ports of entry in return for member companies' adherence to practices that will discourage terrorist intervention in the supply chains of participating firms.

But as the father of C-TPAT, former CBP Commissioner Robert C. Bonner stated: "If you are not a member of C-TPAT during times of crisis, good luck."[6] While membership is not required, strictly speaking, the industry reckons that failure to join risks disfavor with the agency that can help or hurt one's freight flows at ports and border crossings— and Commissioner Bonner has confirmed this impression explicitly.

Amidst this volatility, the lawyer's job is a constant: Help the client to achieve its goals. For the supply chain, these goals typically relate to cost control above almost all else. Perhaps the only other aim that comes close is the fulfillment of customer expectations through business process consistency. However, this new rules climate, by its present ambiguity and unstable prospect for future demands, is likely to at least prompt higher expenditures. And its ad hoc agency interventions may result in less reliable supply chains.

This chapter contends that a lawyer can most effectively mitigate this clash between regulatory pressure and client priorities through a suitable new practice paradigm, at least until this turbulent rules regime settles down.

First, lawyers should pace the frequency of their client interventions to the accelerated rate at which agencies (or Congress) launch these new protocols and mandate technologies to achieve them. Because these post-9/11 directives have a shorter sequence from concept to implementation than does the more typical U.S. DOT initiative,[7] legal advice simply needs to maintain a faster pace to keep up.

---

6. Speech, April 20, 2005.

7. The Federal Railroad Administration (FRA) has been considering electronically controlled pneumatic brake systems for rail cars since the 1990s. Contrast that with the roughly 12 to 18 months estimated for FRA and the Pipeline and Hazardous Materials Safety Administration (PHMSA) to finalize new anti-terror rules on poisonous-by-inhalation chemical rail cars. U.S. Customs and Border Protection (CBP) has been developing the Automated Commercial Environment for trade data since the mid-1990s. Contrast that with the 12 months elapsed between CBP's January 2008 proposal of so-called "10+2" anti-terror data-collection mandates and their final issuance in January 2009. The Federal Aviation Administration (FAA) began the "New York Airspace

Second, post-9/11 logistics regulatory advice needs to reach a lot more people within the client organization than do legal interventions into situations of less operational complexity. The same is true of the contractors and vendors in the client's supply chain as well. Those empowered to cause the client company to succeed or fail at compliance are too numerous, and their value contribution too contingent on the performance of others, for lawyers to rely on the conventional memorandum and conference format more typical of legal advice.

As the freight-train conductor reviews switching orders and waybills prior to accepting a chlorine-laden tank car, he needs to know exactly what TSA will require of the firm sending the chemicals, of his railroad, and of the consignee (intended cargo recipient) under the November 2008–approved "chain of custody" final rule. This is in addition to the numerous long-standing FRA and PHMSA rules.

Similarly, where a U.S. home improvement retailer's purchasing department purchases tools from abroad, its U.S.-based data clerk must give to CBP accurate information about the foreign manufacturer and its incoming cargo under the new anti-terror "10+2" data rules announced in January 2008 and given final status in November 2008. And much of that information may be held by his counterpart in a distinct company and a different time zone.

Those whose actions comprise the supply chain are geographically dispersed, operate at different times around the clock, and report to different companies. Despite their physical and organizational fragmentation, the very interdependency among supply-chain personnel who make recurring operating decisions makes for a multitude of actors, any one of whose respective performance can be decisive in securing—or disrupting—cargo compliance. Given this dispersion of action and responsibility, the lawyer's contribution has to address each actor whose performance can materially help or hurt the firm's standing with DHS, U.S. DOT, and each of their constituent agencies.

Redesign" to mitigate the estimated 75% of nationwide air traffic delays that originate within 150 air miles of New York City during the Clinton administration and is still not finished. Contrast that with the 2007 congressional mandate in the 9/11 Commission Implementation Act to machine-scan freight weighing more than 16 ounces and loaded on scheduled passenger aircraft, required for 100% implementation. In September 2008 the U.S. Department of Homeland Security (DHS) began 100% scanning at Dulles airport, with four more airports scheduled by year-end. DHS plans for 40 such airports eventually.

Third, lawyers need to present their post-9/11 regulatory advice in a format suitable to supply-chain participants. That format should look less like a traditional memorandum or client conference and more like a Six Sigma schematic or management information "dashboard." Why?

Like any other client, those involved in the logistics system need legal advice that they can understand. And they need to be able to implement that advice without much further elaboration by counsel. Because the supply-chain participant's effectiveness tends to depend on multiple other participants in that chain—and, as stated above, those participants are separated by geography, time, and different organizational reporting responsibilities—advice needs to be tailored to this fragmented situation.

To provide meaningful regulatory guidance to one of these participants, the lawyer needs to identify that participant's place in the supply chain under consideration. Then the lawyer needs to both assign responsibility to that participant for the contribution expected of her and describe her duties in a way that describes other, complementary requirements.

For instance, the carrier cannot seamlessly deliver the sea container or aircraft unit load device to the importer unless the nonvessel operating common carrier, freight forwarder, or customs broker has disclosed the prescribed load information to CBP at the specified interval prior to arrival at the U.S. port of entry. The chemical shipper cannot complete the chlorine move to the water treatment plant unless the designated rail tank car is allowed on the designated rail route by the new TSA/FRA rules. Nor will such shipper be able to even originate that load if its railcar fleet does not conform to pending FRA/PHMSA rules for structural integrity.

What this means for the advice format is this: Legal guidance must be given in graphic form and not just verbal, and must be explicit on how each actor to whom that guidance is aimed depends upon others in the supply chain and delivers performance to those others with whom he or she is interdependent.

Most industrial and service firms have long ago translated their day-to-day operations into a pictorial presentation of business process elements. But legal advice still relies heavily on the spoken or written word. And the lawyer's points of contact within the organization tend to be with the legal department or some other functional head—not with each and every person whose own discrete actions may add to or detract from compliance of the entire supply chain.

This proposed shift to a schematic or "dashboard" format for legal advice is more compelling than just catching up with the last decade or two of corporate communications templates used in functions like operations management, finance, and information technology. The dynamic combination of (i) frequent rules changes, (ii) their duplication among federal departments, (iii) a resultant proliferation of agencies to whom the client must answer, and (iv) the numerous additional individuals who need to receive the legal guidance in order for the supply chain to comply with it together call for a mode of transmission more adaptive than the traditional memorandum or lawyer-to-function-head conference.

AN ILLUSTRATION OF THE PRESENT TRANSPORT REREGULATION CLIMATE

This chapter is not designed to exhaustively catalogue this climate's operative requirements. If for no other reason, the first of the three features at work in post-9/11 security-based transportation reregulation—the fast pace of new rules—renders any summary out-of-date after a few weeks or months. But the above summary makes generalizations about U.S. DOT and DHS having parallel "safety" and "security" jurisdiction between them; about overlapping rules on the same activity among TSA, DHS offices, CBP, FRA and PHMSA; and about development cycles between proposal and final status that are faster than is the case with more traditional federal rule-making.

As an illustration, consider recent government demands relating to the hauling of hazardous materials by rail:

- On December 21, 2006, PHMSA and FRA released a notice of proposed rule-making on the routing of rail-borne Poisonous by Inhalation hazmat. On April 16, 2008, they announced that this would take final status on June 1, 2008: "Hazardous Materials: Enhancing Rail Transportation Safety and Security for Hazardous Material Shipments" (Fed. Reg. Vol. 73, No. 74).

- Spelling out 27 criteria on how carriers should select routes for such hazmat, the rule is directed to carriers—but should have impacts on all shippers and recipients of the affected chemicals. Note in particular that the text references both "safety" and "security" as its goals despite its issuance from the legacy safety agencies—PHMSA and FRA.

- Also on December 21, 2006, DHS, through its TSA agency, released a notice of proposed rule-making also addressing Poisonous by Inhalation hazmat carried by rail. This was directed not to routing, but to operational details of handling such hazmat in rail tank cars. And rather than being directed solely to rail carriers, this notice was directed to shippers, recipients, and other parties handling such chemical freight. This proposal was given final status as of November 2008.

- Meanwhile, Congress in 2005 responded to the Graniteville, South Carolina, chlorine release incident by formally conferring jurisdiction over rail tank car safety to PHMSA and FRA by statute (SAFETY-LU, 49 U.S.C. § 20155). This legislation has resulted in a PHMSA and FRA proposal pending final status that would retire within five years most rail tank cars carrying Poisonous by Inhalation hazmat that were built before 1989, and retire within eight years all such cars in favor of new ones built to prescribed heightened structural requirements (April 1, 2008, "Hazardous Materials: Improving the Safety of Railroad Tank Car Transportation of Hazardous Materials"[8]).

    Although the Graniteville incident that sparked the enabling legislation for this proposal was viewed as an accident and not as the result of terrorism, much of the debate around this proposal has focused on the potential for asymmetric attack on the specified hazmat in rail tank cars.

    Note that only PHMSA and FRA—not TSA or any other DHS Office of Chemical Security—have had a formal role in shaping this proposal.

- And separately in Congress, the Implementing Recommendations of the 9/11 Commission Act of 2007 conferred jurisdiction over rail tank car "security" to DHS (H.R. 1)—and its other provisions further complicate the question of who does what among federal agencies.

First, in its section 1519 "Railroad Tank Car Security Testing," 2007's H.R. 1 expressly confers on DHS for "security" what Congress expressly conferred in 2005 on PHMSA and FRA as to tank cars and their "safety" in SAFETY-LU. Each text gives direction to distinct federal agencies—DHS in H.R. 1 and PHMSA and FRA in SAFETY-LU—to prescribe structural and operational requirements for rail tank cars carrying specified chemicals whose unplanned release could harm the public.

---

8. 73 Fed. Reg. 63 (Apr. 1, 2008).

Second, the two statutes provide divergent definitions of the specified chemicals over which Congress expresses security concerns. 2005's SAFETY-LU simply adopts the traditional pre-9/11 definition—those contained in the Hazardous Materials Regulations (HMR) and called "hazardous materials." 2007's H.R. 1 prescribes a new category of "Security-Sensitive Materials" (H.R. 1 § 1501 (13)). As to this new term of art, Congress empowered DHS to define it, albeit with reference to the HMR, and "in consultation to the Secretary of Transportation."

Third, this 2007 H.R. 1 legislation does not take place in a governmental vacuum; the above-described rule-making has been taking place simultaneously. In particular, DHS's TSA unit's final proposal of the rail-borne hazmat rule described above has been delayed due in part to efforts within TSA's Office of Freight Rail Security to include H.R. 1. requirements into its final version.

Note that while the initial TSA rule was proposed in December 2006 prior to H.R. 1's August 2007 enactment, H.R. 1's subsequent enactment is shaping TSA's regulatory proposal in this regard.

WHERE WE HAVE COME FROM: BACKGROUND TO LOGISTICS REGULATORY UPHEAVAL

This chapter invites the reader's attention to something new in the government's relationship to those businesses that move freight or have freight moved for them. The duplicative demands and contentious Congress-agency relationships may be illuminated by some historical context.

Transportation's Economic Deregulation

Legislation in the late 1970s and early 1980s got the federal government out of the business of granting routes and setting rates for motor, rail, and air carriers. Corresponding with this well-publicized economic "deregulation," Congress eliminated the Civil Aeronautics Board and Interstate Commerce Commission as arbiters of who could move freight by air, rail, or highway—and along what routes, for what price, and subject to other specified terms of service.

As government deregulated the business terms under which carriers could operate, it emphatically reassured the public that it was not leaving the business of regulating these cargo modes' physical safety. For instance, the Federal Aviation Administration (FAA) would still have final say on airframe and engine airworthiness and maintenance. The FRA—in a close working relationship with the quasi-official Association of American Railroads—would continue to determine "interchange" standards of all cars allowed to operate on the nation's rail network, and would still prescribe (with the help of PHMSA's predecessor[9]) structural standards for tank cars that haul hazardous materials. And the predecessor[10] to the Federal Motor Carrier Safety Administration (FMCSA) would still determine carrier safety ratings, just as it had before economic deregulation.

Functionally separate and legally unrelated to this deregulation, another agency had long been at work. But its transportation security significance would not take form until after 9/11. U.S. Customs' job was relatively unchanged from the essential function assigned to it at its founding in 1789. Its assignment consisted of keeping specified goods from entering the United States from abroad, and to levy duties and other charges upon imported goods catalogued in a dense set of customs rules. Its job was to regulate economic activity: barring goods of specified origins, admitting others, and collecting excises. U.S. Customs had been, from its founding until shortly after 9/11, an arm of the Treasury Department. It was not considered a part of our government's efforts to secure the public safety or national security.

9/11: The Initial Federal Response to Protect Freight Flows

September 11 recast the public's perception of risk to health and safety, or—more to the point—the sources and directions from which such risks might come. In response, the federal government altered the regulatory landscape by reallocating duties among preexisting agencies, as well as creating a new agency (the TSA). Terrorist violence at the Twin Towers, the Pentagon, and Shanksville, Pennsylvania, altered government's interaction both with the carriers that moved goods and with the goods themselves and the logistics data pertaining to them. Three developments shaped this initial institutional response.

First, within two months of the attacks, Congress established the TSA as an agency of U.S. DOT.[11] While the enabling statute granted authority to protect against asymmetric risks to all transportation modes, the lion's share of policy decisions, budget, and new personnel was allocated to scheduled passenger air operations.

---

9. U.S. DOT's Research and Special Programs Administration.

10. The Interstate Commerce Commission's safety bureau; later the Federal Highway Administration.

11. Aviation and Transportation Security Act of 2001.

As part of DHS's formation in 2002, TSA was transferred from U.S. DOT into DHS. TSA continued to focus on scheduled passenger air operations, with other modes—air cargo, freight rail, and truck receiving only modest attention and resources. During this initial period, DHS placed virtually no tangible constraints on these modes. *Nota bene*: This is not to say that TSA and other arms of DHS were inactive outside of scheduled air passenger service and the airports this sector used. There was considerable study, industry survey work, and calls for voluntary best practices adoption, or, as in the case of rail, creation of so-called security plans whose cost and operational impact was small, if not nonexistent. However, domestic U.S. logistics experienced no constraints that could be characterized as operationally or financially material.

Second—and separate from any activity within TSA—almost immediately after September 11, CBP launched an agenda of vigorous intervention in the physical flow of imports into the United States. Robert C. Bonner, sworn in as Commissioner of U.S. Customs days before the 9/11 attacks, set out in a speech to the Center for Strategic and International Studies (CSIS) on January 17, 2002, an agenda that he would pursue until his resignation from that post in fall 2005. Bonner accomplished all but one of these agenda items—and that uncompleted item he set in motion for his successor's action.

CBP's agenda under Commissioner Bonner was to transform itself from a core activity of policing imports admitted to the country according to their economic and excise payment significance. Under Bonner, CBP took on a second core function: protecting against asymmetric attacks hidden in the international supply chain. For assets, CBP deployed what had been in place before September 11 for its economic mission: agents at CBP-run ports of entry, and a management information system in its Office of Field Operations that was rich in data about the goods physically entering the United States from abroad. The commissioner reengineered CBP into an agency dedicated to defending against homeland security threats that might be delivered to America's population and infrastructure through the import supply chain.

Third, the interdepartmental debate over "safety" versus "security" began during this initial period. While the two words can be synonyms in certain contexts, they were opposite poles in the post-9/11 discussion about hazardous materials. Pursuant to the federal Hazardous Materials Transportation Law[12] and its predecessors, U.S. DOT has regulated the shipment

---

12. 49 U.S.C §§ 5101 *et seq.*

of dangerous goods for decades—now through its PHMSA agency.[13] As traditionally understood, the hazmat threat vector consisted of dangers inherent in the freight itself.

Beginning shortly after 9/11, the federal government witnessed an argument over the implications of domestic terror for protection against these hazardous materials. In its essence, the question was how—institutionally speaking—to protect the homeland from asymmetric attacks on shipments of goods that were themselves inherently dangerous to the public.

One view held that, for instance, an unplanned release of chlorine from a rail tank car might be sparked by terrorist intervention. While the danger was to some degree inherent in the freight itself, the policy concern post-9/11 focused on the threat vector—an individual leveraging such inherent danger by asymmetric attack on the supply chain.

On the other side, some (notably those who had managed these inherent risks for decades within U.S. DOT's predecessor to PHMSA) argued that protection of the public from such unplanned releases—regardless of the intent of whoever caused the release—had been the subject of decades of U.S. DOT and other regulatory attention. PHMSA, this argument went, should have primary responsibility to protect hazardous materials transportation from all threats—whether intentional, in the form of asymmetric attack, or otherwise. There was simply too much institutional learning within traditional U.S. DOT circles to reinvent the proverbial wheel.

DHS and U.S. DOT resolved this debate by allocating to U.S. DOT's PHMSA the job of protecting hazardous materials transportation from dangers inherent to the chemicals being shipped. Correspondingly, they agreed to give DHS's TSA the task of protecting shipments of the same chemicals where those chemicals were the possible subjects of terrorist intervention.

Later (2006–2008) Federal Response to Protect Freight Flows

First, beginning around December 2006, TSA for the first time imposed some tangible constraints on freight moves. For instance, in December 2006, it issued proposed regulations that mandated "chain of custody" legal obligations on those chemical manufacturers who send, on the railroads that carry, and on the distribution intermediaries that handle specified

---

13. And as of Sept. 11, 2001, the Research and Special Programs Administration of U.S. DOT.

Poisonous by Inhalation chemicals that move by rail.[14] This proposal—in contrast to traditional hazardous materials regulation—applied duties directly to participants in the supply chain that were not carriers.

In January 2007, TSA mandated[15] the Transportation Worker Identification Credential (TWIC) for use by specified maritime, trucking, and rail personnel at ocean and inland ports. Without these, a driver, stevedore, or transportation worker will be barred from unescorted access to specified secure areas within covered seaports and inland rail yards. This TWIC biometric credential would require a background criminal check, and has since become informally required by some carriers and facilities engaged in hazmat shipments.

Finally, as to TSA, Congress mandated through legislation enacted in August 2007 that TSA implement 100 percent machine-scanning of all freight (above 16 ounces) loaded onto a passenger aircraft in passenger service (i.e., in the belly-hold, where, it turns out, roughly 75 percent of all U.S. air freight travels)—and provided a flexible deadline for TSA to do so.

Also in 2007, DHS[16] issued a rule for the anti-terror regulation of chemical fixed facilities (as contrasted with their transportation—whose "security" had been assigned to TSA, and whose "safety" had been assigned to PHMSA and FRA, all as described above). While (strictly speaking) not a transportation regulation, this new set of requirements potentially affect all who touch a hazardous materials shipment. In fact, it features the possibility that a railroad or trucking carrier itself can become a fixed chemical facility—when a railcar or truck trailer is detached from "motive power."[17]

Second, CBP rolled out a series of supply-chain security measures. Among the initiatives set forth in Commissioner Bonner's January 17, 2002, speech at CSIS, three would have operative impact[18] on importers and their carriers beginning that year:

---

14. 71 Fed. Reg. 76,852 (Dec. 21, 2006).

15. 72 Fed. Reg. 3491 (Jan. 25, 2007).

16. Note that it is an independent office within DHS that administers this rule (Chemical Facility Anti-Terrorism Standards, or CFATS). As a result, a party sending goods or rail carrier whose activity triggers CFATS' application (see note 17) may find itself answerable to each of the following units for different rules: PHMSA, FRA, TSA, and DHS (Office of Chemical Security).

17. 72 Fed. Reg. 17,688 (April 9, 2007).

18. Note also Commissioner Bonner's Container Security Initiative (CSI), also announced in that CSIS January 17, 2002, speech, which featured place-

(i) Advance manifest requirements for ocean shipping—shortly thereafter required for offshore air cargo, rail freight, and motor carrier traffic entering the United States;

(ii) Addition of dozens of VACIS® X-ray technology scanners at CBP maritime ports of entry; and

(iii) The launch of C-TPAT and a buildup of the rigor and specificity with which CBP required member companies to comply as a condition of C-TPAT membership and its benefits.

CBP's imposition of these constraints on freight flows originating outside the United States for entry at CBP-administered ports varied sharply in both impact and pace from TSA's imposition of security protocols leading up to 2007. Such CBP requirements were a substantial burden long before TSA-administered demands fell heavily on the domestic supply chain.

In addition, 2007 saw the congressional mandate of 100 percent machine scanning of sea containers at CBP-administered ports in the 9/11 Commission Implementation Act.

The third and final development during this subsequent period relates to the "safety" versus "security" distinction worked out earlier between DHS and U.S. DOT. In 2007, Congress gave this departmental duplication its own explicit statutory sanction in the 9/11 Commission Implementation Act: "The Secretary of Homeland Security is the principal Federal official responsible for transportation security."[19]

Following this provision, it is virtually impossible to imagine a DHS intervention against a terrorist threat—however focused on hazardous materials covered by the "safety" provisions of the federal Hazardous Materials Transportation Law—that U.S. DOT's PHMSA would have a legal basis to contest.

A NEW LEGAL ADVICE PARADIGM

The client's operations must not run afoul of any agency as to any particular rule. Given the complexity created by both the traditional background

---

ment of CBP personnel alongside the port security forces of the leading foreign maritime ports. Before his resignation in 2005, the commissioner had announced CBP agreements with over 40 non-U.S. ports—ports that accounted for the lion's share of total volume embarking to the United States by container, and that subjected such U.S.-bound containers to a screening process prior to their sailing.

19. *Id.* § 1310.

and the new requirements, legal counsel needs to help the client meet this challenge.

Distinctive Rules Environment Calls for New Approach

This chapter's purpose is to argue for a distinctive approach to giving ongoing legal advice that responds to those features that define the current federal reregulation of transportation. As summarized above, this environment appears to include the following:

    (i)   A fast pace of new regulatory releases, with a shorter sequence between concept and final status than agencies typically provide for a "safety" rule;

  (ii)   Overlapping jurisdiction between federal departments (and in two cases so far, between congressional demands and those of an agency), with the consequent possibility of parallel demands on a single firm and its activities; and

 (iii)   Regulatory impact that is system-wide—having impact across the client's entire supply chain—and that therefore touches on behavior of employees well beyond legal counsel's traditional circle of senior management and general counsel staffs.

In such an environment, agencies' rapid issuance of new demands, those demands' redundancy as between DHS and U.S. DOT, and their pervasive reach into a client's employee ranks (and the employee ranks of the client's vendors and contractors elsewhere in the supply chain) beset the lawyer. Simply put, for legal counsel trying to support the client's goals of cost containment and business process consistency, today's advice is likely to be materially out of date within weeks or months.

Such advice will pose the question of what other agencies with coordinate jurisdiction such as that between U.S. DOT "safety" and DHS "security" require.

And, unless it is put in direct operational terms, the lawyer's advice will be unhelpful beyond the traditional circle of general counsel staff and managerial function head.

This dilemma relates not to compliance, strictly speaking. If nothing else, the Administrative Procedure Act protects against the rule whose application is immediate upon issuance. But this climate's unwieldy demands strike at the planning cycle and at the process controls that have been a management staple since the introduction of Six Sigma and Balanced Scorecard methodologies. What departs from the routine becomes a point of unnecessary expense—and by definition that same departure interrupts the predictability of business process flow that the client's customers demand.

As a result, the current transportation regulatory environment calls for a new template for the lawyer: client interaction that is tailored to that environment. That template requires an ambitious undertaking quite different from an exhaustive cataloging of the pertinent rules.

Toward a New Legal Advice Paradigm: A Diagram or Chart, Not an Essay

The proposed paradigm's essence is to focus less upon an explanation of a point of law and more on the layout of all of the points of supply-chain operation that legal advice should cover.

For many lawyers, the format for regulatory guidance is little changed from the work pattern absorbed by a junior law firm associate in his early days on the job:

   (i)   Frame a question of law;
  (ii)   Describe the salient facts; and then
 (iii)   Argue pro and con for plausible conclusions based upon authority in case law, statute, administrative rule—or in agency lore.

The complexity of administrative compliance in the supply chain lies more in comprehending all the demands presented, and much less in acquiring any in-depth grasp of regulatory demands on any one functional area. The demands themselves are not all that complex. Obtaining a TWIC credential is fairly straightforward; it is not akin to comprehending SEC Rule 10b-5 and avoiding its prohibitions on fraud-like behavior.

The complexity is experienced at the management level—the individual or team that must ensure that at least one person or business function is assigned to each demand any agency makes of the supply chain. That individual or corporate department may be among management's direct reports or reachable only through contractor or vendor relationships. But the executive's supply-chain challenge is far more about comprehensive coverage of all demands on all supply-chain functions than it is about proficiency in any one (or all) of them.

A Beginning: Work of American Association of Exporters and Importers

Recent work of the American Association of Exporters and Importers (AAEI) embodies this new legal advice paradigm. AAEI sought to illustrate for individual members of Congress the overlapping demands from multiple regulatory agencies in a way that demonstrated those demands' system-wide impacts within a given supply chain. Their "American Traders Guide to Post-9/11 and Homeland Security Programs" charted out 29 federal regulations and initiatives on a vertical line ("Y" axis), against 36 logistics process elements on a horizontal line ("X" axis). AAEI set this matrix out against a process map comprised of 15 commercial elements and 11 regulatory functions included in a supply chain.

Similarly, in its "The American Trader's Guide to Advanced Data Programs," AAEI provided a similarly formatted report on data demands of the international flow of goods. This included a chart on international and foreign government requirements (31 elements on the Y axis, 7 on the X axis), as well as U.S. ones (33 elements on the Y axis, 27 on the X axis).

In the proposed legal advice paradigm, such a dashboard, chart, or process map can concisely frame for a business executive the fast-changing, duplicative new requirements to which his or her enterprise will be subject in a way that captures their impact throughout their business systems and across their supply chains.

CONCLUSION

What AAEI has done is to speak in the chosen language of company management. Executives tend to experience this reregulation as a disruptive proliferation of rules. Legal advice couched in terms of an exhaustive legal memorandum is just not a meaningful response to the question corporate leaders really ask in a dynamic regulatory environment: What steps—if I make sure they are completed—will keep me out of trouble?

The answer many lawyers typically want to give their client is a detailed survey of a carefully circumscribed subject. Their instincts in this connection have been honed by law office culture in which attorneys usually learn their craft.

But the answer that this new regulatory environment demands of lawyers is a comprehensive one. To be actionable, this answer must be robust enough to convey the interdependence and outright overlap among post-9/11 logistics security rules. And it should help such a business manager to evaluate those rules' multiple and possibly simultaneous impacts throughout the supply chain—and across the enterprise's operational, financial, and IT systems.

Until the current reregulation of transportation runs its course back to a more traditional, evolutionary pace and framework, lawyers will need to meet their supply-chain clients live—in complexity and tumult.

CHAPTER 11

Maritime Security Developments and TWIC Tribulations

by Jonathan K. Waldron

This chapter reviews the most significant port-related security changes enacted in legislation following enactment of the Maritime Transportation Security Act of 2002 (MTSA) following the terrorist attacks in 2001. This legislation made a number of significant adjustments to programs within the U.S. port security framework and represented the first major piece of port security legislation since MTSA. In particular, one of the key and most controversial measures undertaken to improve maritime security is the Transportation Worker Identification Credential (TWIC), which, when fully implemented, will be required in order to gain unescorted access to maritime facilities. Accordingly, one of the topics this chapter will focus on is the implementation of the TWIC program, including the problems and delays in such implementation.

INTRODUCTION

Following the terrorist attacks on September 11, 2001, Congress enacted the Maritime Transportation Security Act of 2002 (MTSA) (Public Law 107-295) on November 25, 2002, in recognition that the vulnerability of the nation's ports was equally as important as its airports with regard to preventing and responding to future terrorist attacks. The primary purpose of this legislation was to establish a series of requirements to address port security and infrastructure concerns in an attempt to insulate

U.S. ports from future terrorist activities. The maritime industry has now gained considerable knowledge and experience with the numerous requirements of the MTSA, and in particular with vessel and facility security plan requirements. This landmark legislation, subsequent measures enacted by Congress, and numerous regulatory projects implementing this legislation have established a core port security infrastructure in the last few years. This chapter will address the key developments in this area since MTSA was initially implemented.

Specifically, this chapter will review security plan revalidation requirements and key elements of the Security and Accountability for Every Port Act of 2006 (Safe Port Act) (Public Law 109-347), enacted in October 2006, which made a number of significant adjustments to programs within the U.S. port security framework and represented the first major piece of port security legislation since MTSA. In particular, one of the key and most controversial measures undertaken to improve maritime security is the Transportation Worker Identification Credential (TWIC), which will be required in order to gain unescorted access to maritime facilities when fully implemented. Accordingly, one of the topics this chapter will focus on is the implementation of the TWIC program, including the problems and delays in such implementation. In short, the United States has made substantial security enhancements in implementing MTSA and the Safe Port Act in the areas of overall port security and port facilities, but many questions remain with regard to the TWIC program.

REVALIDATION OF VESSEL AND FACILITY SECURITY PLANS

MTSA requires that vessel and facility security plans be revalidated every five years. 46 U.S.C. § 70102(b)(3). Because the compliance date for the original security plans under MTSA was July 1, 2004, this means that such plans will require revalidation in mid-2009. Resubmittal will require both a security vulnerability assessment of all relevant aspects of vessel and facility operations and a review of the current security plan to address changes to the facility or vessel and the relevant operations. A request for revalidation must be submitted at least 30 days before the expiration of the current security plan. 33 C.F.R. §§ 104.415 and 105.415. Due to the time it likely will take to line up the competent resources to complete this revalidation process, it would be prudent for owners and operators to initiate this process as soon as practicable.

In addition, with regard to facility security plans, the original review and approval was conducted by a single contractor hired by the Coast Guard to review and approve plans. The revalidation of facility security plans will be conducted by the cognizant Coast Guard Captain of the Port (COTP) with jurisdiction over a particular facility. This could result in delays in the review and approval, because each COTP may have differing views concerning what should be required for approval in that particular zone.

SAFE PORT ACT OF 2006

In summary, the Safe Port Act can be divided into three major categories:

(1) Enhancements to overall port security;
(2) Security improvements at port facilities; and
(3) Development of a comprehensive container security program.

The following is a summary of the most noteworthy milestones associated with the implementation of the Safe Port Act since its enactment in the areas of port security and port facilities. Container security will be discussed in a separate chapter in this book under the topic of supply chain, transportation, and logistics security.

Overall Port Security

Section 101. Area Maritime Transportation Security Plans and Salvage Response Plans

Section 101 requires each Area Maritime Security Plan (AMSP) to include a salvage response plan to identify salvage equipment capable of restoring operational trade capacity and to ensure that affected waterways are cleared as quickly as possible after a maritime transportation security incident. The Coast Guard has integrated this requirement into its five-year updated cycle for each AMSP established by MTSA.

Section 107. Long-Range Vessel Tracking

Section 107 requires the Department of Homeland Security (DHS) to establish by April 1, 2007, a long-range automated vessel-tracking system for all vessels operating in U.S. waters that are equipped with the Global Maritime Distress and Safety System or equivalent technology and consistent with international conventions and agreements. Although it did not issue a regulation by the April 1, 2007, deadline, it published its final rule on this issue on April 29, 2008. This rule requires certain ships on an international voyage to transmit ship identification and position information electronically. The types of ships required to transmit these reports are passenger ships, including high-speed passenger craft, that carry more than 12 passengers; cargo ships, including high-speed craft of 300 gross tons or more; and self-propelled mobile offshore drilling units.

Section 108. Establishment of Interagency Operational Centers for Port Security

Section 108 requires the establishment of interagency operational centers for port security at all high-priority ports not later than October 2009. The Coast Guard currently operates approximately 25 operations centers in high-priority ports, but none of the centers reportedly meet the requirements of the Safe Port Act. The Coast Guard reported to Congress in July 2007 that it would take five years and $260 million to upgrade these operations centers to meet this requirement.

Section 109. Notice of Arrival for Foreign Vessels on the Outer Continental Shelf

Section 109 requires the publication of a final rule on notice of arrival (NOA) requirements for foreign vessels operating on the outer continental shelf (OCS) by April 2007. Currently, vessels are required to make such reports when making a port call in the United States but not when arriving to work on the OCS. Despite this statutory deadline, this rulemaking is not expected to be published until 2009.

Section 110. Enhanced Crew Member Identification

This section requires foreign crew members calling at U.S. ports to carry and present on demand such identification as is determined by the Coast Guard, no later than October 2007. The Coast Guard published a final rule defining these requirements on April 28, 2009. Under the new rule, all commercial mariners will be required to carry one of the following identification documents:

- A passport;
- A U.S. permanent resident card;
- A U.S. Merchant Mariner's Document (MMD) or Merchant Mariner Credential, issued by the U.S. Coast Guard;
- A TWIC, issued by the Transportation Security Administration; or
- A Seafarer's Identification Document (SID), issued by any government that has ratified the International Labor Organization's SID Convention, 2003 (ILO 185).

According to the final rule, the Coast Guard believes most crew members already possess and carry acceptable identification. The Coast Guard estimates that the new rule would require only approximately 3 percent of the total number of crew members and vessel operators—both foreign and domestic—whose vessels enter U.S. navigable waters to obtain a new identification document to comply with this proposed requirement.

Section 234. Foreign Port Assessments

Section 234 requires an assessment of the effectiveness of anti-terrorism measures at certain foreign ports not less than once every three years. The Coast Guard has increased the pace of assessments and is expected to complete an initial assessment of all U.S. trading partners in 2008. The Coast Guard will conduct assessments on a two-year cycle thereafter.

Security Improvements at Port Facilities

Section 102. Requirements Relating to Maritime Facility Security Plans

Section 102 requires the owners or operators of MTSA facilities to resubmit their security plans if there is a change in an owner or operator that may substantially affect the security of the facility, and generally requires the qualified individual to be a citizen of the United States. The Coast Guard is initiating a regulatory project to implement these requirements.

Section 103. Unannounced Inspections of Maritime Facilities

Section 103 requires inspection of MTSA facilities at least two times a year, one of which must be unannounced. The Coast Guard is in the process of increasing facility visits to meet these new requirements and is generally conducting unannounced "spot checks."

IMPLEMENTATION OF THE TWIC PROGRAM

Background

Section 102 of MTSA requires DHS to conduct background checks and issue biometric "transportation security cards" to certain individuals. 46 U.S.C. § 70105. Specifically, with certain exceptions, an individual may not enter a "secure area" of a vessel or facility that is subject to MTSA unless the individual holds a transportation security card or is escorted by a person holding such a card.[1] One of the key aspects of an individual vessel or facility security plan is procedures to identify and protect "secure areas." MTSA required DHS to promulgate regulations, without setting a deadline, to prevent unauthorized access to secure areas. Individuals may enter secure areas only if authorized by the individual vessel or facility security plan or accompanied by an authorized individual. In order to enter a secure area, individuals must either possess a "transportation security card" themselves or be accompanied by someone who does. Biometric transportation security cards must be issued to these individuals unless it is determined that the individual poses a terrorism security risk. These biometric transportation security cards are now commonly referred to as a TWIC.

Implementation Responsibilities and Key Actions

The Transportation Security Administration (TSA) and Coast Guard, because of overlapping responsibilities, formally joined efforts to implement the TWIC program in November 2004. TSA is responsible for

---

1. Individuals eligible for a transportation security card include individuals authorized to access secure areas pursuant to approved vessel or facility security plans, licensed mariners, vessel pilots, individuals engaged in towing operations or with access to security-sensitive information, and other individuals "engaged in port security activities" as determined by DHS. 46 U.S.C. § 70105(b)(2).

issuing TWIC cards. As part of this process, TSA is responsible for TWIC enrollment, security threat assessment and adjudication, card production, technology, TWIC issuance, conduct of the TWIC appeal and waiver process as it pertains to credential issuance, and management of government support systems.

TSA contracted with Lockheed Martin (Lockheed) to manage the enrollment process. Specifically, under the contract Lockheed is responsible for operating enrollment facilities. Lockheed staffs the enrollment centers and collects enrollment data from TWIC applicants. This data is submitted to TSA, which is responsible for the background checks.[2] A TWIC is then manufactured and personalized at a federal card production facility and shipped to Lockheed, which issues the cards through the appropriate enrollment center. A TWIC card is valid for five years from the date of issuance.

The Coast Guard is responsible for establishing and enforcing TWIC access control requirements at MTSA-regulated vessels and facilities. The Coast Guard's responsibilities include publishing the rules that will guide the installation of card readers being developed for access control and enforcing the proper use of card readers. The Coast Guard is also responsible for reviewing and enforcing vessel and facility security plans in which secure areas must be designated. The TWIC card program is meant to enhance existing physical access control systems put in place by vessel and facility operators and is not meant to replace any such systems. TWIC procedures do not need to be incorporated into existing facility and vessel security plans until the next regularly scheduled submission, five years from the last plan approval date. Most plans will come up for renewal during the spring and summer of 2009.

As demonstrated in the following time line for key actions taken to implement TWIC requirements, there have been significant delays in the six years since enactment of MTSA in 2002.

- *Enactment of MTSA (November 2002).* Section 102 of MTSA requires DHS to issue a maritime worker identification card that uses biometrics to control access to secure areas of MTSA facilities and vessels.

---

2. This includes a TSA security threat assessment, FBI criminal history records check, and an immigration status and mental history check. Appeals and waivers are available in certain circumstances.

- *Prototype Testing (August 2004 through June 2005).* TSA, through a private contractor, tested a TWIC program prototype at 28 transportation facilities across the country.
- *Dividing the Program into Two Components—Issuance of Cards and Card Readers (August 2006).* Due in part to the difficulties associated with developing a card reader that works effectively, TSA and the Coast Guard decided that the TWIC program would be implemented in the maritime sector under two separate rules. The first rule would cover use of TWICs as a credential for gaining access to facilities and vessels; the second rule would address the use of TWIC readers for confirming the identity of the TWIC holder against the biometric information on the TWIC.
- *Implementation Time Line Established by the Safe Port Act (October 2006).* Section 104 of the Safe Port Act directed DHS to, among other things, implement the TWIC program in priority ports by set deadlines; conduct a pilot program to test TWIC access control technologies, including TWIC readers, in the maritime environment; and allow newly hired employees to work while their TWIC application is being processed. Section 104 also established a deadline for compliance for MTSA facilities of January 1, 2009.
- *TWIC Rule Published (January 2007).* TSA and the Coast Guard issued a rule requiring worker enrollment and TWIC issuance. TSA also awarded a $70 million contract to begin enrolling workers and issuing TWICs to workers. This rule announced September 25, 2008, as the final date by which the new access control procedures must be implemented nationwide for all credentialed mariners and others seeking unescorted access to secure areas aboard vessels. Compliance dates for shore-based maritime facilities and OCS facilities subject to MTSA, however, will be phased in by Captain of the Port zones as published in the *Federal Register* 90 days prior to the compliance date.
- *Implementation Guidance (July 2007).* The Coast Guard issued Navigation and Inspection Circular 03-07 (NVIC 03-07) to provide guidance on how the maritime industry is to comply with the January 2007 TWIC rule and how the Coast Guard will implement TWIC compliance efforts.
- *Delayed Compliance Date (May 2008).* In recognition of the problems associated with enrolling TWIC applicants and acti-

vating the cards, TSA and the Coast Guard published a final rule moving the national compliance date from September 25, 2008 to April 15, 2009. This gave individuals who need a TWIC the opportunity to enroll and gave TSA more time to complete the security assessments of all applicants and issue the TWIC cards.

- *TWIC Reader Pilot Program (June 2008).* As part of the TWIC reader pilot program, TSA issued an agency announcement calling for biometric card readers to be submitted for assessment as TWIC readers.

Escorting/Monitoring in Maritime Transportation Areas

Owners and operators of vessels and facilities subject to TWIC are required to exercise responsibility for controlling access to secure and restricted areas.[3] Non-TWIC card holders entering a restricted area within a secure area must be escorted by a TWIC card holder, and non-TWIC card holders entering a secure area must be escorted or, at a minimum, monitored by a TWIC card holder.

"Escorting" means accompanying the escorted individual continuously while within a secure area to observe whether he is engaged in activities other than those for which escorted access was granted. 33 C.F.R. § 101.105. For a restricted area, this means a live physical side-by-side escort.

Monitoring is allowed in a secure area and can be accomplished by closed-circuit television, security patrols, or automatic intrusion-detecting devices. The monitoring process must provide an owner or operator with sufficient capability to respond quickly if the non-TWIC card holder enters an unauthorized area or engages in unauthorized conduct. An owner or operator always has the discretion to require an escort regardless of whether an individual possesses a TWIC card.[4]

Although the TWIC rule does not alter the MTSA-regulated geographic area of a facility, it does permit those facilities with a significant non-maritime transportation portion to submit for approval an amendment to their facility security plan to redefine their secure area to cover

---

3. Restricted areas are areas within secure areas with additional security requirements because such areas may present a heightened opportunity for a security incident.

4. Newly hired employees are able to gain accompanied access to secure areas for up to 30 consecutive days while awaiting issuance of their TWIC, with an additional 30 days at COTP discretion.

only the maritime transportation portion. The intent of this provision is to limit TWIC applicability to the maritime transportation portion, not to reduce the area over which the Facility Security Plan (FSP) applies.[5] It should be noted that redefinition of non-maritime transportation-related portions does not eliminate the need to implement access control procedures as approved in the FSP. In short, this provision merely limits the facility implementation of TWIC to include those portions with a maritime transportation nexus. All amendments requesting such redesignation were to have been submitted to the COTP no later than September 4, 2007,[6] to NVIC 03-07, enclosure 3.

Personnel Required or Eligible to Obtain a TWIC

Company, vessel, and facility security officers and company, vessel, and facility personnel responsible for security duties are required to obtain a TWIC. U.S. nationals and certain non-U.S. citizens who are lawfully present in the United State are eligible to hold a TWIC. Most foreign nationals in a lawful non-immigrant status with unrestricted authorization to work in the United States are eligible for a TWIC. In addition, the following non-immigrant individuals who have restricted authorization to work in the United States with the following visas are eligible for a TWIC:

- B1/OCS Business Visitor/ Outer Continental Shelf;
- C-1/D Crewman Visa;
- H-1B Special Occupations;
- H-1B1 Free Trade Agreement;
- E-1 Treaty Trader;
- E-3 Australian in Specialty Occupation;
- L-1 Intracompany Executive Transfer;
- O-1 Extraordinary Ability; and
- TN North American Free Trade Agreement

---

5. The Coast Guard will generally consider that the following areas have a maritime transportation nexus and should always be included in the secure area: (a) shore areas immediately adjacent to each vessel moored at the facility, (b) areas designated for loading, unloading, or storage of cargo and stores, and (c) areas containing cargo consisting of dangerous goods or hazardous substances, including certain dangerous cargoes.

6. A facility may request permission from the COTP to submit a redefinition beyond this date. The COTP will consider each request based upon individual circumstances. In any event, the redefinition request may be made as part of the five-year renewal request.

In addition, TSA has the authority to determine that other non-immigrants who have restricted authorization to work in the United States and, although not specifically listed above, who have a legal status comparable to the legal status set forth in this list are eligible for a TWIC on a case-by-case basis.

Personnel who frequently access secure areas in the course of their employment will likely obtain TWICs.[7] For example, although TWIC does not apply to foreign-flag vessels, absent a TWIC, crew members and others aboard foreign-flag vessels moored at U.S. facilities will require escorts when leaving the vessel for any purpose except when working immediately adjacent to their vessels in the conduct of vessel-related activities. Likewise, vessel superintendents needing access to a vessel will need either a TWIC or an escort to pass through the MTSA facility to access the vessel.

Upon expiration of non-immigrant status, a TWIC must be surrendered to the employer and returned to TSA. When a non-immigrant quits or is terminated, the employer is required to provide notification to TSA within five business days.

Personnel convicted of certain crimes listed in the TWIC regulations, or who are found not guilty of these listed crimes by reason of insanity, are permanently disqualified from receiving a TWIC. In addition, applicants are disqualified from receiving a TWIC for the following specified interim periods if: (1) convicted of certain other crimes listed in the TWIC regulations, or who are found not guilty of these listed crimes by reason of insanity, within seven years of the date of an application; or (2) if the applicant was released from incarceration for one of these crimes within five years of the date of an application for a TWIC.

The TWIC Card, Reader Requirements, and Pilot Testing

The physical TWIC card is based on smart-card technology and contains an integrated circuit chip that provides biometric identification without requiring a connection to a central database. The TWIC card can be read either by inserting it into a slot in a card reader or holding it within a short distance of a card reader. Physical contact is not required. In addition, the cards can be read through a stripe reader similar to a credit card,

---

7. These populations include non-credentialed mariners in vessel crew, longshoremen, facility employees who work in a secure area, truckers bringing cargo onto a facility or picking up cargo at a facility, surveyors, agents, chandlers, port chaplains, vessel superintendents, and other maritime professionals.

and the card contains a bar code that can be read by a bar code reader. Before card readers are installed at facilities and on vessels, access to secure areas will be controlled by physical inspection of the card.

The Coast Guard and TSA have initiated work on the second TWIC rule, which will address the requirement for TWIC readers in the marine environment. The Coast Guard and TSA have indicated that the intent will be to apply requirements in a risk-based fashion to leverage security benefits and capabilities. On June 20, 2008, TSA issued an announcement inviting vendors to express an interest, provide information, and demonstrate capability to provide card readers. On August 28, 2008, TSA issued a second announcement and is completing initial capability evaluation testing to assist stakeholders in identifying a choice of readers for use at secure areas in the maritime transportation system. In accordance with the Safe Port Act, the Coast Guard and TSA identified 20 participants at seven diverse port and vessel areas to participate in a TWIC reader pilot testing program. For fiscal year 2008, Congress appropriated $8.1 million to support the card-reader pilots and the testing program.

On March 27, 2009, the Coast Guard published an Advanced Notice of Proposed Rulemaking discussing its preliminary thoughts on potential requirements for use of card readers. Comments were due by May 26, 2009.

Enrollment Status, Compliance Dates, and Enforcement

The first enrollment center opened in Wilmington, Delaware, on October 16, 2007, and additional enrollment centers were opened on a rolling basis around the country. According to TSA, there are approximately 149 fixed enrollment centers, and it estimates that it will open up approximately 275 mobile enrollment centers. Original estimates in January 2007 had projected that approximately 770,000 individuals would need a TWIC. According to the Government Accounting Office, approximately 1.2 million TWIC users have been identified. GAO, Transportation Security: Transportation Worker Identification Credential: A Status Update, GAO-08-1151T (Washington, D.C.; Sept. 17, 2008). As of October 30, 2008, more than 617,000 maritime workers had enrolled for a TWIC and more than 405,000 cards had been activated.

With regard to compliance dates, owners and operators of vessels have until April 15, 2009, to begin requiring the use of TWIC access control procedures. Owners and operators of MTSA-regulated facilities, including outer continental shelf facilities, must begin requiring the use of TWIC access control procedures based on Coast Guard announcements of compliance dates on a rolling basis by COTP zone. The first compliance date of October 15, 2008, was published in the *Federal Register* on May 7, 2008, for the COTP zones of Boston, Northern New England, and Southeastern New England. TWIC compliance dates have been implemented for all of the 42 COTP zones. As of May 2009, over 1.2 million maritime workers have been enrolled in TWIC and more than 1,009,000 cards have been activated. An update of this status can be found at http:///assets/pdf/public_compliance_groupings.pdf.

The Coast Guard has announced a $2.2 million contract for handheld readers that will be used by the Coast Guard to enforce compliance. The contract is for up to 300 readers. Moreover, the Coast Guard has stated that it is now starting to conduct spot checks for compliance.

Future Challenges

At least three substantial potential challenges face the Coast Guard, TSA, and the regulated industry in fully implementing TWIC: (1) enrollment issues, (2) implementation of access control procedures, and (3) development of the card reader.

(1) *Enrollment issues:* TSA and its enrollment contractor have consistently experienced enrollment problems, which have been exacerbated by the fact that the enrollment population of workers is much greater than was previously estimated. Even when workers have completed the enrollment process, in many cases they have been slow to pick up their TWIC cards.

(2) *Implementation of access control procedures:* Although owners and operators of MTSA-regulated vessels and facilities have been given a significant amount of time to plan for the actual implementation of access control procedures, it remains unclear what kinds of delays and other problems will arise when facilities and vessels are required to comply with these new requirements. In particular, many facilities, rather than accept the TWIC card, may decide to shift the burden to visitors and contractors to provide escorts and absorb the attendant costs. In addition, since the implementation of MTSA, the Coast Guard has received reports of MTSA facilities refusing to grant access to seafarers

holding properly issued visas for the purpose of shore leave and other routine visits ashore. Implementation of the TWIC access control procedures could potentially further hinder seafarer access ashore.[8]

(3) *Development of the card reader:* The development of the card reader has been a particularly thorny problem for TSA and the Coast Guard. The future development and implementation of the card-reader technology will need to ensure that TWIC readers can perform effectively in harsh maritime environments and balance security requirements with the flow of commerce. The testing of these devices is still in its infancy stages, and it is difficult to predict when and how the government and industry will ultimately effectively employ TWIC card readers.

---

8. In order to address this problem, the Coast Guard issued a policy notice to COTPs to encourage, support, and facilitate vigorously any accommodations at MTSA facilities, including but not limited to escort provisions, to make shore leave and access to seafarer welfare organizations possible. Coast Guard ALCOAST 529/08, COMDTNOTE 16611, dated Oct. 25, 2008.

CHAPTER 12

Chemical Facility Anti-Terrorism Standards

by James W. Conrad, Jr.*

After a brief historical summary, this chapter describes the elements and operation of DHS's Chemical Facility Anti-Terrorism Standards (CFATS) rule and its current implementation status. In passing, the chapter explains the concept of "inherently safer technology" and the challenges of mandating it. The last part of the chapter briefly discusses the prospects for, and merits of, future legislation.

BACKGROUND

One of the hallmarks of the Homeland Security Act of 2002 was that it gave the new Department of Homeland Security (DHS) no regulatory authority beyond that which it inherited from the 22 legacy agencies that were rolled into it. This was most immediately obvious in the area of critical infrastructure protection, where the new department was limited to "recommend measures necessary to protect the key resources and critical infrastructure of the United States in coordination with other agencies of the Federal Government and in cooperation with state and local government agencies and authorities, the private sector, and other entities."[1]

---

* Portions of this chapter are adapted from *The Security of Chemical Facilities: A Perpetually Moving Target*, 55 FED. LAW. 41 (June 2008).

1. Pub. L. No. 107-296, § 201(d)(6) (Nov. 25, 2002) (amended by Pub. L. No. 110-53, § 531(a)(2) (Aug. 3, 2007)), 6 U.S.C. § 121(d)(6).

This reliance on voluntary action was confirmed in Homeland Security Presidential Directive/HSPD-7, which directed the DHS secretary to "serve as the principal Federal official to lead, integrate, and coordinate implementation of efforts among Federal departments and agencies, State and local governments, and the private sector to protect critical infrastructure and key resources."[2]

Consistent with its initial reluctance to give DHS any new regulatory authority, in the five years following September 11, 2001, Congress enacted only two conventional regulatory programs for critical infrastructure, both in 2002. The first did not even involve DHS; it charged the Environmental Protection Agency (EPA) with overseeing security at public drinking water systems.[3] The other tasked the Coast Guard with regulating security at vessels, ports, and facilities with docks.[4] Significantly, neither was opposed by the prospectively regulated community, primarily because both involved substantial grant programs.

The earliest and strongest countercurrent to this voluntary, cooperative government/industry approach to infrastructure protection was in the area of chemical facility security. Barely a month after 9/11, then-Senator Jon Corzine introduced the Chemical Security Act of 2001.[5] Corzine's bill was hotly contested, as were subsequent bills introduced by other senators and representatives in the intervening years. While the range of disagreement narrowed with time—after DHS was established in 2003, all seriously considered bills on the topic assigned primary jurisdiction to it rather than to EPA—legislation continued to founder on the issue of whether the federal government should be able to mandate the use of less hazardous chemicals or processes, generally (but somewhat misleadingly) referred to as "inherently safer technology."

Finally, as the 2006 congressional elections drew near, the fear of being criticized for having done nothing, and the uncertain prospect of

---

2. HSPD-7, CRITICAL INFRASTRUCTURE IDENTIFICATION, PRIORITIZATION, AND PROTECTION (Dec. 17, 2003), *available at* http://www.whitehouse.gov/news/releases/2003/12/20031217-5.html. (Chapter 6 provides a fuller discussion of the evolution and nature of the federal approach to critical infrastructure protection.)

3. Title IV of the Public Health Security and Bioterrorism Preparedness and Response Act, Pub. L. No. 107-188, 42 U.S.C. § 300i-2.

4. The Maritime Transportation Security Act (MTSA), Pub. L. No. 107-295, § 102, 46 U.S.C. Ch. 701. (Chapter 11 provides a detailed description of the MTSA, which applies to over 300 chemical facilities, including many of the nation's largest.)

5. S. 1602, 107th Cong., 1st Sess. (introduced Oct. 31, 2001).

changes in control of Congress, led that body and DHS to strike a deal in October of that year on a page and a half of text that was added to DHS's Fiscal Year 2007 appropriations bill.[6] That provision (Section 550) is now being implemented as the Chemical Facility Anti-Terrorism Standards or CFATS rule. The next part of this chapter explains that rule and describes its current implementation status. In passing, it explains the concept of inherently safer technologies (IST) and the challenges of mandating it. The last part of the chapter briefly discusses prospects for future legislation.

THE CFATS PROGRAM

Section 550 applies to chemical facilities that "present high levels of security risk."[7] Because the statute is so "bare-bones," the scope of that phrase, and most other important features of the program it established, have had to be defined by regulation. Section 550 ordered DHS to issue these rules within six months, without notice and comment. To its credit, DHS managed to publish a draft rule for comment within a few months of enactment,[8] and then issued an interim final rule (IFR) in April 2007.[9] To meet its six-month deadline, however, DHS deferred the most complicated issue—coverage—to a subsequent rule. That rule, Appendix A to the IFR, was published as a final rule in November 2007.[10] Initial submissions by potentially covered facilities were due in January 2008; implementation and compliance assessment will easily run beyond 2009. This part of the chapter begins by explaining the complicated process of determining whether a facility is potentially subject to the rule. It then runs through the rest of the implementation sequence—that is, determining the applicability of the rule; preparation, submission, and review of security vulnerability assessments and site security plans; and site inspections and enforcement. The discussion focuses on two key topics in the planning process: inherent safety and personnel issues. Finally, it addresses two overarching issues of great controversy: protection of sensitive information and federal preemption.

---

6. Pub. L. No. 109-295, § 550 (Oct. 4, 2006), 6 U.S.C. § 121 note.

7. *Id.* § 550(a).

8. 71 Fed. Reg. 78,276 (Dec. 28, 2006).

9. 72 Fed. Reg. 17,688 (April 9, 2007), codified at 6 C.F.R. Part 27. Subsequent citations to the rule itself will be to Title 6 of the Code of Federal Regulations.

10. 72 Fed. Reg. 65,396 (Nov. 20, 2007).

Applicability

Overview

The IFR's definition of "chemical facility" is extremely broad: "any establishment that possesses, or plans to possess, at any relevant point in time, a quantity of a chemical substance determined by [DHS] to be potentially dangerous or that meets other risk-related criteria identified by [DHS]."[11] As discussed in greater detail below:

- Under the IFR, DHS uses a Web-based screening tool called Top-Screen to determine if a chemical facility is high-risk. If DHS concludes that it is, that covered facility is then subject to other requirements of the IFR. DHS reported that some 30,000 facilities completed Top-Screen by the initial January 22, 2008 deadline and that roughly another 6,000 had filed within the following 14 months.[12]
- DHS reviews a facility's Top-Screen submission and then notifies the facility either (i) that it is provisionally a high-risk facility subject to CFATS and must now submit a security vulnerability assessment, or (ii) that it is not currently subject to CFATS (at least until DHS revises the rule). In June 2008, DHS notified roughly 7,000 facilities that they were provisionally high-risk.

Section 550 and the IFR exempt four categories of facilities whose security is already regulated by other federal agencies: (i) facilities regulated under the Maritime Transportation Security Act (MTSA), (ii) public water systems as defined under the Safe Drinking Water Act, (iii) facilities owned or operated by the Departments of Defense or Energy, and (iv) Nuclear Regulatory Commission (NRC)-regulated facilities.[13] The law and

---

11. § 27.105.

12. Where multiple owners or operators are present at a facility, DHS has said it may conclude that each owner/operator and its associated operations is a separate facility. Co-located owners and operators have some flexibility to define facility boundaries and to identify the person(s) responsible for completing Top-Screen and complying with CFATS. These allocations can be based on operational or contractual relationships among the owner/operators. It would be prudent to make such determinations in consultation with DHS. *See* 72 Fed. Reg. 17,697 & 65,417.

13. Pub. L. No. 109-295, *supra* note 7, § 550(a); 6 C.F.R. § 27.110(b). The presence on an industrial site of a public water system (or an EPA-regulated

rules also exempt wastewater treatment works as defined in the Clean Water Act, even though security at these facilities is not regulated by any federal agency.[14] Also, DHS currently does not require railroad facilities or truck terminals to submit a Top-Screen assessment deferring to regulation of these facilities by the Transportation Security Administration.[15]

Top-Screen and Appendix A

Top-Screen is part of a secure Web-based DHS portal called the Chemical Security Assessment Tool, or CSAT.[16] The CSAT application, which is how potentially and actually regulated facilities file required submissions under CFATS, is one of the major innovations (and headaches) of the rule. DHS maintains an extensive list of over 1,500 CSAT "Frequently Asked Questions," most of which answer subtle interpretive questions arising from the unfortunate complexity of Top-Screen and Appendix A.[17]

A potentially covered facility can be required to complete Top-Screen in either of two ways:

- *Directly.* DHS can notify a facility directly in writing, or through a *Federal Register* notice, that it is a covered facility.[18] Many facilities received written notifications in 2007 as part of DHS's accelerated Phase 1 program.

---

wastewater treatment plant—*see* text accompanying note 15 *infra*) does not exempt the entire site, but the portion of the facility regulated under one of those authorities is to be excluded from Top-Screen calculations. This includes any chemical storage dedicated to those regulated operations. The NRC exemption applies only at facilities where the NRC imposes significant security requirements and regulates the security of most of the facility. The presence at an industrial site of small radioactive sources for chemical process control equipment, gauges, dials, etc., does not exempt the entire site. 72 Fed. Reg. 17,699.

14. *Id.*

15. 72 Fed. Reg. 17,698–99, 65,415. TSA's rule regarding rail facilities was published at 73 Fed. Reg. 72,130 (Nov. 26, 2009) (to be codified at 49 C.F.R. Parts 1520 & 1580).

16. The public CSAT Web page, including registration functionality and the Top-Screen Questions and User Manual, is located at http://www.dhs.gov/xprevprot/programs/gc_1169501486197.shtm.

17. The CSAT FAQs are *available at* http://csat-help.dhs.gov/pls/apex/f?p=100:1:1534993927731333.

18. § 27.200(b)(1).

- *Appendix A*. The Appendix A table lists over 300 "chemicals of interest" (COI) and sets a screening threshold quantity (STQ) for each chemical for each applicable type of hazard scenario or security issue. In general, if a facility possesses an Appendix A chemical at or above one of the STQs for any amount of time, it must submit a Top-Screen assessment.[19] As discussed below, however, this general statement conceals a lot of complexity.

As noted earlier, facilities that possessed a chemical of interest (COI) at or above an applicable screening threshold quantity (STQ) at the time the interim final rule first became effective had to complete a Top-Screen submission by January 22, 2008. A facility that comes into possession of a COI above an applicable STQ on some subsequent date must complete and submit a Top-Screen assessment within 60 calendar days of that date.[20] When a facility make a "material modification," it must submit a new Top-Screen within 60 days.[21] Facilities that think they now fall below any applicable STQ, or that find that they made an error in their initial Top-Screen submission, are encouraged to resubmit to DHS. DHS has dropped facilities from the CFATS program based on resubmissions. Finally, all facilities must update their Top-Screens on a periodic basis, depending on which risk-based tier they are ultimately assigned to.[22]

Commenters urged DHS to base applicability of the CFATS rule on something simple, like the hazard classes set out in the Department of Transportation's (DOT's) hazardous materials (hazmat) regulations.[23] Unfortunately, DHS chose an approach that only an environmental lawyer could love. There are seven Top-Screen security issues, each with one or more STQs:[24]

- *Release chemicals*. There are three kinds of release security issues: *release—toxic*; *release—flammables*; and *release—explosives*.

---

19. § 27.200(b)(2).

20. § 27.210(a)(1)(i).

21. § 27.210(d). This term is only partially defined in the IFR's preamble, but for relevant purposes encompasses the presence of a new chemical, an increased amount of an existing chemical, or any other change that substantially affects the information in the submitted Top-Screen. 72 Fed. Reg. 17,702.

22. See text accompanying note 33, *infra*. Risk-based tiers are discussed beginning on page 223.

23. 72 Fed. Reg. 17,697.

24. As a result, a given chemical at a facility could be subject to more than one STQ.

- *Theft/diversion chemicals.* There are also three theft/diversion security issues: *theft/diversion—chemical weapons/chemical weapons precursors (CW/CWP) chemicals*; *theft/diversion—weapon of mass effect (WME) chemicals*; and *theft/diversion—explosive/improvised explosive device precursor (EXP/IEDP) chemicals.*
- *Sabotage/Contamination.*[25]

The seven security issues have a host of special rules and exclusions regarding what is covered when. DHS created special rules for several very common and economically important chemicals (propane, chlorine, ammonium nitrate, and hydrogen fluoride/hydrofluoric acid) and established a series of generic exclusions (e.g., for COIs in compressed air or in certain hazardous wastes).[26]

Security Vulnerability Assessments

If DHS concludes, based its review of a facility's Top-Screen, that the facility is provisionally high-risk, DHS provisionally assigns it to one of four risk-based tiers, with Tier 1 being the highest risk.[27] The criteria for making high-risk determinations and tier assignments have been classified by DHS.

The first compliance obligation of a covered facility is to conduct a security vulnerability assessment (SVA) and file it with DHS. Facilities in Tiers 1–3 are required to use the CSAT SVA tool, while Tier 4 may use any one of several DHS-approved methodologies.[28] SVAs from the initially regulated group of high-risk facilities were due between September and December 2008. Subsequently regulated facilities generally will have 90 days to complete an SVA.[29]

DHS uses a classified "tiering engine," and some amount of human judgment, to evaluate SVAs. It is supposed to respond to facilities within 60 days of submission to apprise them of its final determination regarding the facility's high-risk status and tier assignment.[30] Facilities that

---

25. *See generally* 72 Fed. Reg. 65,396. The Appendix A final rule contains an additional security-related basis for listing—critical relationship to government mission and national economy—but does not list any chemicals on this basis.

26. *Id.*

27. § 27.220.

28. §§ 27.215(b), 27.235(a)(1).

29. § 27.210(a)(2).

30. 72 Fed. Reg. 17,704.

question these decisions can seek a consultation with the CFATS coordinating official.[31]

Facilities in Tiers 1 and 2 must resubmit an SVA every two years, while Tiers 3 and 4 are on a three-year schedule.[32]

Site Security Plans

Once DHS approves a facility's SVA submission, the facility has 120 days to develop a site security plan (SSP) and submit it, also through CSAT.[33] CSAT contains an SSP template that a facility can use,[34] although a facility can also submit an Alternative Security Program (ASP) in lieu of an SSP.[35] The SSP must describe the facility's security measures and explain how it addresses (i) the vulnerabilities identified in the SVA, (ii) the applicable potential modes of terrorist attack, and (iii) the applicable risk-based performance standards.[36] The modes of terrorist attack, which include vehicle and water-borne explosive devices and ground assault, are not intended to be "design basis threats"; that is, a facility does not have to be able to withstand a particular level of attack for a specified time (unlike nuclear facilities, for example).[37] Risk-based performance standards—in many ways the heart of the CFATS rule—are discussed in the next section of this chapter.

DHS will issue a Letter of Authorization upon its preliminary approval of a plan. After DHS inspectors have visited the facility and found it to be in compliance, DHS will issue the facility a Letter of Approval. If a facility believes it will not be able to fully implement its plan by the inspection date, it can discuss the matter with DHS.[38]

---

31. § 27.120(b).

32. § 27.215(c).

33. § 27.210(a)(3).

34. Only facilities required to complete an SSP have access to the template, but CSAT does make publicly available the SSP Instruction Manual and Questions, as well as screenshots from the template. *See* http://www.dhs. gov/xprevprof/programs/gc-1238784785789.shtm.

35. § 27.235(a). DHS may approve an ASP if it meets the CFATS requirements for an SSP and provides an equivalent level of security. *Id.* While Section 550(a) speaks of ASPs being developed by a variety of organizations, *see* Pub. L. No. 109-295, *supra* note 7, the IFR limits approvable ASPs to those submitted by a covered facility, § 27.235(a).

36. § 27.225(a).

37. 72 Fed. Reg. 17,701.

38. § 27.245.

Tiers 1 and 2 must revise their SSP every two years, while Tiers 3 and 4 are on a three-year review schedule.[39]

Risk-Based Performance Standards

Chemical facilities are a diverse bunch, from huge complexes covering many square miles to small-batch operations. They may be located in remote areas or densely populated urban areas. They may contain vastly differing amounts of chemicals with differing degrees of security sensitivity. What's more, there usually are multiple ways that a facility can secure itself from terrorists. To encompass this diversity in a sensible way, Section 550 adopts a risk- and performance-based approach—its most innovative feature. Rather than specifying (or authorizing DHS to specify) blanket or particular security measures, Section 550(a) states that DHS "shall issue interim final regulations establishing risk-based performance standards for security of chemical facilities and that these regulations shall permit each such facility, in developing and implementing site security plans, to select layered security measures that, in combination, appropriately address the vulnerability assessment and the risk-based performance standards for security for the facility."[40]

To implement this language, the IFR establishes 19 categories of risk-based security performance standards (RBPS) that are intended to become increasingly demanding as one moves from Tier 4 to Tier 1:

1. Restrict Area Perimeter
2. Secure Site Assets
3. Screen and Control Access
4. Deter, Detect, and Delay
5. Shipping, Receipt, and Storage
6. Theft and Diversion
7. Sabotage
8. Cyber
9. Response
10. Monitoring
11. Training
12. Personnel Surety
13. Elevated Threats
14. Specific Threats, Vulnerabilities, or Risks

---

39. § 27.225(d)(2).
40. Pub. L. No. 109-295, *supra* note 7.

15. Reporting of Significant Security Incidents
16. Significant Security Incidents and Suspicious Activities
17. Officials and Organization
18. Records
19. "[A]ny additional performance standards the Assistant Secretary [for Infrastructure Protection] may specify."[41]

Facilities have flexibility to select, and identify in their SSPs, security measures that satisfy the applicable performance standards. CSAT contains a nonbinding guidance document providing DHS's interpretation of what the different RBPS require of facilities in the various tiers.[42] This guidance is likely to be highly significant.

By far, the RBPS that has generated the greatest anxiety among facility owner/operators is number 4, requiring a facility to "[d]elay an attack for a sufficient period of time so as to allow appropriate response through on-site security response, barriers and barricades; hardened targets; and well-coordinated response planning."[43] Most chemical facilities could not feasibly be staffed continuously with armed guards capable of fighting off a terrorist ground attack, as nuclear reactors are, and instead must depend on local law enforcement to provide armed response capability.

INHERENT SAFETY

While DHS cannot compel a facility directly to implement "inherently safer technology," the issue is so central to the future of chemical facility security that it warrants discussion here.

First given a name several decades ago by process safety experts within the chemical industry, "inherent safety" means eliminating a hazard when designing a process so that one does not have to manage the hazard afterward—for example, inflating blimps with helium rather than hydrogen.[44] Deceptively simple in concept, inherent safety can be highly complicated in application, especially as one strives to avoid merely shifting a risk elsewhere or unwittingly creating a new one. And although

---

41. § 27.230(a).

42. *See* note 35 *supra*.

43. § 27.230(a)(4).

44. The best and most authoritative text on the subject of IST is ROBERT E. BOLLINGER ET AL., INHERENTLY SAFER CHEMICAL PROCESSES: A LIFE CYCLE APPROACH (Am. Inst. of Chem. Engineers, Ctr. for Chem. Process Safety, 1996).

inherent safety has become standard practice within the chemical industry and a basic element of chemical engineering education, there is as yet no consensus methodology for comparing the inherent safety of multiple approaches. In some cases, moreover, the exercise is ultimately subjective or arbitrary; for example, how does one weigh the risk of an explosion hazard against the risk of a possible cancer hazard? Most problematic, environmental activists have seized upon inherent safety—which they label IST—as a means of promoting the elimination of particularly hazardous chemicals like chlorine. As a result, the chemical industry has been resolutely opposed to government requirements regarding inherent safety, especially if they empower government officials to second-guess the decisions of process engineers.

Section 550(a) states: "The Secretary may not disapprove a site security plan submitted under this section based on the presence or absence of a particular security measure, but the Secretary may disapprove a site security plan if the plan fails to satisfy the risk-based performance standards established by this section."[45] This means that while a facility must meet the applicable RBPS, it has the discretion to choose among the measures that do so. It follows from this that DHS cannot directly require implementation of IST. DHS has interpreted this prohibition also to preclude it from requiring IST (or any other particular security measure) indirectly; that is, by rejecting a plan unless it contains that measure, or by "engineer[ing] the performance standards to permit only one actual security option" as a practical matter (such as by setting a standard of "no offsite impact in the event of a successful terrorist attack").[46] However, facilities are free to consider IST options to reduce risk and thus meet a performance standard, move to a lower tier, or stop being high-risk.[47] DHS may not agree to recategorize a facility as no longer high-risk, or move it to a lower tier, based on IST if the proposal would shift risk off-site or otherwise not actually reduce risk, or would compromise security.[48]

As the last section of this chapter describes, the inability of DHS to require inherent safety is the single greatest driving force behind continuing congressional efforts to legislate on chemical facility security.

---

45. Pub. L. No. 109-295, *supra* note 7.
46. *See* 71 Fed. Reg. 78,285.
47. 72 Fed. Reg. 17,707 &17,718.
48. *Id.* at 17,707.

BACKGROUND CHECK/PERSONNEL ISSUES

RBPS number 12 requires background checks and identification for facility employees, contractors, and other visitors who have unescorted access to restricted areas and critical assets at a facility.[49] The facility is responsible for determining what criminal background findings would be disqualifying and for checking criminal background and immigration status. DHS intends to establish, in 2009, a fifth CSAT application that will enable employers to submit names for automated evaluation against the National Terrorist Screening Database. According to DHS staff, DHS may respond with "on" or "not on" the list; what an employer does with that information will be up to the employer.

Neither Section 550 nor the IFR establishes a whistleblower system, but DHS has stated that it intends to establish a telephone line through which employees and other individuals can communicate security concerns.[50] Also, neither mandates participation by any particular types of employees in the compliance/implementation process. Organized labor would like to see more on both scores.

INSPECTIONS/ENFORCEMENT

Section 550(a) requires DHS to review and approve each SVA and SSP, and Section 550(e) requires it to inspect covered facilities.[51] If DHS finds a violation, it must give the facility a clear, written explanation of deficiencies and an opportunity for consultation, and may issue the facility an order to comply by a date that DHS determines is "appropriate under the circumstances."[52] If the facility does not comply with the order, DHS may impose a civil administrative penalty of up to $25,000 per violation and may also issue an order for the facility to cease operation until it complies with the order.[53] DHS may choose to notify local emergency responders or other agencies about upcoming inspections on a case-by-case basis, but not necessarily in every case.[54]

The IFR establishes administrative adjudication rules, with an appeal to the under secretary of DHS.[55] The under secretary's decision is

---

49. § 27.230(a)(12).
50. *Id.* at 17718.
51. Pub. L. No. 109-295, *supra* note 7.
52. *Id.* § 550(g).
53. § 27.300(b).
54. 72 Fed. Reg. 17,710.
55. 6 C.F.R. Part 27, Subpart C.

judicially reviewable, but given the amount of discretion that the statute and the IFR accord to DHS regarding the security measures required at a facility, it seems likely that courts will defer heavily to DHS.

The initial focus of DHS's compliance efforts will be reviewing SVAs and SSPs, which will be a centralized, documentary process. Actual site visits will not begin until after the initial tranche of 140 Tier 1 SSPs is approved, in late 2009 or early 2010. This is just as well, because at this writing DHS had only 40 field inspectors, one-third of which had just been hired. DHS will face challenges in the coming years fielding enough inspectors to meet its inspection obligations, and as a result has raised the prospect of a future rulemaking to authorize the use of third-party auditors to conduct inspections.[56]

INFORMATION PROTECTION

Section 550 and the CFATS rule gave rise to a new category of information protection: chemical-terrorism vulnerability information (CVI). The CVI rules and DHS's new procedural manual implementing them are discussed in Chapter 6 of this book.

PREEMPTION

After IST, the most fiercely contested issue in chemical facility security has been the extent to which federal requirements would preempt state programs addressing the same topic. Only three states have any such program,[57] and only one actually imposes obligations on facilities, but the issue has taken on disproportionate importance, mainly because it serves as yet another venue for proponents of IST to promote their cause. The Prescriptive Order issued in New Jersey in 2005 obliged specified categories of facilities, on a one-time basis, to consider IST, although they remained free either to implement it or to explain to the state why

---

56. 72 Fed. Reg. at 17,711–12.

57. Maryland and New York have enacted chemical facility security legislation (*see* MD. ENV'T CODE § 7-701 to 7-709 and N.Y. EXEC. LAW §§ 709–712); New Jersey has issued a "Prescriptive Order" to specified facilities (State of New Jersey Domestic Security Preparedness Task Force, *Domestic Security Preparedness Best Practices at TCPA/DPCC Chemical Sector Facilities*, ¶ 5 (Nov. 21, 2005), *available at* http://www.acutech-consulting.com/acutech-news/2005/BestPracticesStandarsActonChemicalPlantSecurity Nov212005.pdf).

doing so was infeasible. In every other respect, the order was actually less demanding than CFATS. Critics of DHS and IST supporters, however, regularly trumpet New Jersey's "more stringent" program, and have made preemption the second major battleground in the war over chemical facility security.

Section 550 is silent on the topic. DHS's draft rule contained aggressive language implying that the law "occupied the field" and impliedly preempted all state enactments on the subject.[58] After fierce criticism, DHS retreated in the IFR, stating that Section 550 exerted only "conflict" preemption and would only preempt a state program if it conflicted with, hindered, posed an obstacle to, or frustrated the purpose of the federal program.[59] DHS added: "[C]urrently we have no reason to conclude that any [state program] is being applied in a way that would impede . . . Section 550 and this Interim Final Rule."[60] This was still insufficient for its opponents, who succeeded in including, in the fiscal year 2008 omnibus spending law, a provision declaring that Section 550 and CFATS do not preempt state chemical facility security requirements unless there is an actual conflict between the two.[61]

Section 550(f) has a savings clause protecting other federal laws that "regulate[] the manufacture, distribution in commerce, use, sale, other treatment, or disposal of chemical substances or mixtures,"[62] and the IFR declares that it does not intend to preempt existing health, safety, and environmental regulations.[63] It adds, however, that if state or local governments enact security laws or promulgate security regulations under the rubric of health, safety, or environmental protections, they will be measured against the standard described in the rule.[64]

THE INHERENT RISK OF FUTURE LEGISLATION

The price the congressional authorizing committees exacted for allowing Section 550 to bypass their jurisdictions in 2006 was a sunset provision that ends DHS's CFATS authority on October 4, 2009.[65] Multiple Comp-

---

58. 71 Fed. Reg. 78,292 & 78,302.
59. §§ 27.405(a), 27.405(b); 72 Fed. Reg. 17,725–27.
60. 72 Fed. Reg. 17,727.
61. *See* Pub L. No. 110-161, § 534 (Dec. 26, 2007).
62. Pub. L. No. 109–295, *supra* note 7.
63. § 27.405(a)(1).
64. 72 Fed. Reg. 17,727.
65. Pub. L. No. 109–295, *supra* note 7, § 550(b).

troller General opinions support the view that even bare appropriations to fund the CFATS program post–fiscal year 2009 would be sufficient congressional action to supersede the sunset clause in Section 550.[66] However, the issue of chemical facility security has proven to be a more alluring target to legislators than such plants have thus far been to terrorists. Moreover, the issue's appeal seems to arise less from how secure these plants actually are than from the ability of such legislation to effectuate long-frustrated goals of chemical use reduction and elimination. Those most interested in accomplishing those goals have an inherent interest, therefore, in downplaying accomplishments under the CFATS program—no matter how substantial they may be.

From 2001 through 2006, all congressional activity beyond the simple introduction of bills occurred exclusively in the Senate, first in the Environment and Public Works Committee, and then (after its renaming) in the Homeland Security and Governmental Affairs Committee. In 2007, however, action shifted to the House, where the Homeland Security Committee reported a bill that would have made several clear changes and numerous potential ones to CFATS—most prominently, requiring all covered facilities to consider IST and authorizing DHS to require high-risk facilities to implement it.[67]

This bill ground to a halt in the House Energy and Commerce Committee, whose Environment and Hazardous Materials Subcommittee made clear in a hearing on June 12 that it was the body with jurisdiction over the issue of chemical facility security—a claim bolstered by the fact that the House Parliamentarian referred to Energy and Commerce another bill that would do little more than simply strike the sunset clause from Section 550.[68]

Legislative activity in the 111th Congress seems assured, although how far it will progress and the topics it will ultimately address are difficult to predict. Obviously, IST will be a driving issue. Integration with the existing CFATS program should also be vitally important to facilities, which could otherwise face substantial and costly rework. Another issue to watch will be whether Congress attempts, directly or indirectly, to revamp the current one-size-fits-all MTSA program so that it

---

66. *See* Civil Rights Comm'n, 71 Comp.-Gen. 378, B-246541 (Apr. 29, 1992).

67. H.R. 5577, 110th Cong., 2d Sess. (reported Mar. 6, 2008).

68. H.R. 5533, 110th Cong., 2d Sess. (introduced Mar 5, 2008).

also imposes standards upon facilities based on risk. Congress in 2007 passed legislation requiring DHS to regulate the sale of ammonium nitrate.[69] This legislation could easily become a model for regulating transactions involving other hazardous chemicals.

The 111th Congress would do well to bear in mind EPA's experience from a decade ago. When EPA promulgated the Clean Air Act Risk Management Program rule in 1996, some commenters asked it to require facilities to conduct "technology options analyses" to identify inherently safer approaches for chemical processes. EPA declined to do so, stating that:

> [Process Hazard Analysis] teams regularly suggest viable, effective (and inherently safer) alternatives for risk reduction, which may include features such as inventory reduction, material substitution, and process control changes. These changes are made as opportunities arise, without regulation or adoption of completely new and unproven process technologies. . . . EPA does not believe that a requirement that sources conduct searches or analyses of alternative processing technologies for new or existing processes will produce additional benefits beyond those accruing to the rule already.[70]

It should be instructive that Carol Browner's EPA voluntarily took a pass on the opportunity to assess, and make judgments about, the inherent safety of potentially thousands of chemical operations. If IST legislation is enacted next year, DHS will face a task even EPA has shied away from taking on.

---

69. Pub. L. No. 110-161, *supra* note 60, § 563.
70. 61 Fed. Reg. 31,699 (June 20, 1996).

International Trade

CHAPTER 13

CFIUS and Foreign Investment

by Jonathan G. Cedarbaum and Stephen W. Preston[1]

Foreign direct investment in the United States is on the rise and, at the same time, U.S. government scrutiny of mergers and acquisitions potentially affecting national security has never been more intense. In this chapter, the authors examine the interagency Committee on Foreign Investment in the United States (CFIUS) and the process by which it reviews corporate transactions resulting in foreign control of U.S. businesses. That process has been conducted entirely in secret, with the "common law" developed over the years known only to a relative few. CFIUS reform efforts since the Dubai Ports World fiasco—specifically, the Foreign Investment and National Security Act of 2007 and implementing Treasury regulations effective December 22, 2008—have yielded a review process that is more streamlined and substantive standards that, although still very broad and flexible, are better understood. This chapter explores these developments, as well as industry-specific foreign ownership restrictions and investment review regimes in other countries.

Foreign acquisitions of U.S. companies are a routine fact of commercial life. But government and media scrutiny of deals in industrial sectors with potential homeland security implications have become more demanding since September 11, 2001. Although the U.S. is generally open to foreign acquisitions, there are inevitable tensions between pro-

---

1. The authors are very grateful for the extraordinary assistance of Zachary Clopton in the preparation of this chapter.

235

moting open markets, free trade, and competition, on the one hand, and ensuring U.S. national security, on the other. Responsibility for resolving those tensions falls largely on the multi-agency Committee on Foreign Investment in the United States (CFIUS).[2] In addition, several federal departments or agencies oversee industry-specific regimes—in telecommunications, air transport, and nuclear power—that allow government review of direct foreign investment with national security concerns.

Spurred by the weak dollar and booming government revenues in China and several oil-rich countries, acquisitions in the United States by foreign entities reached $407 billion in 2007, up 93 percent from 2006.[3] Foreign buyers accounted for 46 percent of the $230.5 billion of U.S. mergers and acquisitions in the fourth quarter of 2007,[4] the largest percentage of foreign buyers since 1998.[5] Although CFIUS is 20 years old, controversial transactions since 9/11—most notably the outcry over the initial approval of United Arab Emirates–based Dubai Ports World's acquisition of a company operating marine terminals in a number of major U.S. ports—have elevated CFIUS from relative obscurity to the front pages. The increasing investments in the United States by sovereign wealth funds—large pools of investment capital controlled by foreign governments—have also raised new questions in Congress and the executive branch about the regulation of foreign investment.[6] As with investments by other sorts of foreign investors, investments by sovereign wealth funds emanating from countries such as China and the Gulf Arab states, with which the United States has important strategic and geopolitical entanglements, have raised particular concerns.

Responding to these trends, Congress passed the Foreign Investment and National Security Act (FINSA) in late 2007,[7] which brought some

---

2. *See* U.S. Dep't of the Treasury, Committee on Foreign Investment in the United States (CFIUS), http://www.ustreas.gov/offices/international-affairs/cfius.

3. *Weak Dollar Fuels China's Buying Speed of U.S. Firms*, WASH. POST (Jan. 28, 2008).

4. Zachary R. Mider, *International Deals: Americans Sell Out to Foreign Firms at Record Rate*, Bloomberg News Serv., Jan. 9, 2008.

5. *Id.*

6. For helpful brief overviews, see Robert M. Kimmitt, *Public Footprints in Private Markets*, FOREIGN AFFAIRS, Vol. 87, No. 1, at 119–30 (Jan./Feb. 2008); *Asset-backed Insecurity*, THE ECONOMIST 78–80 (Jan. 19, 2008).

7. Pub. L. No. 110-49, 121 Stat. 246 (2007).

significant changes to the CFIUS regime. The president provided additional clarification through an executive order on January 23, 2008.[8] Further clarification has come in the Treasury Department's revised CFIUS regulations, required under FINSA, and effective as of December 22, 2008.[9] Industry-specific regimes managed by various departments and agencies have also continued to develop alongside the CFIUS process.

All of these developments are pointed reminders that, although the United States prides itself on openness to foreign investments, such transactions may raise special regulatory and political issues. Parties to potential foreign acquisitions of U.S. companies or assets need to consider carefully the CFIUS and other regulatory processes in planning—and potentially in valuing—such transactions.

CFIUS

Basic Framework and History

In response to concerns about possible effects of foreign direct investment on national security, in 1988 Congress enacted the Exon-Florio Amendment to the Defense Production Act of 1950. Exon-Florio authorizes the president to investigate the impact on U.S. national security of mergers, acquisitions, and takeovers by foreign persons that result in foreign control over a U.S. company or certain U.S. assets.[10] If the president finds (1) credible evidence that a transaction would impair national security, and (2) that no other provision of law grants him authority to take steps to ameliorate this impact, he may act to block the transaction.[11] The president's findings are not subject to judicial review.[12]

Exon-Florio applies both to proposed mergers and acquisitions and to completed transactions. Unless a party to the transaction voluntarily seeks pre-consummation review, there is no time limit on the president's authority to investigate a completed transaction. A voluntary notice that results in CFIUS clearance grants the transaction a safe harbor from

---

8. Exec. Order: Further Amendment of Executive Order 11,858 Concerning Foreign Investment in the United States, Jan. 23, 2008.

9. *See* 73 Fed. Reg. 70,702 (Nov. 21, 2008).

10. 50 U.S.C. app. § 2170.

11. *Id.* at § 2170(d)(4).

12. *Id.* at § 2170(e).

post-closing review and challenge (except possibly if the parties make material misrepresentations in noticing the transaction or materially breach a condition of CFIUS's clearance approval).[13]

CFIUS is charged with implementing Exon-Florio. An interagency body, CFIUS was initially established by executive order and has now been codified in statute by FINSA.[14] Chaired by the secretary of the treasury, it includes among its members the secretaries of defense, homeland security, and commerce, and the attorney general. The Director of National Intelligence serves as an ex officio member. The committee's review process is confidential, and the process is intended to focus on the true national security implications of particular deals rather than political considerations.[15]

The CFIUS notification process is voluntary, requires no filing fee, and imposes no mandatory waiting period before closing the transaction, although parties to a CFIUS review or investigation typically wait until the process is complete before closing. The CFIUS process involves four steps: (1) a voluntary filing submitted by one or both parties to the transaction; (2) a 30-day committee review of the transaction; (3) a potential additional 45-day committee investigation; and (4) a 15-day period during which the president decides to permit or block the acquisition (or seek divesture after an ex post facto review).[16]

CFIUS had traditionally approved the vast majority of notified transactions during the initial 30-day period, but a growing number of transactions are now being subjected to a second-phase 45-day investigation. Indeed, in 2006 alone, CFIUS launched seven 45-day investigations, as many as had been initiated in the previous five years combined.[17] In 2007, CFIUS conducted six 45-day investigations and parties withdrew at least six voluntary notices.[18] This trend will almost certainly continue,

---

13. *Id.* at § 2170(b)(1)(D)(iii).

14. Pub. L. No. 110-49, 121 Stat. 246 (2007), and Exec. Order 11,858, discussed below.

15. *See* 50 U.S.C. app. § 2170.

16. *Id.* at § 2170(b) and (d).

17. *See* Testimony of Treasury Assistant Secretary Clay Lowery before the House Financial Services Committee, Feb. 7, 2007, *available at* http://www.treas.gov/press/releases/hp250.htm.

18. *See* Government Accountability Office, *Foreign Investment: Laws and Policies Regulating Foreign Investment in 10 Countries*, Report to the Hon. Richard Shelby, Ranking Member, Committee on Banking, Housing, and Urban Affairs, U.S. Senate, GAO-08-320, February 2008, at 6; Council on Foreign Relations, Global FDI Policy Meeting, Washington, D.C., June 26, 2008.

especially in light of increased political pressure from Congress for CFIUS to scrutinize transactions and the general increase in foreign investment in the United States.

Scope and Focus of CFIUS Review

In determining whether to seek "safe harbor" protection by notifying CFIUS of a potential transaction, parties should consider three threshold questions: (1) does the transaction involve a "foreign person" acquiring a "U.S. business"? (2) might the transaction implicate U.S. national security interests? and (3) might the structure of the transaction bring it outside CFIUS's jurisdiction altogether?

The first question can be surprisingly tricky and sometimes requires close analysis of the Exon-Florio provisions and the CFIUS regulations. For instance, under Exon-Florio, the same entity could be a "foreign entity" or "U.S. business" depending on whether it is the target or the acquirer.[19] Any entity is a U.S. business to the extent of its business activities in the United States. Accordingly, the application of the statute could be triggered if a foreign company acquires (directly or indirectly) the U.S. branch office or subsidiary of a foreign company.[20] On the other hand, the same foreign-controlled U.S. branch or subsidiary would itself be deemed a foreign person for Exon-Florio purposes if it acquires a U.S. company or U.S. assets because the new regulations define a "foreign person" to include "any entity over which control is exercised or exercisable by a foreign national, foreign government, or foreign entity."[21]

The second inquiry is extraordinarily open-ended and may be susceptible to changing public policy concerns. The notion of national security interests can be writ quite large. The newly enacted FINSA gives some limited guidance, making clear that national security includes homeland security concerns but not, apparently, economic security.[22] FINSA also makes clear that transactions involving critical infrastructure, critical technologies, and major energy assets may well raise national security concerns.[23] The new regulations, described more fully below, offer

---

19. *See* 31 C.F.R. § 800.216 (2008) (examples 3 and 4); *id.* § 800.226.
20. *See* 31 C.F.R. § 800.226 (2008).
21. *See* 31 C.F.R. § 800.216 (2008).
22. 50 U.S.C. app. § 2170(a)(5).
23. *Id.* at § 2170(f)(6) & 2170(f)(7).

some additional clarity but still leave considerable room for debate and executive branch discretion.

As a practical matter, CFIUS has often shown particular interest in transactions when the target U.S. company has classified contracts with the U.S. government or provides products or services involving U.S. export-controlled technologies; operates or supplies U.S. critical infrastructure, such as the telecommunications network; has significant holdings in strategic natural resources, such as petroleum; or when CFIUS member agencies have specific "derogatory intelligence" about the foreign purchaser. CFIUS may also examine whether the transaction will result in an absence of U.S.-controlled companies that supply technology or products deemed important to U.S. security.

Finally, the limits of CFIUS's jurisdiction have become an increasingly important subject for inquiry as foreign entities have stepped up the pace of investment in the United States. Under the statute, only transactions that "could result in foreign control" are covered transactions subject to CFIUS review.[24] The new regulations, described below, provide additional guidance about the meaning of "foreign control" in the CFIUS context.

Recent Developments

Foreign Investment and National Security Act of 2007

In 2007, Congress enacted the Foreign Investment and National Security Act of 2007 (FINSA). FINSA addresses many of the issues that have been the focus of concern with CFIUS review and codifies elements of CFIUS membership and process.

FINSA established the membership of CFIUS by statute.[25] The secretary of the treasury chairs the committee, but under FINSA other agencies may be appointed "lead agency" with respect to particular

---

24. 50 U.S.C. app. § 2170(a)(3).

25. *See id.* at § 2170(k) (listing the membership as: "(A) the Secretary of the Treasury; (B) the Secretary of Homeland Security; (C) the Secretary of Commerce; (D) the Secretary of Defense; (E) the Secretary of State; (F) the Attorney General of the United States; (G) the Secretary of Energy; (H) the Secretary of Labor (nonvoting, *ex officio*); (I) the Director of National Intelligence (nonvoting, *ex officio*); and (J) the heads of any other executive department, agency, or office, as the President determines appropriate, generally or on a case-by-case basis.")

investigations depending on the nature of the transaction.[26] The departments of Defense, Homeland Security, Commerce, and Justice often take the most active roles in the CFIUS process. Other cabinet departments and economic and national security bodies within the executive office of the president also serve on the committee.[27] An important addition that FINSA mandated is a defined role for the director of National Intelligence, who is now an ex-officio member and must evaluate a transaction's national security implications.[28]

Under FINSA, if CFIUS decides not to clear the transaction in the 30-day review period, then it must commence an additional 45-day investigation at or before the end of the initial review period.[29] FINSA requires an extended investigation whenever the transaction threatens to impair national security, is a foreign government–controlled transaction, or results in foreign control of critical infrastructure.[30] FINSA leaves CFIUS with broad discretion to determine if a transaction threatens national security. The statute also leaves the term "critical infrastructure" defined in only general terms;[31] experience suggests that telecommunications and transportation infrastructure would typically qualify, and the statute suggests that energy assets are a specific form of critical infrastructure.[32] The range of other assets that could fall within this definition seems almost limitless, however.

Among the additional factors CFIUS must now consider in its review are the impact of the transaction on critical infrastructure, broadly

---

26. *Id.*

27. *See* Exec. Order: Further Amendment of Executive Order 11858 Concerning Foreign Investment in the United States, Jan. 23, 2008.

28. 50 U.S.C. app. § 2170(b)(4)(D).

29. 50 U.S.C. app. § 2170(b)(2)(B)(i)(I).

30. *Id.* at §§ 2170(b)(2)(B)(i)(II) and 2170(b)(2)(B)(i)(III). An investigation of a foreign government–controlled or critical infrastructure transaction is not required if the secretary of the treasury (or the deputy secretary) and the head of the lead agency (or deputy head) jointly determine that the transaction will not impair the national security of the United States. *Id.* at § 2170(b)(2)(D).

31. *Id.* at § 2170(a)(6): "The term 'critical infrastructure' means, subject to rules issued under this section, systems and assets, whether physical or virtual, so vital to the United States that the incapacity or destruction of such systems or assets would have a debilitating impact on national security."

32. *Id.* at § 2170(f)(6).

defined, as well as energy assets and critical technologies.[33] In the case of foreign government–controlled transactions—that is, transactions in which the buyer is owned or controlled by a foreign government—CFIUS must also consider the relevant country's compliance with U.S. and multilateral counterterrorism, nonproliferation, and export control regimes.[34]

Reflecting the seriousness with which the U.S. government views foreign investment, FINSA requires high-level sign-off for foreign government–controlled or critical infrastructure transactions that do not proceed to the 45-day investigation stage.[35] In addition, high-level sign-off is required for certifications of completed investigations, which CFIUS must submit to Congress.[36] The act also creates specific authority for CFIUS to enforce mitigation agreements.[37] Furthermore, it explicitly establishes CFIUS's "evergreen" authority to reopen a transaction that has been approved if there has been an intentional breach, and no other remedies will suffice.[38]

Although FINSA preserved the review process's confidentiality requirements, Congress added requirements designed to allow it to exercise increased supervision. CFIUS must now report to Congress at the end of reviews and formal investigations and also report annually about its activities.[39]

As a result of FINSA, companies can expect that more transactions will be reviewed and that more reviews will be exacting, resulting in full, formal investigations. This is inevitable given both Congress's increased attention and the act's expansive view of national security—one that the CFIUS agencies already seem to have adopted. Because of this expected increase in scrutiny, as well as the act's clear support for spontaneous CFIUS review and action if any deal presents concerns, companies should be careful to consider whether any aspect of their transactions might trigger CFIUS's jurisdiction. That question may become more

---

33. "The term 'critical technologies' means critical technology, critical components, or critical technology items essential to national defense, identified pursuant to this section, subject to regulations issued at the direction of the President." *Id.* at § 2170(a)(7).

34. *Id.* at § 2170(f).

35. *Id.* at § 2170(b)(2)(D) (requiring sign-off at secretary or deputy level by Treasury and lead agency).

36. *Id.* at § 2170(b)(3)(C)(iv)(II)(bb).

37. *Id.* at § 2170(l)(1).

38. *Id.* at § 2170 (b)(1)(D)(iii)(I).

39. *Id.* at § 2170(g).

complex as companies employ innovative financial structures for their acquisitions. Companies also should expect more involved mitigation undertakings given FINSA's mandate to CFIUS to use such measures. Finally, they should expect longer-term interaction with, and oversight by, the relevant CFIUS agencies in the wake of any deal that raises national security concerns.

Executive Order

On January 23, 2008, President Bush issued Executive Order 13,456, amending Executive Order 11,858, concerning foreign investment in the United States.[40] The new executive order provides guidance concerning the implementation of FINSA.[41]

The order carefully reiterates the administration's pro-investment policy, stating that the United States unequivocally supports international investment, which promotes economic growth, productivity, competitiveness, and job creation, while stressing that such investment must be consistent with the protection of the national security. That same careful balancing act can be seen in the order's addition of new members and observer agencies to CFIUS: on the pro-business side, the order adds the U.S. trade representative as a member and the Office of Management and Budget, the Council of Economic Advisors, and the Assistant to the President for Economic Policy as observers. On the national security side, the order adds the Office of Science and Technology Policy as a member and, as observers, the Assistants to the President for National Security Affairs and for Homeland Security and Counterterrorism.

At the same time, the order contains several provisions clearly designed to formalize and strengthen Treasury's authority over the CFIUS process. The order expressly delegates to Treasury the president's power to initiate review of a transaction that has been submitted to CFIUS or to initiate a review unilaterally. It also provides Treasury with explicit authority (after consultation with the committee) to request that the Director of National Intelligence prepare an analysis of the risks presented by a proposed transaction.

---

40. Exec. Order 13456: Further Amendment of Executive Order 11858 Concerning Foreign Investment in the United States, Jan. 23, 2008.

41. Whether President Obama will revise the executive order further remains to be seen. Until then, President Bush's Order 13456 will continue to be effective.

Some of the clarifying measures adopted in the executive order may have a more direct impact on transactions subject to CFIUS. For example, the order provides that CFIUS must initiate a 45-day, second-stage investigation of a transaction if even one member agency so requests. Under the order, CFIUS may require a mitigation agreement to remedy "any national security risk"; however, the agency proposing that agreement must provide the committee with a written showing concerning the perceived national security risk posed by the transaction and the risk mitigation measures that will address such national security risks, and CFIUS must decide whether to approve the mitigation proposal. Such agreements should not, except in extraordinary circumstances, require that a party consent to comply with existing law. The order also provides that the provision in FINSA permitting reopening of a previously reviewed transaction should be read narrowly, as the administration expects that it will be triggered only in extraordinary circumstances.

Finally, the order reminds the agencies that will carry out FINSA that they are bound not to disclose information that could impair "foreign relations, national security, the deliberative processes of the Executive, or the performance of the Executive's constitutional duties"—a provision likely designed as a reminder to CFIUS agencies of the administration's emphasis on executive secrecy in the face of FINSA's new emphasis on reports to Congress.

New Regulations

FINSA required the Treasury Department to issue new implementing regulations, and on November 21, 2008, Treasury published the final regulations in the *Federal Register*.[42] The regulations became effective December 22, 2008.[43] The new regulations do not govern transactions where the parties had made a commitment to enter into the transaction before December 22, 2008, whether, for example, by signing a written agreement with material terms, making a public offer to purchase shares, or soliciting proxies in the election of the board of directors of a target company.[44] Transactions noticed to CFIUS before December 22, 2008, will continue to be governed by the prior procedural regulations.[45]

---

42. *See* 73 Fed. Reg. 70,702 (Nov. 21, 2008). For the proposed regulations, see 73 Fed. Reg. 21,861 (Apr. 23, 2008).

43. *See* 31 C.F.R. § 800.210 (2008).

44. *See* 31 C.F.R. § 800.103 (2008).

45. *See id.*

The new regulations address both the process and substance of CFIUS review. Overall, they make the review process a little more streamlined and the substantive standards a little more fully defined, often codifying the CFIUS "common law" that had evolved in secret over the past two decades. Procedurally, the regulations encourage pre-filing submissions,[46] more detailed information in the voluntary notice,[47] and certifications of accuracy (with civil penalties of up to $250,000 per material misstatement or omission).[48] The regulations also authorize the CFIUS chairperson to designate one or more agencies as a lead agency for all or a portion of a review, investigation, negotiation, or mitigation agreement monitoring assignment, as established in FINSA.[49]

The new regulations also address many definitional issues, three of which warrant particular mention. First, the proposed regulations adopt a functional definition of *control*, and avoid a categorical bright-line test.[50] Recall that CFIUS jurisdiction extends only to transactions that involve a change in control. The proposed regulations include a list of 10 "important matters affecting an entity," as well as a list of six minority shareholder protections that are not generally considered to confer control. While the lists clearly expand upon the prior regulations, most of the new provisions simply codify the common law of CFIUS— that is, the practice that often had been followed in particular cases to come before CFIUS. Common minority shareholder protections, such as the power to prevent the sale or pledge of all or substantially all of the assets of an entity and the power to purchase additional shares to prevent dilution, are among the rights that will not, in and of themselves, be deemed to confer control. On the other hand, the ability to select new business lines or ventures that an entity will pursue, and the power to appoint or dismiss officers or senior managers, are deemed to be indicia of control.[51]

Notably, the new regulations preserve the so-called "10 percent rule"— that purchases of no more than 10 percent of voting securities made solely for the purpose of investment are not covered transactions.[52] They

---

46. *See* 31 C.F.R. § 800.401(f) (2008).
47. *See* 31 C.F R § 800.402 (2008).
48. *See* 31 C.F.R. §§ 800.701 and 800.801 (2008).
49. *See* 31 C.F.R. § 800.218 (2008).
50. *See* 31 C.F.R. § 800.204 (2008).
51. *See* 31 C.F.R. § 800.204(a)(5), (a)(8) (2008).
52. *See* 31 C.F.R. §§ 302(b), 800.223 (2008).

do provide useful clarification by reference to examples. Thus, the new version of the 10 percent rule makes clear that a 10-percent-or-less investment does not satisfy the rule where, among other things, the foreign person has contractual rights that give it the power to control important matters or where the foreign person has the right to appoint one or more board seats.[53]

Second, the proposed regulations broaden the definition of *foreign person* to include foreign entities, which are defined to mean companies, branches, trusts, associations organized under the laws of a foreign country "whose equity securities are primarily traded on one or more foreign exchanges" or whose "principal place of business is outside the United States," unless the entity can demonstrate that a majority of its equity "is ultimately owned by U.S. nationals."[54]

Third, the regulations track the statutory definition of *critical infrastructure* as "a system or asset, whether physical or virtual, so vital to the United States that the incapacity or destruction of the particular system or asset of the entity over which control is acquired pursuant to [the] covered transaction would have a debilitating impact on national security," while making clear that this determination is to be made on a case-by-case basis with reference to the particular assets at issue in the proposed transaction.[55] The statutory definition of *critical technologies*, however, is expanded upon to incorporate by reference the definitions from various existing regulatory regimes that deal with the export, trade, or handling of sensitive goods, technologies, and services. Specifically, the new regulations define critical technologies to include, among other things, "[d]efense articles or defense services covered by the United States Munitions List"; "[t]hose items specified on the Commerce Control List . . . that are controlled pursuant to multilateral regimes (i.e., for reasons of national security, chemical and biological weapons proliferation, nuclear nonproliferation, or missile technology), as well as those that are controlled for reasons of regional stability or surreptitious listening"; certain "nuclear equipment, parts and components, materials software and technology specified in the Assistance to Foreign Atomic Energy Activities regulations"; and "[s]elect agents and toxins specified in the Export and Import of Select Agents and Toxins regulations."[56] The regulations state that voluntary notices filed with

---

53. *See id.* (examples 2 and 3).
54. *See* 31 C.F.R. §§ 800.216(a), 800.212 (2008).
55. *See* 31 C.F.R. § 800.208 (2008).
56. *See* 31 C.F.R. § 800.209 (2008).

CFIUS shall identify, among other things, any critical technologies produced or traded by the U.S. business that is the subject of the covered transaction.[57]

Sovereign Wealth Funds

The increasing prominence of sovereign wealth funds has added an extra layer of concern about the possible national security significance of foreign investment. Sovereign wealth funds presently control about $2.5 trillion, and that figure is expected to grow by perhaps $1 trillion per year for the next decade at least.[58] Sovereign wealth funds' present holdings represent only about 3 percent of global assets, but they already top the capital held by private equity firms and hedge funds.[59]

The U.S. government has taken notice. FINSA itself mandates an additional 45-day investigation where the buyer is a foreign sovereign wealth fund or other state-owned enterprise. The executive order described above directs the Department of Commerce to monitor and report on foreign investment trends and significant developments. The Treasury Department has initiated a review of policies related to sovereign wealth funds, has engaged in bilateral talks with governments controlling significant funds, and has encouraged dialogue between investor and recipient countries. The United States has also pushed for the International Monetary Fund, with the help of the World Bank, to develop a set of best practices to encourage transparency and strictly market-based, rather than politically motivated, investment by sovereign wealth funds. At the same time, the United States has supported efforts by the Organization for Economic Cooperation and Development (OECD) to encourage a parallel set of best practices for recipient countries, emphasizing openness to investment and evenhandedness in the treatment of foreign investors.[60]

---

57. *See* 31 C.F.R. § 800.402(c)(4) (2008).

58. Robert M. Kimmitt, *Public Footprints in Private Markets*, FOREIGN AFFAIRS, Vol. 87, No. 1, at 119 (Jan./Feb. 2008).

59. *Asset-backed Insecurity*, THE ECONOMIST (Jan. 19, 2008), at 79.

60. On all these efforts, *see* Kimmitt, *Public Footprints in Private Markets*, *supra* note 58. In September 2008, the International Working Group of Sovereign Wealth Funds, coordinated by the IMF, reached agreement on a draft set of Generally Accepted Practices and Principles (GAPP). *See* Press Release No. 08/04, Sept. 2, 2008, *available at* http://www.iwg-swf.org/pr/swfpr0804.htm. In April 2008, the OECD published a report on recipient country investment

These steps suggest that, for the moment, the executive branch does not see the need for any legislative modifications of the CFIUS process to deal with sovereign wealth funds. But some voices in Congress are already questioning that approach and suggesting that further revision of the CFIUS statute may be necessary.[61]

Investment Review Regimes in Other Countries

The United States is not alone in regulating foreign direct investment with an eye toward national security. In the last few years, at least 11 major recipients of foreign direct investment have approved or are considering new laws that could create barriers to foreign investment. Countries have passed new laws protecting economic security, established new national security review processes for foreign investment, or created additional mechanisms to address investment by foreign governments. According to a Council on Foreign Relations report, three common forces are driving the new investment restrictions: the appearance of new sources of investment, greater governmental ownership and involvement in cross-border investment, and the strong economic positions of host countries.[62]

INDUSTRY-SPECIFIC REVIEW REGIMES

Beyond the general rules of CFIUS and FINSA, the U.S. government has established regulations for foreign investment as it relates to specific industries.

Telecommunications

The Communications Act of 1934 includes various mechanisms by which the Federal Communications Commission (FCC) may review foreign

---

policies, encouraging openness to sovereign wealth fund investment. *See* OECD—Investment Committee Report, *Sovereign Wealth Funds and Recipient Country Policies*, Apr. 4, 2008, *available at* http://www.oecd.org/dataoecd/34/9/40408735.pdf.

61. *See, e.g.*, Hearing of the Senate Foreign Relations Committee, Sovereign Wealth Funds: Foreign Policy Consequences in an Era of New Money, FED. NEWS SERV., June 11, 2008; *Sovereign Funds Need Best Practices, Not New Legislation, Treasury Official Says*, BNA Daily Rep. for Execs. A-28 (Feb. 14, 2008).

62. DAVID M. MARCHICK & MATTHEW J. SLAUGHTER, GLOBAL FDI POLICY: CORRECTING A PROTECTIONIST DRIFT (Council on Foreign Relations Press, June 2008).

participation in the telecommunications industry. First, the FCC can regulate foreign participation in the U.S. telecommunications industry at the license issuance and transfer stages. The FCC must approve any application for any new license. The FCC is required to consider the public interest, which can include national security considerations vis-à-vis foreign applicants.[63] Similarly, any transfer of a license requires FCC approval and includes a public interest factor.[64] As a condition of granting (or approving the transfer of) a license, the FCC may ask applicants to sign Network Security Agreements with various executive agencies, which are designed to mitigate the government's concerns with particular applications.[65] Unlike CFIUS mitigation agreements, Network Security Agreements are generally made public as part of the license.[66]

In addition, the Communications Act regulates the ownership of wireless communication, including radio stations, broadcast television, cellular telephone companies, and most land-line telephone companies (but not cable companies), regardless of whether a technical acquisition or transfer of the license occurred.[67] Section 310(b) proscribes direct ownership by aliens, corporations organized under the laws of any foreign government, and corporations where more than one-fifth of the capital stock is owned of record or voted by aliens, foreign governments, foreign corporations, or their representatives.[68] This section also allows the FCC to deny licenses to corporations that are more than 25 percent owned by aliens or foreign governments if the commission finds that the public

---

63. 47 U.S.C. § 309(a). *See* 47 C.F.R. §§ 20.5, 22.5, 22.7, 24.12, 27.12, 27.302, 73.3564, & 90.1303. A similar requirement and review procedure exists for submarine cable licenses pursuant to 47 U.S.C. § 34–35.

64. 47 U.S.C. § 310(d).

65. The FCC's authority to require Network Security Agreements derives from its various authorities to approve license applications and other communication-related transactions. The FCC may append the Network Security Agreement to a license pursuant to an informal request for commission action under 47 C.F.R. § 1.41. *See also* Rules and Policies on Foreign Participation in the U.S. Telecomm. Mkt. & Mkt. Entry and Reg. of Foreign-Affiliated Entities, Report and Order on Reconsideration, 12 F.C.C.R. 23,891, para. 59–66 (1997) (Foreign Participation Order).

66. *See* FCC Web site, http://www.fcc.gov.

67. Recall that under *Exon-Florio*, CFIUS reviews transactions only if a change in control occurs.

68. 47 U.S.C. § 310(b).

interest will be served by such refusal.[69] No analogous provision relating to foreign ownership or control over wire licenses exists. Still, the FCC may review applications for and the transfer of such licenses.

Air Carriers

The Federal Aviation Act defines an "air carrier" as "a citizen of the United States undertaking by any means, directly or indirectly, to provide air transportation."[70] The act provides that, in order to be a citizen of the United States, an air carrier must satisfy each of the following requirements: (1) the carrier (if a corporation) must be organized under the laws of the United States or a state, the District of Columbia, or a U.S. territory or possession; (2) the carrier's president and at least two-thirds of its board of directors and other managing officers must be U.S. citizens; (3) at least 75 percent of the voting interest in the carrier must be owned or controlled by U.S. citizens;[71] and (4) the carrier must be under the actual control of U.S. citizens.[72]

The first three elements set forth above essentially constitute a bright-line numerical citizenship test. The final element, by contrast, involves an assessment by the U.S. Department of Transportation (DOT) as to whether (assuming a carrier satisfies the numerical test) the carrier is under the actual control of U.S. citizens. DOT review is mandatory.[73] DOT makes its actual control determinations on a case-by-case basis, reviewing "the totality of the circumstances of an airline's organization, including its capital structure, management, and contractual relationships"[74]

---

69. *Id.* This provision is another mechanism by which the FCC has discretion with respect to foreign direct investment. The FCC issued the Foreign Participation Order, which expressed a general policy encouraging foreign applications and provided certain benefits to applicants from World Trade Organization member countries. *See* Foreign Participation Order, *supra* note 65, at para. 29. *See also* Foreign Ownership Guidelines for FCC Common Carrier and Aeronautical Radio Licenses, *available at* http://www.fcc.gov/ib/Foreign_Ownership_Guidelines_Erratum.pdf.

70. 49 U.S.C. § 40102(a)(2).

71. Although the statute only permits non-citizens to own up to 25% of the voting equity in a U.S. air carrier, DOT policy may permit non-citizens to own up to 49% of a U.S. carrier's total equity (as long as the non-citizens' total voting interest does not exceed 25%). DOT Order 91-1-41.

72. 49 U.S.C. § 40102(a)(15).

73. 49 U.S.C. § 41101 *et seq.*

74. 70 Fed. Reg. 67,389 & 67,390 (Nov. 7, 2005) (Docket OST-03-15759).

to ascertain that non-citizens could not "exert any substantial influence" over the carrier's affairs.[75] This interpretation of actual control is sometimes referred to as the "no semblance of foreign control" test.[76] It appears that DOT's definition of control is broader than CFIUS's definition, although neither entity has stated so explicitly. Moreover, it remains uncertain whether a foreign investment in a U.S. airline should ever undergo CFIUS review when, by law, DOT must determine that the airline is under the actual control of U.S. citizens, applying arguably a stricter control requirement than CFIUS.

Nuclear Power

The Energy Reorganization Act of 1974 empowers the Nuclear Regulatory Commission (NRC) to issue licenses for the ownership and operation of nuclear power plants.[77] The act prohibits the NRC from issuing licenses to any entity that the "[c]ommission knows or has reason to believe is owned, controlled, or dominated by an alien, a foreign corporation, or a foreign government."[78] The NRC has adopted fluid standards for determining ownership, control, or domination with "an orientation toward safeguarding the national defense and security."[79]

To implement this proscription, the NRC has adopted a Standard Review Plan.[80] Three aspects of the plan merit attention here. First, the NRC will review each co-applicant for a nuclear power license independently to determine whether it is subject to foreign ownership, control, or domination. Second, where a reviewer "has reason to believe that [an] applicant may be owned, controlled, or dominated by foreign interests,"

---

75. 71 Fed. Reg. 26,425 & 26,426 (May 5, 2006) (Docket OST-03-15759).

76. Memorandum from Jeffrey N. Shane, Under Secretary for Policy, U.S. Dep't of Transp., dated Dec. 15, 2005, at 1 (Docket OST-03-15759). DOT makes its actual control determinations on a case-by-case basis by reviewing "the totality of the circumstances of an airline's organization, including its capital structure, management, and contractual relationships, . . ." to ascertain that non-citizens could not "exert any substantial influence" over the carrier's affairs. 70 Fed. Reg. 67,389 & 67,390 (Nov. 7, 2005) (Docket OST-03-15759); 71 Fed. Reg. 26,425 & 26,426 (May 5, 2006) (Docket OST-03-15759).

77. Pub. L. No. 93-438, 88 Stat. 1233.

78. 42 U.S.C. § 2133(d).

79. NRC Final Standard Review Plan on Foreign Ownership, Control, or Domination, 64 Fed. Reg. 52,355 & 52,358 (Sept. 28, 1999).

80. *Id.* at 52,357–58.

he or she will request additional information to supplement the application. Finally, the plan states that an applicant is foreign owned, controlled, or dominated when a foreign interest has the power to direct or decide matters affecting the management or operations—"the words 'owned, controlled, or dominated' mean relationships where the will of one party is subjugated to the will of another."[81]

CONCLUSION

With the anticipated increase in foreign direct investment in the United States, ever-evolving concepts of national security, and heightened awareness of the clearance process under Exon-Florio, one may expect CFIUS issues to arise more frequently and play a more significant role in M&A transactions for the foreseeable future. Virtually any deal involving foreign interests on the acquiring side and U.S. assets on the acquired side is a possible candidate for CFIUS review. And the wide-open standard as to what may constitute a threat to impair national security makes each CFIUS case a potential act of policy-making. This counsels careful consideration of CFIUS implications early in the negotiations between the parties, attention to the structure of the contemplated transaction as it may affect CFIUS jurisdiction, formulation of a comprehensive strategy addressing the regulatory and political risks associated with the transaction, and effective engagement with the CFIUS staff and stakeholder agencies to identify and resolve any national security concerns, to the extent possible, before the transaction is formally submitted for review.

---

81. *Id.* at 52,358.

CHAPTER 14

Export Control Enforcement Developments

by Thomas E. Crocker

This chapter provides a summary overview of major export control enforcement developments in 2007–2008. This period has seen significant changes in U.S. export control enforcement aimed at stemming illicit defense-related exports and other transfers that implicate the proliferation of weapons of mass destruction (WMD). As a result, both companies and practitioners need to be alert to the changed landscape and to the implications for compliance and the penalty risks that these developments entail.

The most salient developments during the years 2007–2008 include the following:

- Export control violations have become a deliberate and coordinated enforcement priority for the U.S. government as never before;
- Civil and criminal penalties applicable to export control violations have increased steeply;
- The U.S. government has initiated a higher volume of export control cases with a greater emphasis on criminal prosecution and involvement by the Department of Justice (DOJ);
- U.S. enforcement policy has featured increased use of more aggressive enforcement theories and expanding jurisdiction by prosecutors; and
- Higher expectations for export control compliance across the board have ensued.

Each of these developments is discussed in more detail below.

NATIONAL COUNTER-PROLIFERATION INITIATIVE

The groundwork for these major shifts in export control enforcement was laid by the October 11, 2007, launch by the DOJ of the National Counter-Proliferation Initiative aimed at illegal exports of dual-use and military items that could harm the United States or contribute to weapons of mass destruction (WMD) proliferation.[1] Initially led by Assistant Attorney General for National Security Kenneth Wainstein (who has since moved to O'Melveny & Myers LLP), the initiative is an interagency effort. Coordinated by the National Security Division at the DOJ, it involves U.S. Attorney offices across the country, plus the Federal Bureau of Investigation (FBI), Immigration and Customs Enforcement (ICE), the Department of Commerce's Bureau of Industry and Security (BIS), the Department of Defense's Criminal Investigative Service, the Department of State's Bureau of Politico-Military Affairs, and other agencies on an ad hoc basis.

The concerns that underlie the initiative include a 2006 Department of Defense report that found a 43 percent increase in suspicious foreign contacts with U.S. defense firms, as well as intelligence reports that concluded that some 108 countries have entities that focus on trying to acquire controlled U.S. technology, with China and Russia predictably leading the pack. The FBI has publicly cited targeted U.S. industries as including biotechnology, pharmaceuticals, nanotechnology, quantum computing, advanced materials, communications and encryption, and weapons systems. Specific targeted technologies have included components for nuclear weapons systems, guidance systems, basic ingredients for chemical and biological weapons, military aircraft components, warship data, and night vision equipment.[2] Transshipment hubs, such as Singapore, the United Arab Emirates, and Hong Kong, also have been cited as sources for concern.

---

1. *See* DOJ Press Release, Justice Department and Partner Agencies Launch National Counter-Proliferation Initiative, 07-806, Oct. 11, 2007. The launch of the DOJ initiative had been presaged by the appointment of a National Export Control Coordinator at DOJ (*see* DOJ Press Release, Justice Department Appoints National Export Control Coordinator as Part of Enhanced Counter-Proliferation Effort, 07-440, June 20, 2007).

2. Remarks of FBI Special Agent Joel Moss before the BIS Update 2007 Conference on Export Controls and Policy, Oct. 31–Nov. 2, 2007.

The centerpiece of the initiative is to increase and provide more focus on export control enforcement by applying the lessons learned in combating terrorism. A major element of the initiative has been to train assistant U.S. attorneys (AUSAs) nationwide to bring export control cases (in the past, AUSAs often have been reluctant to bring export control cases because, among other things, they have had limited understanding of the applicable laws, the factual proof often turned on complicated technological end-use questions, and the cases sometimes involved multiple international jurisdictions). The approach of the initiative also has been to create multi-agency counterproliferation task forces throughout the United States similar to ongoing counter-terrorism task forces. It has brought together prosecutors, investigating and export licensing agencies, and the intelligence community to coordinate these efforts. It focuses in particular on geographic areas with concentrations of high-technology businesses and research facilities. As stated by former BIS Assistant Secretary for Enforcement Darryl W. Jackson, the drivers underlying the initiative are that "national security and fostering trade must be mutually reinforcing," "prosperity depends on security," and "broader implementation of effective compliance" must take place.[3]

The bottom line is that the likelihood of enforcement action has dramatically increased at the same time that compliance with U.S. export controls is becoming more complicated in light of global sourcing and supply chains.

INCREASED PENALTIES

At the same time, liability for violations of the export control laws has increased sharply. U.S. enforcement authorities continue to implement dual-use U.S. export controls contained in the Export Administration Regulations (EAR)[4] pursuant to the International Emergency Economic Powers Act (IEEPA)[5] because of the lapse of the EAR's prior statutory authority under the Export Administration Act of 1979 (EAA), as amended.[6] Civil penalties under IEEPA, which also serves as the statu-

---

3. Remarks of BIS Assistant Secretary Darryl W. Jackson before the BIS Update 2007 Conference on Export Controls and Policy, Oct. 31–Nov, 2, 2007.

4. 15 C.F.R. § 730 *et seq.*

5. 50 U.S.C. §§ 1701–1706.

6. 50 U.S.C. app. §§ 2401–2420 *et seq.*

tory authority for most sanctions programs administered by the Department of the Treasury's Office of Foreign Assets Control (OFAC), remained steady for many years at $11,000 per violation. However, in 2006 Congress raised the per violation civil penalty to $50,000 and subsequently with the IEEPA Enhancement Act (Pub. L. No. 110-096), passed October 16, 2007, raised the civil penalty to the greater of $250,000 or twice the amount of the transaction. Thus, within the space of less than two years, civil penalties increased almost 25-fold.

As part of the same act, Congress raised criminal penalties from $50,000 and 10 years' imprisonment to $1 million and 20 years' imprisonment. Further, the IEEPA Enhancement Act expanded the scope of persons liable for civil or criminal penalties in connection with exports by including "conspiracy" and "aiding and abetting" violations. Although this expanded scope could potentially apply to any person, its impact is likely to be of most concern to customs brokers, shippers, and trade finance providers. Further, the Bush administration indicated interest in seeking even higher penalties from Congress as part of legislation it has sponsored to renew the lapsed EAA.[7]

ENFORCEMENT TRENDS

Recent cases demonstrate that both criminal and civil enforcement of export controls for sensitive goods and technology is among the U.S. government's top priorities starting even before the launch of the National Counter-Proliferation Initiative.[8] While criminal cases arguably have attracted the most attention, civil enforcement also has proceeded at an accelerated pace. For example, by one count, BIS brought some

---

7. *See* the administration-sponsored Export Enforcement Act of 2007, currently pending before Congress, which would increase civil penalties to $500,000 and criminal penalties to the greater of $5 million or 10 times the value of the export per violation.

8. The pace of export control matters handled by DOJ picked up considerably in 2007. According to a DOJ Fact Sheet, DOJ handled some 32 major export-related criminal cases and prosecutions between Oct. 5, 2006, and Oct. 5, 2007. The cases involved a wide variety of factual scenarios, including exports of F-4 and F-14 fighter jet components, the export of products with nuclear and missile applications to Pakistan, the sale of military night-vision goggles to various foreign parties, the export of sensitive aircraft components to Iran, etc. *See* DOJ Fact Sheet, *Major U.S. Export Enforcement Actions in the Past Year*, 07-807, Oct. 11, 2007.

95 civil enforcement actions in 2007 and 41 such actions through September 30, 2008.

A few of the more prominent enforcement cases during the 2007–2008 period are summarized below.

The ITT Corporation Case

On March 27, 2007, ITT Corporation, whose NV division is a leading manufacturer of high-technology night vision equipment, pled guilty to multiple criminal charges of violations of the Arms Export Control Act (AECA).[9] ITT is currently the twelfth-largest supplier of defense systems to the U.S. military. The plea deal included a $100 million settlement, one of the largest penalties ever in a criminal case.[10] ITT NV was also prohibited for three years from exporting defense articles or furnishing defense services by the U.S. State Department's Directorate of Defense Trade Controls (DDTC), which administers the International Traffic in Arms Regulations (ITAR).[11]

The first charge against ITT arose from its export of classified technical data related to night vision goggles to China, Singapore, and the United Kingdom without a license or authorization from DDTC.[12] In the late 1990s, ITT possessed classified specifications for filters that prevent lasers from causing damage or degradation to night vision goggles. ITT originally subcontracted to obtain parts of the classified filter from a California-based company. According to the Statement of Facts filed with the plea agreement, in early 2000 ITT began to explore offshore manufacturing options as a way to reduce costs. In 2001, despite its awareness that it could not share the classified filter specification with any foreign country, and despite its awareness that it had no export license, ITT sent the classified drawings and specifications to a Singapore supplier.

---

9. 22 U.S.C. § 2778 *et seq.*

10. For a summary of the terms of the settlement, *see generally* DOJ Press Release, ITT Corporation to Pay $100 Million Penalty and Plead Guilty to Illegally Exporting Secret Military Data Overseas, 07-192, Mar. 27, 2007.

11. 22 C.F.R. Parts 120–130.

12. The facts presented regarding ITT's export control violations are based on the Statement of Facts that was appended to the plea agreement filed with the U.S. district court for the Western District of Virginia. According to the plea agreement, ITT agreed that "the Statement of Facts . . . is true and accurate to the best of its knowledge and belief and establishes an adequate basis for ITT's plea to Counts One and Two."

Based in part on a recommendation from an ITT manager in the United States, the Singapore supplier exported the controlled drawings and specifications to a facility in China to begin low-cost production of certain filter components. As part of the same project, ITT also turned to a U.K.-based sister company of its Singapore supplier as a source of coating technology used in the classified filter. In early 2001, ITT sent the classified filter specifications to this U.K. company to obtain a quote on the production of the coating. ITT never obtained an export license for this transfer and failed to verify the security clearance status of the U.K. company.

Offshore production plans for the classified night vision filter components were quite advanced—and the classified technical data had been shared with multiple offshore entities—before ITT finally submitted a license application to DDTC for offshore production in June 2001. However, the DOJ's investigation later concluded that the application was not only late, but also contained false information.

Shortly after ITT submitted its export license application for the night vision filter technology, an ITT employee mentioned to a Department of Defense employee that ITT had been obtaining some of the filter parts offshore. This statement prompted the U.S. government to request that ITT recover all of the technical data that it had exported to offshore suppliers. ITT failed to comply with this request. In addition, ITT continued to push forward with the unauthorized foreign production of the night vision filters. At a time when the government was already aware of ITT's illegal exports, ITT issued additional purchase orders. Over 1,000 filter parts were already produced in the U.K. and an additional 20,000 filter components were produced in China before ITT told these offshore suppliers to cease production in February 2002. In October 2002, the government executed a search warrant on ITT's facilities.

Material Omissions in a Voluntary Disclosure

The second charge against ITT arose from ITT's apparent omission of material facts during the course of a voluntary disclosure made to DDTC. This voluntary disclosure was unrelated to the technology transfer that led to the first criminal charge.

According to the Statement of Facts, ITT regularly lent or consigned night vision equipment to foreign customers for evaluation and testing. ITT held a license for these temporary export consignments, but the license required the company to verify the return of the exported equipment after four years. However, throughout the 1990s, ITT failed to ensure the return of the consigned night vision equipment.

ITT compiled a list of these past-due consignments by March 1998. However, the company failed to take any corrective action until nearly two years after the list of violations was compiled, when ITT's outside law firm prepared a Preliminary Notification of Voluntary Disclosure in April 2000. ITT's preliminary disclosure indicated that the consignment license violations were "recently discovered," and in the final disclosure letter sent in May 2000, counsel described several forms of corrective action that ITT supposedly had undertaken.

According to the DOJ, the Department of State relied on the representations made during the voluntary disclosure ultimately to elect not to refer ITT for criminal prosecution. Instead, ITT and DDTC entered into a civil penalty consent agreement in October 2004 under which ITT agreed to pay an $8 million penalty. However, based on its further investigation, the DOJ concluded that ITT made numerous false statements and withheld material facts regarding the consignment violations in an attempt to minimize the civil penalty it would receive. Among the false statements and omissions cited by the DOJ was the statement by ITT's outside counsel that the violations were "recently discovered," when in fact the evidence obtained by the government established that ITT delayed the voluntary disclosure for at least two years. The DOJ also cited the statements in the disclosures that ITT had taken immediate corrective action when most of the corrective action did not take place until the time ITT filed its final disclosure.

Exceeding the Scope of an Existing TAA

Prosecution of a third charge—which related to the unlicensed and unauthorized exports of night vision technical data to China, Singapore, and Japan—was deferred under the plea agreement. According to the Statement of Facts, ITT for years had been sharing export-controlled technical specifications with its Singapore-based supplier. ITT did so first without a license and then continued to do so in violation of the "build to print" limitations set forth in a Technical Assistance Agreement (TAA) that DDTC had approved. Indeed, contrary to the narrowly defined limits of the TAA, ITT brought engineers who were Singapore and Chinese nationals into close collaborative efforts with its own engineers to share and develop controlled night vision technology. According to the Statement of Facts, ITT was aware of these violations and chose not to disclose them.

Failed Corporate Compliance Culture

The Statement of Facts also provides numerous examples of executive and managerial-level disregard for the company's export control responsibilities. For example, an export license manager hired by ITT in May 2000, shortly after the initial disclosure of the consignment violations, resigned after just seven weeks on the job when he realized that ITT's management disregarded export compliance.

Also, in November 1998, an ITT employee told an ITT manager that she was not willing to violate export license requirements. The manager ordered the employee to make an illegal export anyway. After the employee informed high-level executives of this violation, ITT promoted the manager to a position of even greater responsibilities regarding export compliance. While many of these internal weaknesses cited in the Statement of Facts were not themselves violations of law, they appear to have influenced the government's aggressive stance toward the case and the severity of the punishment imposed.

The ITT Plea Agreement

The plea agreement between the government and ITT imposed $100 million in fines, forfeitures, and other payouts. The U.S. attorney described the agreement as the "first of its kind." The first portion of the penalty was a $20 million fine to the Department of State. Second, ITT agreed to pay the statutory maximum criminal fine of $2 million as part of its guilty plea. Third, the company agreed to forfeit $28 million, which amount was deemed to be proceeds traceable to the violations, to various law enforcement agencies to reward their work in the investigation. Fourth, ITT agreed to pay $50 million in "restitution to the victims of their crimes—the American soldier."[13]

This $50 million restitution penalty is perhaps the most unusual aspect of the massive settlement. Over the five years following the settlement, ITT is required to invest the $50 million to accelerate the development of the most advanced night vision equipment for U.S. military use. The Army's Night Vision and Electronic Sensors Lab must approve every dollar spent as part of this project. Further, the U.S. military retains Government Purpose Rights to all technology that emerges from this effort. The Government Purpose Rights enable the U.S. military to

---

13. *See* Statement of U.S. Attorney John Brownlee on the Guilty Plea of ITT Corporation for Illegally Transferring Classified and Export Controlled Night Vision Technology to Foreign Countries, Mar. 27, 2007.

share the technology with ITT's competitors. Finally, any of the $50 million that remains after five years will be immediately paid to the government.

The plea agreement also required ITT to implement several export control compliance measures, including the hiring of an independent export monitor and staff, annual audits, mandatory reporting of violations, extensive export compliance training, and the submission of annual compliance certifications. The plea agreement's $50 million investment requirement will give ITT the opportunity to maintain its role as a developer and producer of sophisticated night vision equipment for the U.S. military. However, ITT's industry-leading night vision division suffered a three-year DDTC debarment. Persons subject to DDTC debarment are prohibited from participating directly or indirectly in the export of defense articles, including technical data.

The Axion Indictment

Two days after announcing the plea agreement with ITT, the DOJ announced indictments in the Northern District of Alabama against Huntsville-based Axion Corporation. The charges arose from the firm's alleged unlicensed export of technical drawings to overseas manufacturers, as well as Axion's submission of false test reports with regard to the supply of helicopter and Bradley assault vehicle parts. Axion's owner was indicted, too. He faced up to 30 years in prison and $1.75 million in fines if convicted on all five counts.

The indictment charged that beginning in September 2003, Axion Corporation exported technical drawings for the Blackhawk helicopter to China without first obtaining a required license from DDTC.[14] The indictment accused the owner and the company of defrauding the government of millions of dollars and compromising U.S. Army secrets. In a statement similar to the announcement of the ITT plea agreement, the DOJ described this indictment as "a warning to companies seeking to enhance their profits at the expense of America's national security."

---

14. In addition, according to the indictment, in January 2004 Axion submitted an allegedly false document to the U.S. government in connection with a military contract. The document reported that certain testing of a defense article had been performed, when the defendants allegedly knew that the test reports were false. Then, in February 2004, Axion and its owner made an allegedly fraudulent representation to the U.S. Army concerning the origin of an aircraft part it supplied pursuant to a military contract.

However, the DOJ did not prevail in this first case tried after the launch of the National Counter-Proliferation Initiative. On December 28, 2007, following a bench trial, the defendant corporation and its owner were acquitted of all charges and were reinstated as government contractors in good standing.[15]

Indictments and Arrests for Selling Electronic Components to Entity List Companies

On April 3, 2007, just days following the announcement of the Axion indictments, the DOJ indicted four persons and arrested two of them in connection with alleged exports of electronic components to Vikram Sarabhai Space Centre and Bharat Dynamics, Ltd., both Indian companies on BIS's Entity List (Supp. No. 4 to Part 740 of the EAR).[16] Under the EAR, exports to any party on the Entity List normally require an export license from the BIS, regardless of the nature of the articles exported. One of the arrested defendants was denied bail. Two defendants were not arrested because they resided in Singapore and India.

The first set of criminal charges in the indictment alleged EAR violations in the form of the export to Entity List buyers of commercial electronic components, including SRAMs (Static Random Access Memory), capacitors, semiconductors, rectifiers, and resistors. These items allegedly have missile guidance and firing systems applications. The defendants did business through a company named Cirrus, with offices in South Carolina, Singapore, and India. The South Carolina defendants were alleged to have obtained orders from Entity List companies and then negotiated with commercial vendors in the United States, sometimes deceiving the vendors by preparing false end-user certificates. The defendants would then arrange for initial export through their Singapore office, thus concealing the actual destination from U.S. authorities.

The remaining charges of the indictment asserted violations of the ITAR in connection with exports of certain microprocessors and capaci-

---

15. DOJ Press Release, Alexander Nooredin Latifi and Axion Corporation Acquitted, Dec. 28, 2007. For more detail on the *Axion* case, see article prepared by Axion's defense attorneys, James F. Barger, Jr. & Henry I. Frohsin, *The Axion Case: How a Rare Defense Victory May Shape the Future of Arms Export Control Act Prosecutions and Defense Trial Strategies*, 3 WHITE-COLLAR CRIME REPORTER NO. 2, Jan. 18, 2008.

16. DOJ Press Release, Two Indicted and Arrested on Charges of Supplying Indian Government with Controlled Technology, 07-217, Apr. 3, 2007.

tors allegedly covered by the United States Munitions List (USML). The indictment stated that these items were sold to an enterprise affiliated with India's Ministry of Defence for use in light combat aircraft.

One of the defendants subsequently entered a guilty plea and was sentenced to 35 months in prison.[17]

Prosecutions of Academic and Others for Deemed Export Violations

Deemed exports are exports of technical data to non-U.S. persons in the United States that would require an export license if exported from the United States to that person's country of origin. Deemed exports have long been a source of concern to BIS and to U.S. companies and academic institutions that employ research and technical staff who are not U.S. citizens or resident aliens. Enforcement of the deemed export provisions (found at 15 C.F.R. § 734.2(b)(2)(ii) of the EAR and at 22 C.F.R. § 120.17 of the ITAR had been restrained until the launch of the National Counter-Proliferation Initiative. Now that is changing.

In a case that should attract the attention of the academic community across the United States, on September 3, 2008, a federal grand jury convicted a retired University of Tennessee professor of illegally exporting military technical information relating to plasma technology for use in drones operated as weapons or surveillance systems pursuant to a U.S. Air Force contract. Professor J. Reece Roth was convicted of one count of conspiring to export technology relating to 15 different defense articles to a Chinese citizen who was a graduate research assistant at the University of Tennessee, as well as 15 counts of violating the AECA and one count of wire fraud. The maximum punishment for the conspiracy conviction is five years' imprisonment and a fine of $250,000, while the maximum penalty for each of AECA offenses includes up to 10 years' imprisonment and a criminal fine of $1 million.[18] The conviction was the result of a multi-agency investigation of the type being pursued by the

17. *See* DOJ Press Releases, Businessman Pleads Guilty to Supplying Indian Government with Controlled Technology, Mar. 13, 2008, and Businessman Sentenced for Supplying Indian Government with Controlled Technology, June 16, 2008.

18. *See* DOJ Press Releases, Retired University of Tennessee Professor Convicted of Arms Export Violations, 08-774, Sept. 3, 2008, and Physicist Pleads Guilty to Conspiracy to Violate Arms Export Control Act, 08-299, Apr. 15, 2008.

National Counter-Proliferation Initiative and involved elements of the FBI, ICE, BIS, and U.S. Air Force.

In an earlier case, BIS also pursued deemed exports through a civil settlement with Ingersoll Machine Tools of Rockford, Illinois, which resulted in a $126,000 civil fine. In that case, the company settled allegations that it had committed eight unlicensed deemed exports to Italian and Indian foreign nationals in violation of the EAR. The allegations involved deemed exports of production and development technology for vertical fiber placement machines and production technology for five axis milling machines to Indian and Italian nationals in the United States. The technology was controlled for National Security and Missile Technology reasons to India and Italy and was also controlled to India for nuclear nonproliferation reasons.[19]

Reexport Violations Prosecuted

In a further development, BIS and the DOJ have pursued both civil and criminal penalties extraterritorially against foreign companies that engage in unauthorized reexports of U.S.-origin goods or technology. For example, on August 14, 2008, BIS announced a $119,250 civil penalty against Reson A/S (RAS) of Slangerup, Denmark (as well as separate additional civil penalties against its UK, South African, and U.S. subsidiaries), for 29 violations of the EAR in connection with reexports of underwater navigation equipment.[20]

Likewise, on April 10, 2008, Cryostar SAS, a French company, pled guilty to conspiracy, illegal export, and attempted illegal export of cryogenic submersible pumps to Iran. Cryostar's plea agreement resulted in payment of a $500,000 criminal fine and two years' corporate probation.[21]

IED Conspiracy Indictments

Following an extensive interagency investigation into the use of U.S.-made goods in the construction of improvised explosive devices (IEDs)

---

19. *See* BIS Press Release, Illinois-Based Firm Settles Charges of Deemed Export Violations, Apr. 12, 2008.

20. *See* BIS Press Release, Danish Company and Subsidiaries Settle Charges for Illegal Exports and Reexports of Underwater Navigation Equipment, Aug. 14, 2008.

21. *See* BIS Press Release, French Corporation Pleads Guilty to Conspiracy, Illegal Export and Attempted Illegal Export of Cryogenic Submersible Pumps to Iran, Apr. 10, 2008.

in Iraq and Afghanistan, on September 17, 2008, BIS and the DOJ jointly announced the indictment of eight individuals and eight corporations for their participation in conspiracies to engage in illegal U.S. exports of dual-use commodities to Iran through middle countries, including the United Arab Emirates, Malaysia, England, Germany, and Singapore. The indictments came as a result of a coordinated investigation, again bearing the hallmarks of the National Counter-Proliferation Initiative, involving DOJ, BIS, OFAC, the Department of Defense's Criminal Investigative Service and ICE. In a related development on the same day, BIS added 75 names to its Entity List because of their involvement in the global procurement network that was the subject of the indictment.[22]

HIGHER EXPECTATIONS FOR COMPLIANCE

These cases, and others brought over the last two years, highlight a number of issues that warrant attention from the exporting community, particularly in the defense and technology sectors.

First, these cases underscore the importance of implementing export control compliance mechanisms with high-level management support. For example, if ITT's management had not displayed such disregard for export compliance, the government may not have pursued a record-breaking $100 million penalty.

Second, executives, owners, and individual employees are not immune from prosecution. The prosecution of the Axion Corporation owner, as well as of the alleged IED export violators and the Entity List exporter to India, all illustrate an increased willingness of the DOJ to prosecute responsible individuals.

Third, the India export case and possibly the Axion case raise questions about what goods and technologies are properly covered by the USML and about DDTC's and DOJ's aggressive interpretation of the scope of the USML. These cases should focus exporters' attention on the utility of DDTC's Commodity Jurisdiction procedure under which exporters can obtain binding rulings on whether their goods or technology are subject to the ITAR or the EAR prior to exporting.

---

22. *See* DOJ Press Release, Sixteen Foreign Nationals and Corporations Indicted on Charges of Illegally Exporting Potential Military and Explosives Components to Iran, 08-828, Sept. 17, 2008, and BIS Press Release, Commerce Department, Government Partners, Break Up Iranian Ring Charged with Procuring IED Components, Sept. 17, 2008.

Fourth, virtually all of these cases demonstrate the myriad challenges that arise when exporters simultaneously deal in controlled articles and work with foreign manufacturers or foreign purchasers. Such business initiatives increase the need for internal controls over technology and the careful management of export licensing and the TAA processes.

Fifth, the prosecution of deemed export cases, especially the one involving the University of Tennessee professor, means that companies and academic institutions must exercise heightened care in their technology-sharing programs and research departments. Academic institutions which up to now thought they were insulated from export control concerns because they had entered into contracts with elements of the Department of Defense or, worse yet, because they supported and practiced "academic freedom," would now be well advised to disabuse themselves of such notions and to substitute sound export control compliance programs for wishful thinking.

Sixth, the range of penalties pursued by the U.S. government in the two deemed export cases cited above (criminal conviction versus a $126,000 civil fine for essentially similar violations), as well as the varying penalties sought and obtained in the other cases, make risk assessment difficult for U.S. exporters.

Seventh, the DOJ's new willingness to prosecute companies outside the U.S. for reexport control violations brings home to non-U.S. persons the extraterritorial reach of U.S. export control laws. Although these laws have had extraterritorial reach since their inception, there is a newfound aggressiveness on the part of the DOJ in prosecuting such cases. Non-U.S. companies that obtain their goods or technology from the United States may want to pay particular attention to their compliance with U.S. reexport control requirements.

Eighth, the ITT case raises significant questions regarding the proper approach to voluntary disclosures. In ITT's case, outside counsel helped prepare a preliminary voluntary disclosure, followed by an internal investigation and, eventually, a more complete final disclosure to the U.S. government. Statements made in the preliminary disclosure, however, were cited by the U.S. government as evidence of ITT's willful disregard of export control laws. Thus, the prospect of having every word in disclosure submissions subject to scrutiny, or interpreted as misstatements, should give companies and their counsel pause—especially since ITT still had to pay an $8 million penalty as part of its voluntary disclosure. Thus, the ITT case illustrates a new level of care that must go into preparing and presenting voluntary disclosures.

Finally, exporters and their service providers should exercise particular caution regarding activities that could be deemed to be aiding, abetting, or conspiracy in relation to other people's activities.

* * *

In conclusion, the U.S. government over the last two years has come to view export controls, especially as they relate to the proliferation of WMD, as an essential component of homeland security. Further, the government has elevated that concern to the political level within the DOJ and has implemented a coordinated interagency program to address it by applying lessons learned from another homeland security front, counterterrorism. Whether this initiative will be sustained in the new administration remains to be seen. However, a solid groundwork has been laid, and the exporting community should approach its compliance responsibilities with an understanding and appreciation of the changes that have occurred.

TABLE OF CASES

269

Nash v. Port Auth. of N.Y. & N.J., #129074/93, 2008 N.Y. App. Div. LEXIS 374, 2008 N.Y. slip op. 03991 (1st Dept.); 164

Nat'l Parks & Conserv. Ass'n v. Morton, 498 F.2d 765 (D.C. Cir. 1974); 101

Nielsen v. George Diamond Vogel Paint Co., 892 F.2d 1450 (9th Cir. 1990); 170, 171

People v. Haneiph, 191 Misc. 2d 738 N.Y.S.2d 405 (N.Y.C. Crim. Ct., 2002); 26

Pierce County, Wash. v. Guillen, 537 U.S. 129, 147 (2003); 36

Riggs Bank, N.A., FinCEN Assessment of Civil Money Penalty, *In re,* 2004-01 (May 13, 2004); 71

Sigue Corp. and Sigue LLC, FinCEN Assessment of Civil Money Penalty, *In re,* 2008-01 (Jan. 28, 2008); 72

South Dakota v. Dole, 483 U.S. 203 (1987); 41

Southern Ry. Co. v. United States, 222 U.S. 20 (1911); 36

Stone v. Ritter, 911 A.2d 362 (Del. 2006); 156

Tighe v. Osborne, 149 Md. 349 (1925); 23

United Haulers Ass'n, Inc. v. Oneida-Herkimer Solid Waste Mgmt. Auth., 127 S. Ct. 1786 (2007); 24

United States v. Lopez, 514 U.S. 549 (1995); 37

United States v. Morrison, 529 U.S. 598 (2000); 38

INDEX

271